THE
MULFUZAT TIMURY
OR
AUTOBIOGRAPHICAL MEMOIRS
OF THE
MOGHUL EMPEROR TIMUR

THE MULFUZAT TIMURY,

OR,

AUTOBIOGRAPHICAL MEMOIRS

OF THE

MOGHUL EMPEROR TIMUR:

WRITTEN IN THE

JAGTAY TURKY LANGUAGE

TIMUR

TRANSLATOR

CHARLES STEWART

GYAN

Published by

Gyan Publishing House
5, Ansari Road
Daryaganj, New Delhi-110002
Phone: 011-47034999, 9811692060
E-mail: books@gyanbooks.com

Distribution Network
gyanbooks.com
India, USA, Canada, UK, Australia

ISBN: 978-93-6920-177-8 (HB)

First Published, 1830

2nd Impression 2025

Printed at: Gyan Press, Delhi.

THE MULFUZAT TIMURY, OR, AUTOBIOGRAPHICAL MEMOIRS OF THE MOGHUL EMPEROR TIMUR

Author: TIMUR, Translator: CHARLES STEWART

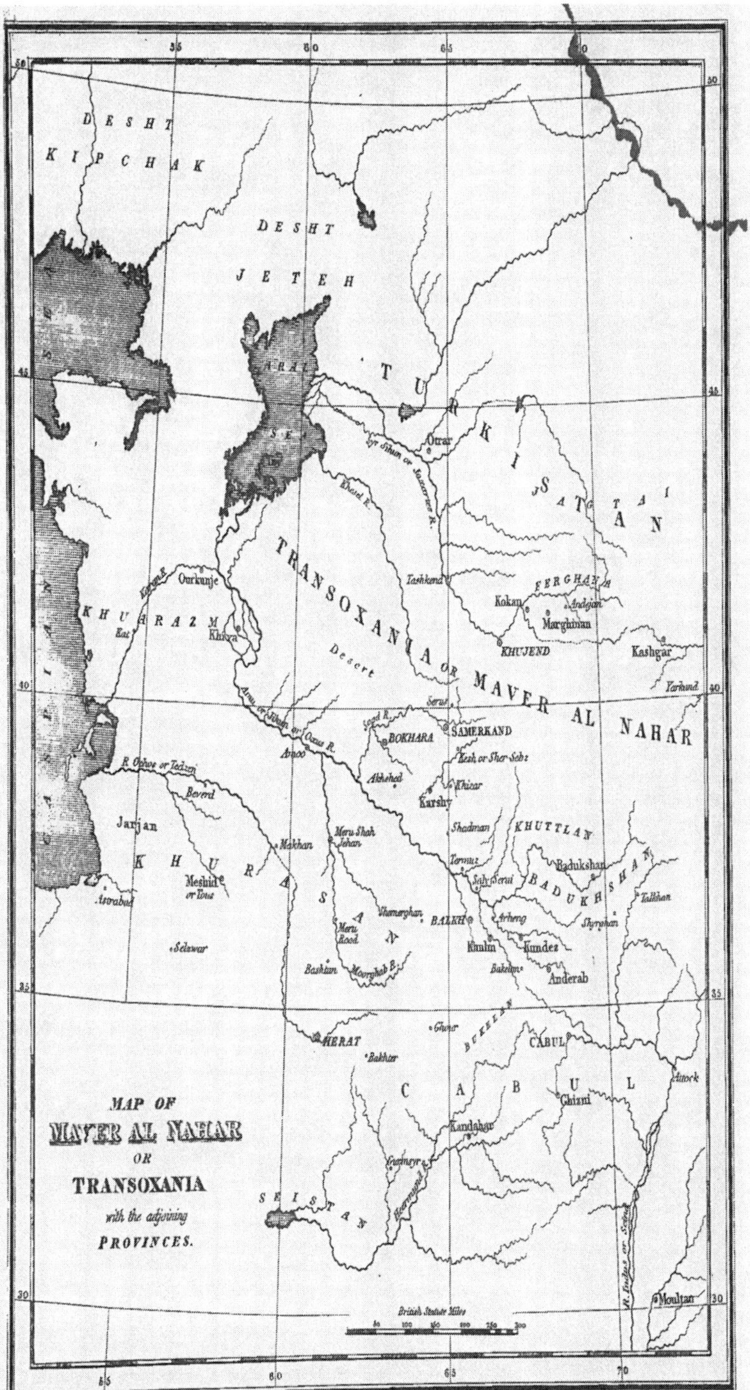

DESHT KIPCHAK
DESHT JETEH
ARAL SEA
TURKISTAN
JSATGTAI
TRANSOXANIA OR MAVER AL NAHAR
KHUARAZM
Ourkunje
Khiva
Otrar
Tashkend
FERGHANA
Kokan
Andjan
Marghinan
KHUJEND
Kashgar
Yarkund
Desert
BOKHARA
SAMERKAND
Kesh or Sher Sebz
Akhshed
Khizar
Karshy
Amol
R. Oxus
Beverd
Jarjan
KHURASAN
Makhan
Meshid or Tous
Astrabad
Selswar
Meru Shah Jehan
Meru Rood
Bashtan
Moorghab R.
BALKH
Shadman
KHUTTLAN
Termuz
Badukshan
BADUKHSHAN
Talkhan
Arheng
Khulm
Kundez
Bakelan
Anderab
Ghour
HERAT
Bakhtir
CABUL
Ghizni
Kandahar
SEISTAN
Heermund R.
Attock
Moultan
British Statute Miles
MAP OF MAVER AL NAHAR OR TRANSOXANIA with the adjoining PROVINCES.
Engraved by Josiah Neele 352 Strand.

THE

MULFUZĀT TIMŪRY,

OR

AUTOBIOGRAPHICAL MEMOIRS

OF THE

MOGHUL EMPEROR TIMŪR,

WRITTEN IN THE

JAGTAY TŪRKY LANGUAGE,

TURNED INTO PERSIAN BY

ABU TALIB HUSSYNY,

AND

TRANSLATED INTO ENGLISH BY

MAJOR CHARLES STEWART,

LATE PROFESSOR OF ORIENTAL LANGUAGES

IN THE HONOURABLE EAST INDIA COMPANY'S COLLEGE.

1830.

TO

COLONEL DAVY,

TRACEY PARK, SOMERSETSHIRE.

DEAR SIR,

As the Public are indebted to your late Father not only for his able Translation of the Institutes of the Emperor Timūr, but also for his having with much perseverance procured and first brought to Europe an authentic copy of the Memoirs of that Monarch, I have much pleasure in dedicating to you my Translation of those Memoirs, in hopes of assisting in some degree to transmit to posterity so meritorious a name.

I have the honour to be,

Dear Sir,

your obedient humble servant,

CHARLES STEWART.

Bath, May, 1830.

PREFACE.

The fame of Timūr, erroneously called Tamerlane, although long known to some persons in Europe, was more generally communicated to the Public in the year 1722, by the labours of the indefatigable Orientalist, Petis de la Croix, who translated from the Persian language the History of that Monarch, denominated *Zuffer Namēh*, or *Book of Victory*, by Sherif Addyn Aly of Yezd.

In the year 1723, the French edition was turned into English by Mr. John Darby, who dedicated his work to His Royal Highness Frederic Prince of Wales, but these histories commence only with the twenty-fifth year of Timūr's age. Iben Arab Shāh's Arabic History of Timūr, called the *Ajaib al Mukhlukāt*, *Wonders of the Creation*, was translated into Latin by Golius in 1636, and again by Manger in 1767 and 1772, but, being more of a coarse satire on that Prince than his real history, it is little worthy of credit, and has consequently fallen into disrepute.

In the year 1783, Professor White of Oxford, published a Persian Edition of the *Institutes* of Timūr, with an English translation by Major William Davy of the Honourable East India Company's Service,* which was deservedly much admired, and as it was the cause of producing the Translation of the following Memoirs, I shall take the liberty hereafter of subjoining a portion of its Preface.

In the year 1787, the late Professor Langlés of Paris, published a French translation of the *Institutes*, under the title of

"Instituts Politiques et Militaires de Tamerlane proprement appellé
" Timour, ecrits par lui-même en Mogol, et traduits en François sur
" la version Persane d'Abou Taleb al Hosseini, avec la Vie de ce
" Conquerant, &c. &c."

William Erskine, Esq. in his Preface to the Memoirs of Baber, pub-

* See Note at the end of the Preface.

lished in 1826, (in praise of which work too much cannot be said) informs us, that he had seen at Bombay, a complete Persian translation of the Autographic Memoirs of Timour, the original of which had been found in the library of Jaafer Pashā of Yemen, and that it appears by Astley's Collection of Voyages, that a person of that name was Pashā of Yemen in 1610. This is of importance, as it nearly fixes the date of the Persian Translation, which is confirmed by the dedication of the work to the Emperor Shāh Jehan of Hindūstan.

Having thus premised, I proceed to give a description of the Manuscript brought from India by Major Davy, which I have undertaken to translate: it is an Octavo volume, written in the common Persian hand, and as it has never been bound, was probably copied for that gentleman in Calcutta, it is enclosed in an old cover, on which is written in Major Davy's hand; "This Manuscript, which is a fragment of Timūr's, is very valuable, therefore preserve it with care. N. B. It is to be put in the little black writing box."

The Manuscript contains four hundred and fifty-seven pages; after the Persian Translator's Preface, it commences with the *Institutes*, which nearly agree with the printed edition; these are succeeded by the Designs and Enterprizes of the printed copy, after which follows the Book of *Omens*, mentioned in the 8th page of Dr. White's Preface, and which I might probably also have omitted in my translation, did I not fear the reproach of having left part of my work undone.*

The History commences at the 188th page, with the birth of Timūr, A. H. 736, (A. D. 1336,) and is continued in the form of annals till A. H. 777, being the forty-first year of his age, omitting the last thirty years of his life.

It is written in a careless manner, occasionally obscure, with much tautology, and some repetitions, but without any break in the detail, except at the commencement of a new year, evidently evincing that the art of book-making has not been employed to set it off, and that it is a

* Monsieur Langlés says in the sixth page of his Preface; "ces superstitions sont, pour le philosophe, des renseignemens certains sur les mœurs et sur l'esprit des hommes. J'engage donc M. M. Davy et White à faire cette restitution, si ce n'est pas à l'érudition, du moins à la Philosophie."

translation from some language less polished than the Persian.* I have however found it requisite to divide the Translation into Books and Chapters.

In comparing Major Davy's Translation with Petis de la Croix's, I have found so much discrepancy between their spelling of Oriental names, that one can hardly suppose the same persons, or places are meant, I have therefore ventured to make an innovation in Anglo-Oriental orthography, by making use of such of our letters as agree with the Persian Alphabet.

The *exact* pronunciation of a proper name is of little consequence to the European reader, while the Oriental student will be thus enabled to transpose it into the Persian character; some of the names of places have been so long settled, that I have not interfered with them, but take this opportunity of stating that *Kund* or *Kend*, in the Tūrky language, signifies a town, and therefore forms the termination of the names of many cities; Turān, called by the Greeks, Transoxiana, and by the Arabs, Maveralneher, should properly be spelled Ma-verā-al-neher: *that which is beyond the river.* Khurasān being the Eastern province of Persia, was called the Region of the Sun.

We are very much indebted to the French Literati for information on Oriental subjects, but they have led us into a very false orthography by their partiality for the letter C, which does not exist in the Persian language, and their alteration of several important letters.

Almost all Arabic names have meanings, and are derived from a root of three letters, thus from H. M. D. *praise*, is derived Muhammed, *the greatly praised*, consequently the writing of it Mahomet, as is frequently done, destroys the etymology; Amr, signifies *command*, whence Amyr, *Commander*, which should always be written with the first letter of the alphabet, although frequently written *Emir* and *Umeer*; Amyr al Mumenyn, *Commander of the Faithful*, must be in the recollection of every person who has read the Arabian Nights' Entertainments.

* The Tūrky language differs as much from the modern Turkish, as the Saxon does from the English.

Some of the French authors write,

Dragoman	for Terjūmān,	an Interpreter;
Chagān	for Khakān,	an Emperor;
Chacan	for Shegun,	an Omen;

whilst the letters j, y, t and d are constantly interchanged.

The Persian short vowel called *Zubber*, is sounded in Persia as short a, in Turkey as short e, in India as short u, and causes a difference in the pronunciation of the natives of these countries; but as the letter E has six sounds in French, and at least three in English, the variation is not greater than is to be found in the dialects of England, Scotland, and Ireland.

I am aware that it is impossible to fix the pronunciation of any language, but as it is desirable that Translators should observe an uniform system, and the mode suggested by Sir William Jones having failed of success, I venture to propose a more simple one, which will save most of the diacritical points, so troublesome both to the writer and to the reader; viz. that of using such of our consonants as agree with those of the Persian Alphabet.

With respect to the vowels,

let the short e represent the Persian vowel	Zebber.
short i, - - - ,,	Zere.
short u, - - - ,,	Pysh.

Let our ā, ū, and y, represent the corresponding long vowels, alif, vau, and ye, this latter to be generally sounded ee, or as the French i of *Dire*, *Lire*, &c.

Our slender *a* in *Slave*, &c. does not exist in Persian, and the only word in which the open *o* occurs, is in *Koh*, a mountain, therefore probably a misnomer. In Arabic it is formed by the letters *Ain* or *Alif* with the vowel Pysh, as عُمْر *age*; اُمَرا *nobles*. The Arabic K may be sometimes used for C, but as it adds to the number of letters, without an adequate advantage, I think it better omitted.

Note, referred to at page 1. Mr. William Davy went out to India as a Cadet, about the year 1767, and having early applied himself to the study of the Persian language, was selected by Sir Robert Barker, Commander-in-Chief of Bengal, to be his Secretary and Persian Interpreter; in this situation he was in constant habits of associating and transacting business with many of the principal natives, and even with the Great Moghul, or Emperor of Delhy; after a residence of twelve years, he returned to England. When the late Lord Macartney was appointed to the government of Madras, he requested Major Davy to accompany him; they sailed in 1781, but on their arrival found the whole of the Carnatic overrun by the armies of Hyder Aly, and the Major seeing there was no field then open for his abilities, proceeded to Calcutta, and was immediately taken into the family of the Governor General, Warren Hastings, where he employed himself in the duties of his office, the pursuit of his studies, and collecting information.

In the year 1784, he again embarked for England, but died on his passage home; his books and papers were however carefully transmitted to his executors, and by them made over to his son, now Colonel Davy of Tracey Park, near Bath, in whose library, the MS. of which I have undertaken the translation, remained unexamined till last year, when in consequence of my report of it to the Royal Asiatic Society, it was recommended to the Oriental Translation Committee. The following extract of a letter respecting the authenticity of the Institutes, was written by Major Davy, previous to his return to India, and was published with the Preface to that work.

Extract of a Letter from the late Major Davy, to the late Doctor White, Laudian Professor of Arabic in the University of Oxford, dated October 24, 1779.

"The History of Timour, written by himself, carries with it the strongest proofs that he wrote for posterity only; and that he could not, in prudence, or in policy, make his work public during his life: for it contains not only the same accurate detail of the facts and occurrences of his reign, as are found in other authors, but it goes much further. He gives you that which he only had the power to give, the secret springs and motives which influenced his conduct in the various political and military transactions of his life, the arts by which he governed, as well as the power by which he conquered. He acknowledges his weaknesses, honestly owns his errors, describes the difficulties in which he was occasionally involved by those errors, and the policy by which he surmounted and overcame those difficulties. In a word, it is a compleat Index to his head and his heart; and though, take it all in all, it redounds to the honour of both the one and the other, yet it was a work by no means calculated for the perusal of his enemies, or even his subjects during his life; since it would have enabled those who chose it, to combat him with his own weapons, or, in other words, to have turned his arts and his policy against himself. Hence it is reasonable to suppose, that the work in question was entirely unknown during his life; and its subsequent temporary obscurity may, I think, be plausibly accounted for, by the probability of one copy only existing at the time of his death, by the uncertainty into whose hands that copy fell, and by the divisions which followed in his family after the death of Shaahroch.

"Abu Taulib ul Husseini, in the Dedication of his Translation to Sultaun ul Audil, says, that in the library of Jafir, Haukim of Yemmun, he met with a manuscript in the Turki or Mogul language, which, on inspection, proved to be the History of Timour, written by himself; containing an account of his life and actions from the seventh to the seventy-fourth year of his age, &c. &c. He then proceeds to give the Translation of the said History, in which are included the Institutes.

"It may appear remarkable that the Translator should say so little, or in fact nothing, to prove the authenticity of the valuable work, which he was about to translate. It has an extraordinary appearance, I allow; but, I think, the following inferences only can be drawn from it: either that he thought the work itself contained sufficient proofs of its own authenticity, or that at the period when he translated it, it was so well known, as not to admit of doubt, or dispute. For my part, I think his inattention to this point is a very strong, if not the strongest possible proof, that the History and Institutes of Timour are genuine.

"An European critic may say, that this same Abu Taulib might have wrote the work himself in the Persian language, and have imposed it upon the world as a Translation from the Royal Mogul author. This I take to be impossible. Authors in the East neither sold their works to booksellers, nor published by subscription, nor depended for support on the applause, the generosity, or the credulity of the public: they were patronized by Princes, who rewarded their labours in proportion to the value of their works. And therefore, if Abu Taulib had been capable of writing such a work, he never would have been guilty of so dangerous and foolish an artifice, which could tend only to diminish both his fame and his profit. The applause and the reward due to the Translator of an excellent work, must, whatever his merit, be inferior to those which are due to the author of such a work; if therefore he had been master of abilities to write the Life and Institutes of Timour, as there written, he would have spoke in the third person instead of the first (no other alteration being necessary,) and have stood forth as the author of the first and best History of the Life of Timour, that ever was wrote; for which he must have obtained both applause and profit tenfold. The same mode of reasoning will hold good to prove that the *Turki* copy could not be wrote by any *Mogul* author, but him to whom it is ascribed, Timour himself.

"The noble simplicity of diction, the plain and unadorned egotism that runs through the whole of the Institutes and History of Timour, are peculiarities which mark their originality and their antiquity also. The Orientals, for some centuries past, have adopted a very different mode of writing; the best of their historical works are filled with poetical and hyperbolical flowers and flourishes, which are so numerous, and occur so frequently, that many a *folio* volume, weeded and pruned of these superfluities, would be reduced to a very moderate *octavo*.

"The only work bearing the least resemblance to the Life and Institutes of Timour, which has fallen under my observation, is the History (or Commentaries) of Sultaun Babour, written by himself.* Babour was descended from Timour in the fifth degree; he was the son of Omer, the son of Abu Saeed, the son of Mahummud, the son of Meraun Shaah, the son of Timour. About eighty years elapsed between the death of Timour and the birth of Babour. Babour in the twelfth year of his age, and the 899th year of the Hejra, sat upon the throne of his father, in the kingdom of Furgauneh. The earlier part of his life very much resembled that of his great predecessor, Timour: and his abilities in the field and in the cabinet, his fortitude in distress, his activity and courage when

* See Memoirs of Baber, published by William Erskine, Esq. in 1826, the Preface, Introduction, and Notes to which, contain a vast deal of information, and the whole of the work is highly creditable to the learned author.

surrounded with difficulties and danger, and the glory and success with which his enterprizes were finally crowned, make the resemblance between these two Princes still more striking. Like Timour, Babour wrote an accurate History of his own Life and Actions in the *Turki* language; which though by no means equal to the admirable composition of his renowned ancestor, is a work of infinite merit. Yet this history, great as the Royal Author was, remained in obscurity till the middle of the reign of his grandson Acbur, when it was translated into the Persian language by one of his Omrahs, Khaun a Khaunaun. It is more difficult to account for the temporary obscurity of this valuable work, than for that of Timour's; for at the death of Babour it must have fallen into the hands of his son Humaioon, and on his death, into those of Acbur. Yet till the middle of his reign it remained unknown and untranslated: and if Acbur had, in the early part of his life, been driven from his throne, if divisions had taken place in his family, and his posterity had been scattered abroad, this valuable manuscript might have fallen into private hands, and have remained unknown for a century longer; possibly, have been totally lost. No critic, either Oriental or European, pretends to dispute the authenticity of Babour's History; and, as far as I have been able to discover, the learned of the East consider the Institutes and History of Timour as equally genuine.

"I was acquainted with several great and learned men in India, both natives and Persians: on perusing the works of Timour, I was led to make the same enquiry which you have made, whether they were, or were not authentic? The answers I received were always in the affirmative, and attended with some tokens and expressions of surprize, that I should, or could, doubt their being genuine. Shaah Aulum, the present Mogul, has a beautiful copy of the History and Institutes of Timour; which he holds in such esteem, and of which he is so exceedingly careful, that though he granted me the use of any other book in his possession, this he positively excepted by name, as a work so rare and valuable, that he could not trust it to the care of any person whatever.*

"Upon the whole, if the learned of the East, for several generations,

* Times are since altered, and I have now lying before me two authentic transcripts of the Emperor's copy, an account of which will be hereafter given; CHARLES STEWART.

have been induced to give implicit credit to the Institutes and History of Timour, which is certainly the case, I do not see how Europeans can, with any degree of propriety, doubt their authenticity. The Oriental critics have the very best materials on which to form their opinions; our small stock of knowledge in the language, and still smaller stock of Asiatic Historians, render us very incompetent judges of the point in question. There are a great number of Oriental Manuscripts in the libraries of the learned; but I am convinced, that there are still many, very many, which never have found, and possibly never will find, their way into Europe; and therefore, though no *historical* evidence can be produced to prove the authenticity of the works of Timour, yet no one can pretend to say, that such *historical* proofs do not exist. The learned of the East must be the best judges whether they do, or do not merit their belief and veneration; and they have thought proper to bestow upon them both the one and the other. It is much to be regretted, that the Life of Timour, written by himself, is not to be found in Europe: if that, and the Institutes could be translated and published together, such is the accuracy of the narrative, such the importance of the matter, and such the lights that they would mutually reflect on each other, that it would, I conceive, be impossible for any one to read them, without acquiescing in their authenticity from the *internal* evidence alone.*

Yours, most assuredly,

WILLIAM DAVY."

* See also Dr. White's Preface to the Institutes, page 6.

INTRODUCTION.

The extensive region, formerly called Scythia, and now generally denominated Tartary, has been inhabited from a very early period by Nomade nations, who wandered with their flocks and herds from one part of the continent to another, frequently migrating from the shores of the Eastern Ocean, to the midst of Europe, where they were known by the appellation of Goths or Getes, Vandals, Huns, Turks, Tartars, &c.* These nations were subdivided into various tribes and hordes, consisting of from five thousand to seventy thousand families, who took their names from some celebrated chieftain, and were subject to their respective leaders under the title of Khāns (Kings); but when a number of these nations were united under one leader, he assumed the title of Khākān, (Emperor).†

In the tenth century, a person named Tumenāh Khān, whose descent has been traced by the Oriental historians from Noah, commanded a horde of Moghuls then dwelling to the north-west of China, this person had twin sons, Kubel Khān and Kajuly Behader, whom he prevailed on to sign an agreement, that the dignity of *Khān* should continue in the posterity of the former, and that of *Sepah Salar,* Commander-in-Chief, in the descendants of the latter.

From the first of these sons was descended, in the fourth degree, Zingis, called by the Persians, Jengyz Khān, born A. D. 1154, and from the second in the eighth degree, the hero of the following Memoirs, who was born in the district of Kesh, province of Maveralnaher, A. D. 1336.

* An ample detail of all these nations will be found in Gibbon's History of the Decline and Fall of the Roman Empire.

† See printed copy of the Institutes of Timūr, pages 131 and 285: Gibbon following the French orthography, calls him Chagan.

Jengyz or Zingis died in A. D. 1227, having divided his vast dominions between his four sons, called Jūjy or Tūchy, Jagtay, Auktay, and Tūly; to the first of these was assigned the extensive kingdom of Kipchāk or Great Tartary; to the second, Tūrkestān and Maveralnaher, (Transoxiana); to the third, Mughulistān and Northern China; to the fourth, Persia, and that part of India, west of the river Indus. Their descendants reigned over these countries till the time of Timūr, who subdued them all; but as neither Jengyz or Timūr assumed the title of *Khākān*, (Emperor) there probably existed a more ancient and honourable family than either of them.* An ancestor of Timūr, named Kerachār Nuyān, was married to a daughter of Jagtay Khān, second son of Zingis, by which means the two families became doubly connected; in consequence of which, Timūr bore the title of *Gūrgān*, son-in-law of the Khān; it also signifies a great Prince. The continuation of the family history will be given by himself.

P. S. I fear that the number of proper names which occur in this work will tire my readers, but such is the style of Oriental history; the reason assigned for it is, that it may serve as a record of the actions of each chief, and should the author omit any persons, he might be called to account by the heirs. Mirza Abu Talib, who wrote his Travels through Europe, in 1803, apologized to his countrymen for the number of *barbarous* names he was obliged to relate to them, so that the complaint is mutual.

* Since writing the above, I have been informed by one of our best Chinese scholars, that the Mandarins of that country are called *Kwans*, but that the title of Jengyz was *Ching-sze Kho-han*.

MEMOIRS OF TIMŪR.

PREFACE

TO THE PERSIAN TRANSLATION.

In the Name of the most merciful God,

Eternal praise is due to the Almighty, who, through his special favour, said to Adam, Verily we have made thee our vicegerent over the earth;—

He, who fixed the nest of the Phœnix (Ankay) with expanded wings of victory of the everlasting dominion of his Majesty (Timūr) on the pinnacle of the lofty mountain of *Kāf*, commanding the world;—

Boundless thanks be also to the Omnipotent, who has exalted above all the sovereigns of the world the dignity of the *Khelāfet* and the family of the Prophet, in order to disseminate the glorious religion of Muhammed, and renovate the luminous law of *Mustafā*;—

Glory to the Creator, who, having formed the circumference of the heavens, with all the elements, around the axis of the earth, established the circle of supreme sovereignty in the blessed person of his Majesty, confirming the sacred verse of the Korān,

"A just monarch is the Shadow of God, and the guardian of his kingdoms."

The unworthy and sinful Abū Talib al Hussyny represents to those who stand at the foot of the royal throne, that during my residence in the two sacred cities of Mecca and Medina, I saw in the library of Jāfer, Governor (Hākim) of Yemen, a book, in the *Tūrky* language, dictated (mulfuzāt) by his Majesty, who now dwells in paradise, Timūr *Sahib Kerāny,* may God pardon him all his offences, in which are inserted all the occurrences of his life from seven to seventy-one years, and in which he narrates the means by which he had subdued so many countries, and had become the sovereign of so many dominions, in hopes that this book may become an exemplar for posterity, and the cause of promoting religion.

But as the work was written in the Tūrky language interspersed with Arabic, and therefore difficult to be understood, I have translated it from Tūrky into easy Persian, that it may be useful to Princes in administering their affairs and in preserving their authority. Ministers and Generals may also derive great benefit from the perusal of it in conducting the business of Government.

May the Almighty God preserve and protect his Imperial Majesty *Sahib Kerany Sany** (Shāh Jehān) from all the vicissitudes and evils of life, and keep extended over the heads of mankind the Shadow of his Sovereignty and Justice through the (intercession) of the Arabian Prophet, his illustrious descendants, and his beneficent companions.—The Text will be found in Appendix No. I.

* Sahib Kerān, signifies Lord of the Auspicious Conjunction; Sany, the second. Shāh Jehān mounted the throne of Hindūstan, A. H. 1037, A.D. 1628.

MEMOIRS OF TIMŪR.

BOOK I.—TEZŪKĀT.

CHAPTER I.

Be it known to my victorious and fortunate Sons, to my noble and princely Grandsons and others, that,*

Tūrky.

* * * * * * * * *

* * * * * * * * *

I have written my Memoirs in the *Tūrky* language, in order that each and every one of my posterity, who, by the divine aid, and the protection of Muhammed, (upon whom and upon his descendants be the peace of God) shall ascend my Throne and succeed to my Sovereignty, which I obtained by much labour, toil, marches and wars, (having understood them) may put in practice those rules and regulations, by which their Sovereignty and Dominion may be preserved safe from ruin or decay.

N. B. Here follow Books 2d and 3d, being the Institutes and Designs translated by Major Davy and edited by Professor White, 4to. edition, Oxford, A.D. 1783; and which also appear in the French edition of the Institutes, by Monsieur Langlès, Paris, A.D. 1787. In some of the MSS. that I have examined, the Memoirs precede the Institutes, but in Col. Davy's copy they follow them.

* The following two lines are in the ancient Jagtay Tūrky, the words of which are not to be found in Meninski's Dictionary. The lines will be found in Appendix No. 2.

MEMOIRS OF TIMŪR.

BOOK IV.—MULFUZĀT.

CHAPTER I.

Be it known to my fortunate Children, to my intelligent Ministers, to my faithful and zealous Nobles, that Almighty God, on account of the Twelve following Rules, which I have constantly practised, hath conferred greatness on me, and hath made me the Shepherd of his flock, and hath assisted me by his celestial aid so that I have attained the high pre-eminence of Sovereignty;—

1st. Having taken in hand the Scales of Justice, I have neither increased nor decreased (the portion of any one) but weighed equally to all;

2d. I have administered strict justice to mankind and endeavoured to discriminate between truth and falsehood;

3d. I paid obedience to the orders of God and respected his holy laws, and honoured those whom he had honoured;

4th. I had compassion on mankind and conferred benefits on all, and, by these qualities, I gained the affections of God's creatures, nor did I ever vex a single heart by injustice, I never turned away a supplicant from my court, but whoever took refuge with me I assisted;

5th. I ever gave the affairs of religion precedence over worldly affairs. I first performed my duty towards God and then attended to my worldly concerns;

6th. I always spoke the truth, and ever listened to the truth, and with sincerity performed my religious and secular duties, and avoided the paths of crookedness. For I have heard that, when God created Adam, the Angels said to each other, "a creature has been formed whose posterity will be liars, breakers of their promise, and guilty of wickedness." The Lord said to the Angels, I will send a Sword among them, which shall cut in pieces every perverse or unrighteous person it encounters, as I have heard that the Sword there meant is (the power of) Princes, it is therefore incumbent on every Monarch to speak and listen only to truth;

7th. I have always performed whatever I promised to any person, nor ever deviated from my agreement. I was never guilty of Tyranny nor Injustice, nor ever permitted myself to fall into vice or infamy, nor, on any occasion, did I cut the cord of affection due to my children, grand-children, relations, or connexions;

8th. I considered myself as the Treasurer of the property of God, and never expended any of his sacred property without the sanction of his deputies (the clergy). In collecting the revenues from his servants, I observed lenity and discretion, nor did I ever take the wealth or possessions of any person unjustly, neither did I employ myself in accumulating riches or substance, but ever looked to the welfare and happiness of my soldiers and subjects: thus I did not touch the accumulations of my Father's nobles, nor was I covetous of the property of any person; for it is known to me, by experience, that Amyr Hussyn having cast the eyes of covetousness upon the property of his soldiers and subjects, and seized upon the wealth of his Father's nobles, his prosperity was soon annihilated;

9th. I considered obedience to God as consisting in submission to his prophet, and therefore acted according to the Law of Muhammed, and did nothing contrary to that sacred code: I always considered the Descendants of Muhammed (on whom be the peace of God) and the companions of his Holiness as my friends, and performed to them the duties of affection;

10th. I gave currency to the faith of Islam through all my dominions, and supported religion, by which means I gave stability to my Government;—for I had heard that Church and State are twins, and that every Sovereignty that is not supported by religion soon loses all authority, and its orders are not obeyed, but that every person, worthy or unworthy, presumes to meddle therewith;

11th. I gave free admission to the *Syeds*,* to the learned, and to the prelates of religion, and always treated them with great respect, and never turned any of them away from my court, so that they constantly attended my assemblies, and induced the people to pray for my prosperity; I constantly associated with the learned and religious, and heard from them many anecdotes, both of sacred and profane history;

Thus they related to me that the King of Constantinople, once invaded the dominions of the King of Ry, but having heard that his Court was attended by numbers of Syeds, and many learned and devout personages, he refrained from subduing his country, but wrote to the Ministers and Nobles, "I have read in the Heavenly books, that whatever Court is attended by learned, devout, and religious persons, that Government cannot be overturned, and having been

* Descendants of Muhammed.

informed that such is the case of your country, I am convinced it cannot be subdued." He also wrote to the King, "Whereas I have discovered that your disposition resembles that of our former just Monarchs, I have not injured your country, but having withdrawn my army, have ceased from attacking you. Farewell."

12th. I asked the blessings of the Hermits, of the other inspired and holy persons, and besought their prayers; I also protected the Anchorets and the Dervishes, I never vexed them, but captivated their hearts; I exerted myself in arranging the affairs of the Musselmāns, and avoided killing any of their people; I paid particular respect to the descendants of the Prophet, and was cautious never to degrade or injure any of that noble race; I also shunned the discourse of the wicked and ungodly;

For I had heard that when God elects a person to the government of a country, and places in his hands the reins of authority over mankind, in order that he may rule them with justice, if he conducts himself with equity and propriety, his kingdom endures, but if on the contrary, he is guilty of injustice and tyranny, and commits unlawful actions, the Lord renders him childless, and takes away his Dominion and Sovereignty, to give them to another;—

Wherefore in order to preserve my Sovereignty, I took Justice in one hand, and Equity in the other hand, and, by the light of these two lamps, I kept the palace of Royalty illuminated;—

As I had heard that just Kings are the Shadow of God, and that the best King is he who imitates the disposition of the Lord, in forgiving sinners, I followed the examples of those just Kings, and forgave my enemies.

CHAPTER II.

I appointed four righteous Ministers to govern my dominions, the first of these was the praiseworthy Mahmūd, commonly called the *Meteor of Khorasān*, the next was Nasir Addeen; I gave them positive orders that they were never to advise me to do any thing that was unjust, that they themselves should never deviate from the path of rectitude, nor mis-represent evil for good, that they should always tell me the truth, and never deceive me by falsehood, and that they should not pry into the wealth and property of my subjects.

For I had been informed that whenever God Almighty exalts any person to the throne of Sovereignty, he confers on him special dignity and wisdom, by means of which he renders mankind obedient to him, this virtue is a ray of the Grace of God which shines on the Monarch, and as long as he is grateful for that favour, his fortune and dominion continue to increase.

Thus when I reviewed my army in the plains of Anatolia, and found that it extended fifteen miles in length, I considered that this innumerable host were all obedient to me, and returned thanks to God, for having made so many of his creatures subservient to my will, although but a weak mortal like themselves.

When I mentioned this subject to the learned of my court, they said, the Grace of God has thrown on you a Divine ray, which is called "the Shadow of God," as the Prophet hath said, "a just King is the shadow of God," by means of which shadow a just Monarch keeps mankind in subjection, and from the dread of that shadow, the people are obedient, and his power and authority become current over the empire; wherefore as long I have been seated on the throne of Sovereignty, I have been ever grateful for that favour, and have constantly paid respect to the orders of God, by shewing kindness to his creatures, and have always conducted myself with equity and justice.

In consequence of this determination, when I had reached my twenty-first year, I resigned the guidance of my conscience into the hands of the Pole star of religion, Shaik Zyn Addeen Abu Beker, *Tatyabady*, upon which occasion he bound round my loins his own shawl-girdle, he then placed his *own* cap on my head, and put on my finger a ruby ring, on which was engraved, (Rāsty va Rūsty) Righteousness and Salvation, and said, "the aurora of your good fortune will shortly dawn, for I have seen by inspiration, that in obedience to the orders of the chief of the descendants of the Prophet (Aly) a man of God will become your tutelar Saint, it is not convenient that you should *now* see him, but, the time will come, when he shall see you, and you shall see him." Thus when I was seventy years of age, and was returning in A. H. 806, from the conquest of Anatolia, I paid my respects to the Kutb al Aārifyn, (Pole star of Wisdom), Shaikh Sudder Addeen Ardebelly,* and having begged his blessing, requested that he would allow one of his disciples to accompany me, to be my spiritual guide; he replied, "in the Mountain of *Salaran*, there is a fountain, the water of which is sometimes cold, sometimes warm, go thither, and the first person that shall come there to perform his ablutions, and say his prayers, will be your guide:" in compliance with the commands of the Shaikh, I went up to the fountain, performed my ablutions, and having said my prayers, waited with anxiety to see who should come; to my great surprise, the first person who came to the fountain in the morning, made his ablutions and prayed, was my Head Groom, (Myr Akhūr);

* See Appendix IV.

the second and third day, the same circumstances were repeated, I was astonished and said to myself, surely the Shaikh has made a mistake, but addressing myself to the man, I said, " O Syed, I have hitherto considered you as one of my inferior servants, how is it that you have attained this dignity and honour;" he replied, by order of the *Kutb al Aktab*, (Star of Stars), even from the very commencement of your Sovereignty, I have been the firm supporter of your government; he then began to say his prayers, in which I joined him; during this religious act, I experienced both delight and inspiration. When we had finished our prayers, he said, " O Prince you are at this moment the Guest of God, whatever the guest asks of his host, is gratuitously given;" accordingly I wished for Faith, he replied, " the faith in Muhammed is eternal;' it is a city where those who encompass it proclaim, ' there is no God but God,' and those in the interior reply, ' it is known there is no God but God;' That city is the Gate of Gates, and those who enter or come forth from it, are constantly repeating those words;" at this time I bent down my head in prostration, when I again raised my head, I saw that my companion had resigned his soul to his Creator; I was much affected. When I reported the circumstances I had seen to the Shaikh, he replied, " the arrangement of the affairs of every country, and the power of placing and displacing of Monarchs, with the bestowing of Kingdoms on the Worthy, and taking them from the Unworthy, is in the hands of the True Worshippers, who are the Agents of God; every country has its peculiar Guardian, or Patron Saint, appointed by the *Kutb al Áktab*, whilst the Guardian supports the Monarch, the country flourishes, but otherwise it falls to decay:* as long as the Guardian exists, the State prospers, but whenever he is withdrawn it declines, and if another Patron is not appointed in his stead, that dominion is shortly subverted." The Shaikh continued, " the Man of God, who had charge of the Kingdom of *Kyser*,† died this year, on which account you have been easily victorious over him." I considered this was a warning, that my turn would soon come, but as I had still hopes that another Patron would be appointed in the room of my deceased saint, I made an offering to the Shaikh of four thousand captives, natives of that country, (Rūm)‡ in order to supplicate his intercession.

* The Shaikh must have received some imperfect information of the Patron Saints of Europe, unless the invention is Asiatic, but I fear this passage will be thought very obscure.

† *Cæsar*, being the title assumed by Bajazet and other Ottoman Emperors.

‡ See Appendix IV.

CHAPTER III.

In the year 771, A. H. (A. D. 1378), when I had driven the Jetes* out of Tūran, and mounted the throne (of Tartary), and had directed the royal proclamation *(Khutbeh)* to be read from all the pulpits, the Syeds, the learned, the prelates, the rich, and the poor, all raised their hands (to heaven) in prayer for my prosperity; but Khuajē Abyd, who was the most celebrated prelate of that time, forbade them to pray for me, saying, " do not pray for this murderer and blood-thirsty Tūrk, who has put to death an innumerable number of Musselmāns, nor repeat blessings on him." On that very night the Khuajē dreamt that he saw me standing in the presence of his Holiness the Prophet, that he entered, and several times made his obedience to Muhammed, without his salutation being returned, at length he called out, " O Messenger of God, do you permit this wretch Timūr, who has murdered hundreds of thousands of your followers, and who has destroyed the habitations of so many Mūsselmāns, to stand near you, whilst you do not return the salutation of me who am the zealous supporter of your religion, and the establisher of your law?" his Holiness replied to him in an angry manner, " although Timūr has shed much of the blood of my followers, as he has been the friend, the supporter, and respecter of my posterity and descendants, why dost thou forbid the people to pray for and bless him?" The Khuajē having awoke, came even during the night to me, and asked pardon: when this intelligence reached the people, they all raised their hands in prayer for my prosperity, and, considering me as supported by the Divine favour, bore witness to my right: in gratitude for this favour, I day by day shewed more respect, attention, and affection to the descendants of Muhammed, and esteemed myself as the elect of God.

Another circumstance which confirmed me in my opinion, that I had the Divine support, occurred in the year 804, when I invaded the country of Anatolia with four hundred thousand cavalry, and Bayazid had drawn out his army to oppose me; whilst I was reviewing my forces, a party of three hundred of the Arabs of Irāc, and Syeds of Kerbela and Nejef, commanded by Syed Muhammed Miftah, came to my assistance, I ordered them to be admitted, considering their coming as an auspicious omen, and a proof of the Divine aid. Syed Muhammed, who was also the standard bearer, advanced and said, " the fourth Khalif (Aly) appeared to me in a dream, and said to me, carry my white standard to the young Tūrk:" having consulted the principal persons of Nejef, they agreed that,

* The Translator has sometimes made use of the name Uzbek, by anticipation.

"you the Prince Timūr, who have just invaded this country, are the person meant." I returned thanks to God for this special favour, and commanded that the history of the white standard should be recorded in the Royal Journals.

Soon after this, Aykē-Timūr having come near me, called out, "may the victory be propitious;" I took the word *Victory* as an omen, and gave him charge of the white standard, with orders to go and commence hostilities: on seeing the white standard, he was much affected, and set out to comply with my commands.

Another of the omens which afforded me much pleasure was this, when Tugleck Timūr Khān, the descendant of Jengyz Khān, the first time he invaded Maveralnaher, and had crossed the Sihūn (Jaxartes), summoned all the chiefs to meet him. Hajy Berlas was afraid, and preferred emigration to remaining, therefore set out for Khorasān. I was also divided in my opinion what I should do, I therefore wrote to my Counsellor (Peer) for his advice, whether I should go and meet Tugleck Timūr, or, having collected all my horde and tribe, proceed to Khorasān. He wrote me this answer:

"It was asked of the fourth Khalif Aly, 'if the heavens were bows, and the "earths the strings of those bows, and calamities were the arrows, and mankind "the butt of those arrows, and the archer should be God, to whom ought mankind to flee for succour, the Khalif replied, that they should flee to God.' It is "therefore your business to advance towards Tugleck Timūr, to embrace him, "and to pluck the bow and arrow from his arms. Farewell."*

From this letter I received much consolation, and I went and met Tugleck Timūr on the banks of the Khojend river; he was much rejoiced at my coming; he made me one of his counsellors, employed me and consulted me on all occasions, until he received intelligence that his chiefs had raised the standard of rebellion in the Desht Kipchāk,† on this subject he consulted me, whether he should go himself to quell them, or should send another army to do so; I said to him, "in your going there is only one danger, but in sending, there are two, the wise man is he who chooses the lesser danger;" hereon he praised me exceedingly: again he consulted me respecting the government of Maveralnaher, I said to him, "your government resembles a tent, let the poles thereof be made of the wood of equity, and let the rope pins be firmly fixed in the ground of justice, so that every person, who enters the tent, may pass out in safety."

"Act kindly to the Syeds, the learned, and the prelates of that country, and preserve the people under the shadow of your justice, do good to the good, and

* See first Design, page 15, Davy's Institutes and Sequel.

† An extensive region situated to the north of the Caspian Sea, bounded on the west by the Volga.

use policy with the bad, so that you may restrain the soldiers in the bonds of kindness."

But he disgusted his chiefs by confiscating the property they had collected from the people of Maveralnaher, and compelling them to pay it into his treasury; he consulted me again on this occasion, I told him "that the minds of the Tūrks were narrow like their eyes, that it was requisite to satiate them in order to gain their attachment, and to tie up their tongues."

As he much approved of my advice, he set out for the Desht Kipchāk, in order to quell the rebels, and left me in charge of Maveralnaher: he further wrote an agreement, stating that he had divided the kingdom with me in a brotherly manner, but this was a mere pretence to keep me quiet while he was engaged with the rebels.*

CHAPTER IV.

Another of the auspicious omens predicting my future greatness, was this: in a dream I saw the Prophet Muhammed, "on whom be the Grace of God," who congratulated me and said, "in consequence of the support you have given to my descendants, the Almighty has decreed that seventy-two of your posterity shall sit on the throne of Sovereignty." When I awoke, I wrote all the particulars of this dream to my *Peer*, he replied by letter, "I congratulate you on this "dream, your having seen the Prophet, (on whom be the grace of God) proves "that you will certainly obtain numerous victories, and that many happy con-"sequences will arise from this dream." As the Emperor Subuktageen, in "consequence of his pity to a doe, (whose fawn he had caught and released) "was honoured by a vision of the Prophet, who said to him, 'in recompense of "the pity that you this day shewed to the animal, the Almighty will bestow "sovereignty on your posterity for many generations;' how much more so will "he bestow on you, who through compassion to the Syeds and other inhabi-"tants of Maveralnaher, have delivered them from the cruel hands and slavery "of the Jetes; doubtless your descendants shall reign for seventy-two gene-"rations." To elucidate the circumstance, it becomes requisite to mention, that, when Tugleck Timūr Khān invaded Maveralnaher a second time, he sent me a friendly invitation, I therefore went to meet him, but he broke his promise (of confirming me as Governor of the province), and gave the country to his son Alyas Khuajē, and made me his Commander in Chief (Sepah Salar); but when he saw that I was dissatisfied, he produced the agreement engraven

* See first Design, Institutes.

on steel, between my ancestor Kajuly Behader and Kubyl Khān, wherein it was stipulated that the dignity of *Khān* should for ever continue in the posterity of Kubyl Khān, and that of Sepah Salar with the descendants of Kajuly Behader, and that they should never oppose each other;* when this agreement was read to me, in order to comply with its contents, I accepted the appointment of Commander in Chief; but as Alyas Khuajē had no talents for governing, and permitted his soldiers to extend the hand of rapine, the inhabitants of Maveralnaher came to me, and complained that the Jetes† had carried off nearly one thousand of their virgin daughters from Samerkand and its neighbourhood, and that the orders of Alyas Khuajē were not listened to by his followers; again a number of the Syeds of Termuz came and complained to me, that the Tūrkish soldiers had carried into captivity seventy of their brethren and children, all descendants of the Prophet (on whom be the grace of God): on hearing of this my honour was roused, I pursued the plunderers, defeated them, and recovered the captives; on this account the Jetes bound up the loins of animosity against me, and carried their complaints to Tugleck Timūr Khān, and wrote to him that I had raised the standard of rebellion, in consequence of which he issued an edict for putting me to death, which edict fell into my hands; it was at this time that I had the dream above mentioned.

Another happy omen was this, my *Peer*‡ wrote to me, he had seen in a vision, that the Almighty had appointed me his treasurer, and that the keys of the treasury would be consigned to me by his Vizier Mustafā; this good news exalted my ideas, and induced me to expect success from fate.

Another time when I was very much annoyed by the oppressions of the Jetes, and knew not what to do, I received the following letter from my *Peer*.

" The supported of the Lord, may God continue to protect him; I have seen " in a vision, the messenger of the Lord of all worlds, who has promised to make " you his vicegerent, and support you, and therefore be not afraid, nor despond, " for he is with you."

I was much rejoiced by this letter, and became strong of heart, although I was in daily expectation of the arrival of Tugleck Timūr's edict to put me to death; and when the edict did arrive, (the Saint) Amyr Kelan, sent me this verse of the traditions of the Prophet, " Flight is proper for him who has not the power to oppose." I therefore fled to Khuarizm, with sixty horsemen, and wrote a description of my situation to my *Peer*, and received the following answer to my letter; " may God protect Abul Munsūr Timūr; let him lay down these four

* See second Design, Institutes, page 25. † See Note to page 9.

‡ See Zyn Addeen (ornament of religion), page 7.

" rules for his conduct, that with the arm of magnanimity he may be successful
" and prosperous through life, as is recorded in the traditions.

" 1st. Be determined in whatever you undertake, place your undertakings
" on faith in God, and do not relax your exertions.

" 2nd. Invest yourself with the robe of honour, and permit not fornication or
" adultery to be committed in your dominion: It is related that a Crane once saw
" in her nest, a young Raven associating with her young ones, and for several
" days and nights she permitted it to remain, at length a number of Cranes col-
" lected and tore the owner of the nest to pieces with their beaks and claws: the
" honour of a man should far exceed that of birds, especially that of Princes,
" which should ever protect the respectability and reputation of their subjects.

" 3rd. Do not neglect consultation, prudence, and caution, for every dominion
" which is void of these is soon overturned.

" 4th. It is a tradition of the illustrious Khalifs, that stability is better than
" perturbation, therefore endue yourself with bravery and magnanimity;—grace
" be with him who follows the true direction."*

Another presage of my good fortune was this, a celebrated Astrologer waited on me, and delivered a plan of my Horoscope, stating that at the time of my birth, the planets were in so favourable and auspicious conjunction as certainly to predict the stability and duration of my good fortune and Sovereignty; that I should be superior to all the Monarchs of the age; that whoever were my enemies should be subdued, and whoever were my friends should be prosperous; that I should be the protector of religion, the destroyer of idols, the father of my people; that my descendants should reign for many generations, and that they should be prosperous as long as they continued to support the Muhammedan religion, but if they should deviate therefrom, their dominion would soon be annihilated.

CHAPTER V.

About this time I also had an extraordinary dream, I thought I was seated on the sea-shore, and that I had in my hands a large net, which I dexterously threw, and caught a number of crocodiles and other large fish; this dream I interpreted thus, that the net was my dominion, which shall spread over the face of the globe, and that all mankind will become subject to me.†

* Here he relates another instance of his good fortune, in escaping from Aly Beg, which appears in the History.. See page 37 of the Institutes, therefore omitted here.

† Two other Anecdotes have been passed over, as they will again occur in the History.

Another circumstance which strengthened my faith in the Divine aid, was this; at the time that I approached the Jete army, under Alyas Khuajē, and had drawn up my own forces, and put on my armour, whilst I was considering the plan of the battle, the hour for prayer arrived; after having made my devotions, I again looked at the plan of the battle, and then lay down on the spot where I had said my prayers; soon after, I dreamt that I heard a voice say, "Timūr, victory and success is thine:" when I awoke, I could not see any body, nor were there any of my servants or attendants near, I was therefore convinced that the voice was the voice of an angel, (Hatif Ghyb) or invisible spirit, which I had heard, and in gratitude, prostrated myself, and returned thanks to God.

From amongst the encouraging circumstances that occurred, was this; at the period that I invaded Fars, Shāh Munsūr came unexpectedly on me with five thousand horse, I called out for a spear, but none of my attendants were in readiness; suddenly I saw a Spearman in the form and dress of an Arab at my side, who gave into my hand a lance, and said, "O God assist Timūr," at this instant Shāh Munsūr fell from his horse, and (my son) Shāh Rūkh came up with him and wounded him. When I made inquiry for the Arab, he was no where to be found, but I subdued the province of Fars.

Another extraordinary event was this, at the time that I dispossessed the Ruler (Vạly) of Balkh of his country, my Peer wrote to me, "may the victorious Timūr consider this note as auspicious; the Guardian Angel of Khorasān has given the key of that country into your hands, it is requisite that you shall deliver that province from the injustice of Sultān Ghyās Addeen." I was rejoiced by this intelligence, and immediately set out for Khorasān, and having crossed the Jihun, I subdued Ghyās Addeen, and took all his stores and treasures.

Another of the proofs of Divine aid which I received, was this, Syed Mahmūd *Gēsūderāz** waited on me, and congratulated me that Amyr Syed Aly Hamdāny (another Saint) had deputed him to tell me, that the Holy Prophet had taken me under his care and protection, in order that I might propagate the faith of Islam in the extensive region of India: on receipt of this message, I bound up my loins in the service of Amyr Syed Aly, because previous to this time while I was at Samerkand, he had used very harsh expressions towards me, which had very much affected me, but for which he afterwards apologized. I was however afraid that he was still incensed against me, till I received this message, when I was convinced that these people (the Saints) do not harbour malice, I therefore recovered my spirits.

Soon after this notice, I began to destroy the temples of India, and to give

* See Appendix V.

currency to the Muhammedan religion in that country; when I destroyed the temple of *Kukel*, which was one of the greatest in that region, I broke the images with my own hands, previous to which the Brahmans brought me several loads of gold, and requested me to spare their gods; I said to them, "I will break your gods, to give them an opportunity of performing a miracle by healing themselves." Amongst the images, was one the size of a man, which they begged me not to break, and even threatened me with his vengeance, saying, "amongst the miracles, which the original of this performed, was, his getting sixteen hundred women with child in one night." I replied, "the cursed Satan debauches several thousands of persons in a very short period, therefore this miracle is of no weight."

Another extraordinary circumstance was this; whenever I undertook any thing, I cared not whether it was deemed a lucky or an unlucky hour, but placing my faith on God, I commenced it, yet the Astrologers always affirmed that whatever I had undertaken, the hour had been propitious for the event.

CHAPTER VI.

Another very encouraging presage, was this; when Tugleck Timūr Khān advanced into Maveralnaher, I was doubtful whether I should go and meet him; I dreamt that a Falcon came and sat on my hand, and a number of cattle gathered around me;* among the cattle was a Lion, which I seized, and put a collar on him: the interpretation of this dream was thus explained; viz. The Falcon was the emblem of good fortune and sovereignty, the cattle signified abundance and prosperity, the Lion typified the Monarch, on whom I should place the collar, and subdue him; being thus encouraged, I went and met Tugleck Timūr Khān.†

When I invaded Fars, I saw in a dream, that a number of bottles of wine had been presented me, and that I broke them in pieces with my sword, by which means I much injured the sword; the interpretation of this dream was, that I should suffer some misfortune. It was shortly after this that Shāh Munsūr attacked me suddenly with five thousand horse, and although I completely defeated him, nevertheless at that time my troops were defeated in the desert, by

* The late Tippoo Sultān probably took the idea of his dreams from this work. See the Sultān's Letters published by Colonel Kirkpatrick in 1811.

† He here relates two other dreams respecting his brother-in-law, Amyr Hussyn, and Tukel Behardur, the circumstances of which belong to the History, and will be related.

Tucktumush Khān, who forgetting my kindness to him, and my raising him to be King of the *Desht Kipchāk,* had watched his opportunity, and attacked me with an army as numerous as the drops of rain; I therefore wrote to him, "Whoever returns evil for good, must be a bastard, and will certainly receive his reward; when you fled from Aurūs Khān, did I not give you an asylum, I released you and made you King of the *Desht:* as you have not been sensible of my kindness, but have taken this opportunity to attack me, be assured you shall suffer for your bad intentions."

About this period I dreamed, that the sun arose in the east, and having ascended over my head, became suddenly eclipsed, it then retrograded and sunk in the east: the interpretation of this dream was, that Tucktumush Khān was typified by the sun, that he should advance against me, that he should be defeated, and compelled to retreat by the same road he came; thus it was that Tucktumush Khān came against me with a numerous army, but my troops attacked him with the fierceness of lions, and destroyed them, by which means the tribe of *Jujy* were plundered and put to shameful flight, and I returned successful and victorious.*

When I was about to invade Arabian Irāc, I dreamed that I had entered a valley, in which I saw a number of lions, that they came close to me, and in fact surrounded me: afterwards when I entered that country, I found that the inhabitants of it, although Arabs by descent, had very much the features of lions; they however brought me valuable presents, and I subdued the kingdom of Irāc Arab.

When I was about to invade Hindūstan, and my chiefs, by their backwardness, rendered me doubtful whether I should proceed; I dreamt that I was in a large garden, and saw a number of people who were pruning the trees, and sowing seeds; that the garden was full of trees, both great and small, on the tops of which the birds had built their nests; I thought that I had a sling in my hand, and that I destroyed the nests with stones from the sling, and drove away all the birds: this dream was realised when I took that country, by my expelling all the Sultāns, and taking possession of the kingdom.

Again, when I invaded Syria, the armies of Egypt and Constantinople both joined the Syrians, on which occasion my nobles came to me, and said in a desponding manner, "to contend with three nations, and to defeat three armies, requires a greater force than we have;" I was then engaged in prayer, and soon after having fallen asleep, I dreamt that I ascended a mountain, and that when

* Jujy, called also Tucky, the eldest son of Jengyz Khān, died six months before his father, but his sons obtained the kingdom of Kipchāk, as their portion of his dominions.

I arrived at the top, I was overwhelmed in black and white clouds, and caught in a whirlwind of dust, this was succeeded by a heavy shower of rain, which soon laid the dust; the learned of my court expounded the dream in this manner; viz. "The mountain is the kingdom of Syria, the black and white clouds are the armies of Egypt and Syria, the rain is the army of your Majesty, which will shortly annihilate your enemies, and settle all these disturbances." I placed much faith in my dream, persevered in my intentions, and shortly defeated the armies of Syria and of Egypt, and was successful and victorious. Again when the *Kyser Bayazid* (Bajazet) advanced against me with four hundred thousand warriors, and the shouts of the *Rūmians* were excessive, I addressed myself to the Prophet and his descendants, and employed myself in prayer that night; I dreamt that I was travelling through a wilderness, and that I saw a number of people on all sides, at this time I observed a great light, which seemed attached to the horizon of the heavens; I went towards the light, but was interrupted by three mounds of earth, which fell before me, and from which there arose a great smoke; I also saw five persons, who having taken the hands of each other, proceeded before me; from seeing these persons, I felt a degree of awe and dread, and I heard some one say, this is the Prophet who is going with his friends to heaven; upon which I hastened, and having overtaken them, made my obeisance to Muhammed, "upon whom and upon his descendants be the grace of God." The prophet made a sign to one of his four companions who had a club in his hand, to give it me; when I took it in my hand, it became very long; when I awoke from my sleep, I found myself exalted and exhilirated by this dream, and became strong of heart, as if I had been strengthened and aided by the *white standard* of Aly; and it was in consequence of this dream that I was enabled to take from the *Kyser* the kingdom of Rūm.

After this, when I called to mind the toils and labours I had undergone, in subduing so many countries of the world by the arm of courage, I considered whether it was likely that my good fortune and sovereignty should endure, and was anxious to discover which of my sons or descendants, the Almighty would place upon my throne, in order to preserve my fame and glory: shortly after this I saw in a dream the Prophet of God, who told me "that *seventy-two* persons of my descendants should be rulers of the earth."

Still I was anxious on this subject, till I saw in a dream, that I was sitting under a shady tree, having innumerable branches and leaves, the top of which reached to the heavens; from the leaves and branches of this tree, there fell, like a heavy shower of rain, various kinds of fruit, immediately all sorts of reptiles, birds, cattle, and other animals, surrounded the tree, and voraciously began eating the fruit; afterwards they violently attacked each other with their claws and beaks; when I had tasted the different kinds of fruit, I found some of them sweet, some sour, some bitter, some insipid, at this time I heard a voice proclaim, "this is the tree which you yourself have planted;" when I awoke, the interpreters expounded the dream thus, "you are the tree, the leaves and branches are your posterity, who shall be the supporters of your state and sovereignty, and will benefit mankind by their benevolence."

CHAPTER VII.

Another time when I had reflected on the past, I repented and was ashamed of many of my doings and sayings, and soon after dreamt that I was sitting in a desert, overgrown with thorns and thistles, and that I was surrounded by dogs, hogs, demons, men and women with frightful and horrid countenances; I was so terrified by their appearance that I awoke, and was so much impressed by this dream, that I wrote the circumstance to my *Peer*,* and received from him the following answer, "that which you saw in a dream was the representation of "your vices and evil actions, such as tyranny, passion, lust, injuring the creatures of God, avarice, covetousness, envy, and pride, which are all of the worst "quality; therefore change your habits, and you will receive the reward of good "actions and virtuous morals." In consequence of this advice, from that time I refrained from injuring mankind, and from all enmity and strife.

Another time I dreamt that I entered a garden filled with flowers and odoriferous herbs, in it were also many fruit trees, and running streams, it was inhabited by beautiful young persons and charming songsters, also by handsome boys and girls, all of whom came and paid their respects to me; I was much delighted with them, and so pleased with my dream, that I again wrote all the particulars to my *Peer*, who wrote me in answer, "return thanks to God, for "the Almighty has shewn you the representation of your good actions and virtuous deeds, and know that the Prophet (on whom be peace) hath said 'every "man at his birth has two devils in attendance;' I also had them, but by the "grace of God, I have subdued them; it is therefore incumbent on every man "to imitate the conduct of the Holy Prophet, and endeavour to subdue his "animal and brutal passions, and invest himself with good qualities and praiseworthy morals, by which he may attain eternal felicity. Farewell."

At the time that I determined on a holy war against the unbelievers of China (Khāta), and having made my preparations, and marched from Samerkund, I

* Spiritual Counsellor.

became doubtful whether my life would last the accomplishment of this design, and whether I should proceed on this sacred expedition, or relinquish it; I dreamt that I had climbed a high tree, and that I was sitting on one of its numerous branches, when the branch broke, and I fell to the ground; I also thought that I was carrying a pitcher of wine on my head, and was going along the road, suddenly the pitcher fell from my head and was broken, and the wine spilt; I then thought that my Father Teragay took me by the hand, and led me into a meadow, and having left me there, went away; the interpreters expounded this dream in a manner that was not satisfactory, I, therefore, resigned myself to the decrees of Providence.

Also about this time, I dreamt that I was in a frightful desert, and that I was quite alone, but that after travelling some distance, I came to a green plain, in the midst of which was a garden; I entered the garden and found it delightful, it contained fountains and rivulets of pure water, and trees inhabited by sweet singing birds; in the middle of the garden I saw a lofty palace, and a stately looking man was seated on a throne in the hall of the palace, and on his right and left hands stood numerous attendants, and they had in their hands, papers and pens, and several volumes were lying before them; I asked what is this man writing, I was answered, in these volumes the destiny and period of life of all mankind is written; I wished to inquire how long I had to live, and what was to be my destiny, but I awoke from my dream.

At the time I invaded the province of Fars, the people of Shirāz took part with Shāh Munsūr, and having joined him, put my Governor (Hakim) to death, I therefore gave orders for a general massacre of the inhabitants of Shirāz, on which, the very religious Syed Abul Ishāk waited on me, and requested that I would cancel the cruel order, I however would not listen to the request of the Syed; that very night I dreamt that I saw the Prophet, (upon whom be the grace of God), who frowned on me and said, "one of my posterity came to your court and interceded for a number of culprits, why did you not attend to his petition, that I might have interceded for you at the court of the Almighty;" when I awoke, I perceived my error, and immediately mounting my horse, I rode to the residence of the Syed, and begged his pardon; I also put an immediate stop to the slaughter, and ordered that Shirāz should in future be annexed to the royal exchequer, and an annual allowance made to several of the inhabitants; and I also bestowed on Khuajē Mahmūd, the district of Mehrjān, and conferred a title on him; I then made a vow that I would never again reject the petition of a Syed, that I would never be deficient in respect to them, but that I would always do honour to the descendants of Muhammed, and the companions of his

Holiness; that being convinced of the obligation of aiding and befriending them, I would more and more extend my favour towards them.

I communicated all these circumstances to my *Peer*, who immediately wrote on the margin of my letter, "may God grant all thy desires, and may this lesson "prove auspicious to the posterity of the Prophet, through the intercession of "Muhammed and the Divine grace; in obedience to the orders of God, and "for his sake, you must befriend this class; do you not see that by honouring "and respecting them, you draw down blessings on your own posterity, and as "long as the conduct of the latter shall be proper, they may hope for aid in "this world and the next; let your kindness to them increase and increase; sal-"vation to him who follows the true guidance."

But of all the presages of my future greatness, that which gave me the most pleasure, and confidence in the Divine aid, was a circumstance that my Father Teragay told me, he said, "sometime previous to your birth, I dreamt that a person of a luminous countenance, resembling, in figure and dress, an Arabian, presented me with a naked scymitar, with which when I began to fence, there issued from it numerous sparks which illuminated the whole earth, after which there spouted from my hand a *jet d'eau*, which threw the water into the air, and which fell in large drops on the ground; the interpreters being consulted, thus expounded my dream; of your sons, one will be a world-subduing sword, who will purify the earth from the defilement (of idolatry), and spread the true religion over the face of the globe, and will generally benefit mankind, and his descendants and posterity shall be numerous."

This omen rejoiced me extremely; I was convinced that Sovereignty was written in the page of my destiny, but resolved to be contented with whatever of good or evil might occur to me, and to be satisfied with the decrees of Providence.

MEMOIRS OF TIMŪR.

BOOK V.

COMMENCEMENT OF THE HISTORY.

CHAPTER I.

My Father Teragay related to me the following circumstance relative to my name, "soon after your birth, I took your virtuous mother to pay our respects "to the celebrated Saint Shaikh Shems Addeen, when we entered his apartment, "he was reading aloud the 67th Chapter of the Korān, and was repeating this "verse; 'Are you sure that he who dwelleth in heaven, will not cause the earth "to swallow you up, and behold *it shall shake*," (Tamurū). The Shaikh then stopt and said, "we have named your son, Timūr." *

I was much delighted by this anecdote, and returned thanks to God that my name was taken from the sacred volume; it was also a great inducement for me to learn that chapter by heart.

When I had attained my seventh year, my father took me by the hand, and led me to the school, where he placed me under charge of Mullā Aly Beg, the Mullā having written the Arabic alphabet on a plank, placed it before me, I was much delighted with it, and considered the copying of it as an amusement.

When I reached my ninth year, they taught me the daily service of the Mosque, during which I always read the 91st Chapter, denominated the *Sun*.

While seated in the school-room, I always took the chief seat, and often fancied myself the commander of all the other boys. One day a subject of conversation was started, on which was the best mode of sitting, each boy gave some answer to the question, when it came to my turn, I said, the best mode of sitting is on the knees, for Muhammed has commanded, "whilst in prayer sit on your knees;" on which all the spectators praised me exceedingly. When we came out from school, we began to play as children, but I assuming the command, stood upon a high mound, and having divided them into two armies, caused them to fight a sham battle, and when I saw one of the parties worsted, I sent them assistance.

* See Appendix VI. also Sale's Translation of the Korān, page 437.

At twelve years of age, I fancied that I perceived in myself all the signs of greatness and wisdom, and whoever came to visit me, I received with great hauteur and dignity.

At this time I selected four amiable companions, with whom I constantly associated, and when I attained the sovereignty, I remembered their claims, as well as those of my other play-fellows and acquaintances, and promoted each of them according to his deserts.

By the Divine grace, from the time of being nine years old, till I had reached seventy-one years, I never dined alone, and never walked out without a friend, and whenever I put on new clothes, on taking them off,* I gave them to my companions; and whatever they asked from me, I never refused, but gave it without humiliating intreaty.

At fourteen, I had formed an intimacy with a very handsome youth, and passed great part of my time with his tribe; he was sensible of my partiality, and also shewed great affection for me, at length a blackguard of Maveralnaher, who was called *Mullāchē*, and who under the semblance of a student, had been admitted into the circle of our acquaintance, took a liking to the youth; but as this fellow was an entertaining companion, I was pleased with him; this circumstance made him very vain, and he used to talk in a familiar and obscene way: one day having given him admission into our society, I overheard the boy say to him in a familiar manner, "I dont want your kisses;" I was quite nettled at these words, and resolved never to allow such impropriety of conduct, either in myself or others.

At sixteen, my father took me by the hand, and brought me to his own Monastery, he there addressed me; "my boy, our ancestors from generation to generation, have been commanders of the armies of the Jagtay and Berlas family. The dignity of (Sepah Salar) Commander in Chief, has now descended to me, but as I am tired of this world, and consider it no better than a golden vase filled with serpents and scorpions, I mean, therefore, to resign my public office, and retire from it, in order to enjoy the delights of tranquillity and repose; but as I have founded this village, and erected this monastery in my own name, to perpetuate my fame, and that of our family, I must particularly request that you will not diminish ought of its revenues or privileges."

My father then related to me the genealogy of our family, extending to Tumuneh Khān, whose genealogy is carried back in history to Japhet, the son of Noah,† he added;

"The first of our family who had the honour of conversion to the faith of *Islām*,

* It is said that the Afghans never change their clothes till worn out.

† See Introduction.

was Kerachār Nuyan, who was the Gurgān (son-in-law) of Jagtay Khān, as he was a sensible man, he of his own accord adopted the faith of Muhammed, and said to his family and people, 'when I look around me in the universe, I see 'but one world, yet I am of opinion that there are other worlds besides this;* 'but I am also convinced, that there is one only God who hath created all these 'worlds, and who is all sufficient to rule, and direct all these worlds; but as 'he has chosen this world as his special dominion, he has deemed it requisite 'to have ministers (to instruct mankind): he hath therefore chosen Muhammed 'to be his *Vizier* in this world, and as it was requisite that Muhammed should 'have ministers (to extend his religion), he hath appointed the holy race of '*Khalifs* to this dignity."

"Now my son, as this speech of our ancestor is quite conformable to my judgment, I also have become a sincere Musselmān; I request, O Timūr,

1stly. That you will imitate the example of your illustrious progenitor in conforming to the sacred religion of Muhammed, (on whom, and on his posterity and companions, be the peace of God), I intreat you never to deviate from his law, but ever to respect and honour his descendants and followers in the persons of the *Syeds*, the learned, and the prelates of his religion; associate with them, and constantly ask the blessings of the dervishes, the hermits, and the righteous upon all your undertakings; obey the commands of God, and have compassion upon his creatures.

2dly. That you will encourage and give currency and support to the religion of the Prophet.

3rdly. That you will believe that we are all the servants of God, and appointed by his decree to inhabit this terrestial globe; that our destinies are predicted, and that whatever is written on our foreheads, must come to pass; as it is decreed that we shall all do so and so, and have not the power of quitting this world, we must be content with whatever *fate* determines, and be satisfied with whatever God shall give us; we should also assist our poor brethren, and constantly, by every means in our power, befriend all the creatures of God; let us always acknowledge the unity of God, and by our practice, strengthen the four pillars of the law; viz. prayer, fasting, pilgrimage, and alms.

4thly. Be affectionate to your relations and connections, injure no person, nor keep any one in bonds, unless the bonds of kindness; deprive no man of his rights by fraud or tyranny; clothe yourself in the robe of justice; avoid the society of the bad and wicked; keep no man in prison more than three days, and distribute provision to the poor and hungry; and plant yourself in the hearts of

* See Appendix VII.

your subjects by beneficence, otherwise you will fall from your power and prosperity."

When my father had finished his discourse, I promised faithfully to follow his counsel, and to comply with his advice.

When I attained the age of seventeen, my father being indifferent about worldly affairs, and in delicate health, I took upon me the charge of his private affairs, and made the following arrangements; I formed every hundred sheep into a separate flock, and appointed a shepherd to each flock, whose profits were to be one fourth of the milk, the butter, and the wool; I did the same with the goats, separating the wethers from the females; I likewise denominated every twenty horses a stable, separating the horses from the mares; also the camels in the same manner.

Of the various omens which predicted my future greatness, one which most tended to raise my hopes was this; one day I went to pay my respects to the famous Saint Amyr Kelāl, and when I entered the assembly, I seated myself at the very lowest end of the room, (literally where the shoes are taken off); the Saint looked at me and said, "although this boy is in appearance so little and young, he is in fact, a great personage;" he then made room for me near himself, and after looking at and conversing with me for some time, he fell into a slumber; after he awoke, one of his servants presented to him a tray of bread and sweetmeats, he stretched out his hand, and having taken seven cakes and sweetmeats, gave them to me, saying, "eat a mouthful of each of these, in consequence of which, the *seven regions of the world* shall become subject to you;"* I was astonished at these words, and the people of the assembly looked first at each other, and then on me, but through awe of the Saint, no one ventured to speak; I therefore folded up the cakes, and carried them to my father, who said to me, "Kelāl is a great personage, a descendant of the Prophet, a seeer of visions, and a worker of miracles, whatever he has told you of his visions, will certainly come to pass; take care of these cakes, and do not give of them to any body, but regard them as the greatest blessing from the blessings of that holy personage."

Some time after this event, my father went with me to pay his respects to the Saint, who said to him, O Prince;

(Here follows a line in the Jagtay Tūrky.)

at this time there was a basket of nuts before him, he ordered my father to count them; after he had done so, he informed him that there were three hundred and seventy nuts, the Saint said, "each of these three hundred nuts signifies a year,

* Many of these Santons were considered as deranged, but their predictions were not the less credited.

the remainder are the number of Timūr's posterity, which shall reign for three hundred years;" he then presented the basket to my father, which I took, and placed the nuts with the cakes; when I mentioned these circumstances to my mother, she took my head between her hands and blessed me: the cakes and the nuts remained in my possession for many years, during all which time my prosperity encreased.

Some time after the affair of the nuts, my mother went also to pay her respects to the Saint, and was most graciously received, at length he said to her,

(Here follows a verse in the Jagtay Tūrky.)

" Seventy of Timūr's sons, grandsons, and descendants, shall reign for the " term of three hundred years, provided that they make no change of (the " Muhammedan) religion, but give currency to the faith of Islām; neither shall " they vex nor injure the descendants of the Prophet, but do every thing in their " power to give him satisfaction for the blessing he conferred on mankind; " bounty shall be heaped upon bounty, and prosperity added to prosperity, as " long as they continue to shew kindness to the relatives and descendants of his " Holiness."

When my mother reported to me the conversation of the Saint, although then only seventeen years of age, I made a solemn vow to the all merciful God, that I would never neglect the descendants of the Prophet, but do every thing in my power for their honour.

CHAPTER II.

When I had entered my eighteenth year, I became vain of my abilities, and thought no person superior to myself, or any thing too difficult for my undertaking; I was at this time very fond of riding and hunting, one day having pursued a deer, while at full gallop, I came suddenly to the brink of a ditch, more than five *guz* (ten or fifteen feet) in breadth, and four *guz* in depth, I attempted to turn my horse, but he was obstinate; I therefore tried to make him jump over the ditch, he reached the opposite bank with his fore feet, but not being able to clear it, fell, while he was struggling, I had slipped my feet out of the stirrups, sprang from the saddle, and reached the bank, the horse tumbled into the ditch, and was disabled; my companions soon after came up, and congratulated me on my good fortune and happy escape; I said, " it was God who had preserved me, who is also the bestower of fortune;" my friends not being able to jump the ditch, I went round to them, and having mounted a led horse, proceeded homewards. When we had gone some distance, it became dark, and began to rain, in consequence of which, we lost the road, and as the night was extremely cold, we thought we should have perished (in the desert).

About this time we saw some black (felt) tents or huts, upon which my companions said, "these are hillocks of sand and dust," so we gave ourselves up for lost; I therefore threw the reins on my horses neck, and took hold of the mane, the horse raised his head and began to neigh, and stretched his neck. When we arrived near the tents, we saw a light shining through one of the doors, which gave us courage; I therefore alighted from my horse, and entered the tent, the inhabitants of which supposing I was a thief, hallooed out and prepared to attack me; but when I told them all the circumstances, they were ashamed, and having cleared out a room which was constructed under ground, lighted a fire for us, on which my companions entered, and we took possession of the room; the good people shortly brought us some *Temakh Keruny* soup, of which I eat a great quantity, and was quite refreshed; they also brought us some blankets, upon which we lay down, but they were so full of fleas, that I could not sleep a wink all night. After I had mounted the Imperial throne, I recollected all the circumstances of my hunting excursion, of the cold and frost of the night, and of our society in the cellar, in consequence of which I sent for the family, (and made them *Terkhan*), i. e. amply rewarded them.

During this year, I was very ill for four months, and they could not find out any cure for my disorder, I therefore gave up all hopes of life; for a week I could eat nothing, but on the seventh day, they gave me a pomegranate; soon after I became quite languid and insensible, and while in the swoon, I fancied that they had bound me on a wheel, and were bearing me towards heaven, and afterwards descending to the earth; I did not recover from the fit, till they had burned me between the fore finger and the thumb, when I felt the heat of the iron, I opened my eyes, and saw the servants and my father and mother standing around me crying aloud, I also joined in lamentation; soon after this I became hungry, and the physicians having asked me what I would like, and they would bring it, I called for *Yekhny*, and some of the *Temakh* broth; I eat a whole plate full of the latter, and during the night fell into a deep perspiration, and from that time recovered.

Another of the auspicious omens predicting my sovereignty, was this; one day during this year, I was seated in my father's monastery, and was reading the 67th Chapter of the Korān;* when a gray-haired Syed entered the monastery, and having looked attentively at me, demanded my name, (having told him) he compared it with the chapter I was reading, and said, "God Almighty has given the sovereignty of the earth to this boy and his posterity;" I looked upon this

* See Appendix VI.

circumstance as a mere dream, but when it reached the ears of my father, he encouraged my hopes, and shewed my Horoscope to one of the Astrologers of Tūrkestān, who said, "he will be superior in his own dominions, in dignity, and authority, to any of his predecessors, and he will add other countries to his own dominions, and will be an ornament to religion:" he then said to me, "your descendants and posterity shall rise to the very highest dignity:" when I had heard these words, I gave him a handsome present.

At this period, I passed much of my time in reading the Korān, and playing at chess; I was also much employed in charitable actions, and soliciting the blessings of the hermits and dervishes.

I was also fond of horsemanship, and I employed a celebrated riding master to teach me the art, and also to instruct me in the science of manœuvering an army; I frequently assembled my companions, and having taken upon myself the title of Commander, made them all obedient to me; and whenever we rode out, I used to divide them into two armies, and taught them how to advance, and how to retreat in the field of battle.

CHAPTER III.

About this period, I asked my father to tell me the history of our family from the time of Yafet Aghlān, which he did, nearly in the following manner:

"It is written in the Tūrkish history, that we are descended from Yafet Aghlān, commonly called (Abu al Atrāk) Father of the Tūrks, son of (the Patriarch,) Japhet, he was the first monarch of the Tūrks: when his fifth son Aljeh Khān ascended the throne, the all gracious God bestowed on him twin sons, one of which was called *Tatar*, the other *Moghul*; when they were grown up, Aljeh Khān divided the kingdom of Tūrkestān between them during his life-time; after they were seated on their respective thrones, they became proud of their authority, and forsook the religion of their ancestors, placing their feet in the paths of infidelity: Tatar had eight sons, from whom are descended eight (Oulous) tribes. Moghul had nine sons, from whom are descended nine clans: these two parties frequently disagreed, and fought many battles in the plains of Tūrkestān.

Till at length, after the establishment of the *Islām* faith, Tumenāh Khān was seated on the throne of dominion of the region of Tūrkestān; he had two sons by one birth, one of which he named Kajuly, the other Kubel Khān; when Kajuly had arrived at the age of manhood, he dreamt one night, that he saw two stars rise from the breast of Kubel Khān, and shortly after set; again he thought he saw a star, equal in splendour to the sun, which illuminated the whole world; when he awoke, he related his dream to his father, who expounded it in this manner; 'from the posterity of your brother, a boy shall be born in the third generation, who shall be the conqueror of the world:' Tumenāh Khān then gave orders for a grand feast, to which he invited all the nobles and principal persons; during the feast the brothers, having embraced each other, entered into an agreement, which was drawn up in the Tūrkish language, and engraved on a plate of steel, and which was deposited in the treasury; the subject of the agreement was this, 'that the posterity of the two brothers should never quarrel with each other; that the dignity of *Khān* should for ever remain in the descendants of Kubel Khān, and that of (Sepah Salar) Commander in Chief, and prime minister in the family of Kajuly.'*

In A. H. 549, Mungū Behadur, son of Kubel Khān, had a boy, born with his two hands full of blood, to whom he gave the name of *Timujy*; when this personage arrived at the age of forty-nine, after much toil and danger, he was seated on the throne of Tūrkestān

On the day that he took the title of Khān, a dervish entered the assembly, and proclaimed, "the Lord hath said to me, 'I have given the surface of the earth to Timujy,' and I confer on you the title of Jengyz Khān, that is to say, King of Kings." But Jengyz abandoned the duty of a conqueror, by slaughtering the people, and by plundering the dominions of God, and put to death many thousands of the Muselmāns.

On the morning of the day that he died, he bestowed the sovereignty of Maveralnaher on his eldest son Jagtay Khān;† he appointed Kerachār Nuyān, son of Ayzdumjyn Berlās, son of Kajuly Behadur, who is my fourth and your fifth ancestor, to be generalissimo and prime minister; and caused the agreement entered into by Kajuly and Kubel Khān, to be brought from the treasury, and given to them; Jagtay having perused it, delivered it to Kerachār Nuyān, and conferred on him the title of Gurgān or Kurkān (Great Prince).

When God had bestowed on Kerachār Nuyān a son, he called him Anchel Nuyān; Kerachār was not at first one of the true believers, but followed the religion of the (Majusy) Materialists, who say that God is in every thing, and in every person; he was however anxious to acquire a proper knowledge of God, and therefore sought the acquaintance of all holy men, at length he asked the opinion of one of those learned personages, who was descended from Muhammed,

* See Institutes, page 25.

† This name is spelled in Persian both Jagtay and Chagtay, a large portion of Tūrkestān is called after him.

what do the Muselmāns say respecting the true knowledge of God; the holy man replied, 'the faith of the Muselmāns is this, that from all eternity there has existed an Omnipotent and Omniscient Being, he is our God, and he is the God of all creatures, it is therefore not proper to say, as the Materialists do, for there is only one God, the creator of all things; we deny a plurality of Gods, and assert that there is only one:' Kerachār after some reflection, said, 'it is true, God can have no partner, he is all sufficient.' He then submitted himself to the holy man as a convert, and repeated the Creed after his preceptor; viz. 'there is no God but God, Muhammed is the Messenger of God;' glory be to him who is eternal, omniscient, and omnipotent, the all seeing, the all hearing, the giver of speech, the causer of all events.

Praise be also to his Messenger Muhammed, who by the miracle of dividing the moon, evinced he was the true Prophet, he is the minister of the glorious God, and the Khalifs are his Viziers.

From that time Kerachār became firm in his faith, and invited all the people to imitate his example, in consequence of which, the religion of Muhammed encreased and became current through all that region.

He also divided the country of Irān equally between the *(Ayelat)* different clans, and appointed the plains of Kesh for the residence of the tribe of Berlās, (his own tribe) giving them the water, the grass, and pasturage of that and several other places for their support; Kerachār then took on him the business of generalissimo, and subdued the countries of Kashgār, of Badakhshān, Andejān, and Hassar, also parts of Khorasān, which he retained as his own private territory.

When Kerachār departed this life, he was succeeded by his eldest son Amyr Ayltekuz, as generalissimo, who conquered several countries; when your grandfather Amyr Burkul succeeded as *Sepah Salar*, finding that there were dissentions among the tribes and clans, (Alusāt va Kushunāt) he was disgusted, and having retired from his office, contented himself with the government of his own clan of Berlās: he however possessed an incalculable number of sheep and goats, of cattle, of slaves and servants.

On the death of your grandfather Amyr Burkul, I succeeded to his possessions, but I preferred the company of the learned and the religious persons, and associated mostly with them, frequently soliciting their blessings and prayers, that the Almighty God, would bestow on me a son, which should raise the fame and encrease the dignity of the tribe of Berlās.

About this time, a celebrated Astrologer came from Fars to Maveralnaher, and one day when seated in the assembly of the learned personages, he said, 'from the revolution of the heavens it is well known to me, that, in the year seven hundred and thirty, (of the Hejira) a child shall be born, who will prove the conqueror of the world.' Verse, 'In the year seven hundred and thirty, on the 9th of the month, Rejeb, a star of auspicious title shall arise;' God hath bestowed this boy on you."*

When my father had related all these circumstances to me, I was convinced in my own mind, that I was born to succeed to the sovereignty, and believed myself endued with all the requisite abilities; I became however very religious, constantly prayed to God for success, and made numerous offerings of cattle and sheep to the Syeds, the learned, and devout personages.

Thus I sent an offering of twenty sheep to the (Saint) Amyr Kelal, but in consequence of heavy rain, they missed the road, and I thought were lost; but some days after having gone to pay my respects to him, I saw the sheep standing at his door, and returned thanks to God, that my offering had been accepted. As soon as the Saint cast his eyes on me, he said to the by-standers, "the sovereignty of the territories of God has been bestowed on this young Tūrk;" he then began to say his prayers, I also imitated his example: after he had finished his devotions, he said, "good fortune and royalty is to be your fate, provided that you support the religion of Islām."

At this time I repented (of my follies), and left off playing chess; I strictly adhered to the law, and followed the dictates of religion; I also made a vow never to injure any creature, and whenever I did so by chance, was very sorry for it; thus one day having unintentionally trodden on an Ant, I felt as if my foot had lost all its power; I constantly begged the intercession of the first Khalifs, and was benevolent to all mankind.

A. D. 1355. In the year 756, I attained my twentieth year, and having reached the age of maturity, my father Teragay made over to me a number of tents, sheep, camels, slaves, servants, and attendants, from which during this year I gained much profit. The first arrangement I made of my private affairs was this, I gave the command of eighteen slaves to one slave, to whom I gave the title of *Aun Bashy*, and I named every twenty horses a (Tavyleh) stable, and every hundred camels a (Kuttar) string, and every thousand sheep a (Gileh) flock, and gave each of these in charge of a particular slave, and allotted to each of them, a certain share of the profits. During this year I was again very unwell, and a physician of Samerkund having administered pomegranates to me, I was seized with a violent palpitation, and became quite insensible, upon which

* The date here mentioned is supposed to be a mistake either of the Persian translator, or of the copyist, as all other authorities fix the birth of Timūr on the 25th of Shabān, A. H. 736, corresponding with the 7th of May, A. D. 1336.

my father and mother, and all the attendants wept bitterly; after this, a physician of Tūrkestān seared me with a hot iron, upon which I came to myself; they afterwards gave me some *Yelmak* broth, and other food, and I became convalescent. In gratitude for my recovery, I made valuable offerings of sheep and horses; thus I gave an hundred camels in honour of the Prophet, and fifty more in honour of the illustrious Khalifs, and gave ample charities to the poor, the hermits, and dervishes, through whose prayers I entirely recovered.

CHAPTER IV.

In this year A. H. 756, Amyr Kezān Sultān, son of Sūr Aghlān, held the standard of sovereignty over the tribe of Chagtai,* and for fifteen years had extended the hand of oppression over the people of Maveralnaher, and placed his feet out of the path of justice and equity: in consequence of his tyranny, his subjects were in a state of despair, confining themselves to their houses, and praying for his death.

I was also much incensed by his bad conduct, and felt every inclination to rebel against him, and take revenge of his cruelty, but I could not find any body of consequence to join me; nor until I had distributed all my wealth among them, could I prevail upon any person to unite with me, whilst I was very much affected at the sight of their oppressed state.

At length Amyr Kūrgen, who was one of the greatest chiefs of the tribe of Jagtay, rebelled against him, and in the year 746, (A. D. 1345) fought with him in the desert of Derreh Zengy, but was defeated.

The tyrant having been successful, renewed his oppressions, and returned to Kershy; this astonished the people, who expected that Providence would have interfered in their behalf.

In consequence of such evil conduct, a Syed of Termuz said, " that as long as Amyr Kezān retains these habits, he will never be conquered;" the people therefore began openly to curse him, which only stimulated him to fresh acts of injustice. Some of the effects of the malconduct of this worthless monarch were:

1stly. A very severe frost, which destroyed the cattle.

2ndly. A total want of rain, in consequence of which the cultivation was quite dried up, and the fruits were annihilated.

3rdly. A famine which swept off the people.

During the following year, Amyr Kūrgen having again recruited his army,

* See Note to page 28.

advanced towards Kershy, and having engaged the tyrant, defeated and took him prisoner; he at first confined him, but at the end of two years put him to death, and relieved the kingdom of Maveralnaher from his oppressions.*

Amyr Kūrgen then took possession of the kingdom, restored much of the property that had been unlawfully seized, and conducted himself with equity; but as the nobles would not acknowledge his authority, I had some intention of taking the sovereignty upon myself;† however the chiefs anticipated my design, and raised Danishmundchē Aghlān, one of the descendants of Jengyz Khān, to to the dignity of *Khān,* to whom they vowed fidelity, and made him monarch of all Maveralnaher.

Amyr Kūrgen, with the title of Commander, ruled the kingdom in the name of Danishmundchē Khān, for the term of ten years, with great propriety; re-established the laws, and gave encouragement to the Muhammedan religion.

A. D. 1356. When I had attained my twenty-first year, I wished to have united all the tribe of Berlās, and to have rebelled; I was joined by forty of my school-fellows, and we consulted upon taking possession of the mountain of Kāān; but at this time my mother was called to the divine mercy, and my sister Tūrkān Akā took charge of my household; I was for some time very melancholy, and gave up my ambitious intentions. After the days of mourning for my mother were accomplished, my father betrothed me to the daughter of Amyr Jakū Berlās. About this time, my father deputed me to Amyr Kūrgen, on some business respecting our tribe and clan, by which means I became acquainted with the Amyr, who took a great liking to me, adopted me as his son, and gave me one of his grand-daughters in marriage, with great honour and much wealth, and seated me near himself in the assembly.

After the death of the Amyr, as his son was not equal to the duties (of Vizier), I had some wish to take the office myself, and had got the consent of several of the chiefs; but recollecting my debt of gratitude to the father, I said to myself, "better be patient," and took patience.

In this year, I one day went into the desert to hunt, when we came to the hunting ground, a violent storm of both snow and rain came on; afterwards the snow being very deep, I lost my road, and wandered about; at length I saw something dark, when I approached it, I found it was a hill, at the bottom of which there was a great cave, in which some families of the Arlāt clan had

* He was the last of the descendants of Jengyz Khān, who actually reigned over Transoxiana, although several young men had the empty title of Khān conferred on them, but they were mere puppets in the hands of the powerful chiefs.

† This was a boast of Timūr, as he was then very young; Aghlān signifies both a boy and a Prince.

taken shelter from the inclemency of the weather, had formed chambers in the rocks of the cave, and had pitched their tents in its vicinity; as I was nearly dead with cold, I got off my horse, and entered the cave without ceremony; I there saw a good fire, with a pot well filled with broth hanging thereon; as I was very hungry, the sight of it delighted me; the owner of the room was very kind, he pulled off my coat and boots which were wet through; he also unbound my quiver, and bringing some horse rugs, made a bed for me; he then brought the hot soup, of which I eat a quantity, and became warm and refreshed: I passed the night there, and in return to the family for their kindness, I took their eldest son home with me, and introduced him to the Amyr.

Another time I went a hunting and met with a very serious accident; I was pursuing a deer at full speed, when I unexpectedly came to a dry well, the horse was very active, and attempted to jump the well, but although his fore feet cleared it, his hind legs fell in; I vaulted from the saddle, and tried to get over, but did not succeed, and both horse and man went down; my companions thought I was killed; but when they found me alive, they were much rejoiced, and made offerings for my lucky escape, which was considered as a fortunate omen, and gained me many followers.

In the year 757, an army from Irāk invaded Maveralnaher, and A. D. 1357. collected much plunder; I was then just twenty-one, and was sitting with Amyr Kūrgen, when intelligence of the invasion was brought; he instantly ordered me to take command of a detachment, and pursue the enemy; I followed the Irakians twenty-three (Fersukh) parasangs, and having made a forced march, came up with them at mid-day; the enemy were divided into two parties, one of which protected the plunder, while the other prepared to oppose me; my officers advised me to attack the plunder, but, I said "no, let us defeat the fighting part, and the other will soon disperse;" I then gave orders to charge, and putting spurs to my horse, rushed on; the Irakians stood their ground, and we came to blows; but after a few cuts on each side, they fled, upon which I took possession of the plunder, and having restored it to the owners, waited on the Amyr, who praised me exceedingly, presented me with his own quiver, and appointed me (Beglerbeg) Commander of the tribe.

At this time, I was very anxious to rebel against the *Khān*, and to assume the power myself; but when I mentioned it to Amyr Kūrgen, who was then very busy, he said, "cannot you wait, it will be yours some time or other:" I therefore relinquished my intention.

About this time, I went again to pay my respects to the *Kutb al Aktab* Shaikh Zyn Addeen Shādy; at the time of my arrival, he was seated with some of his disciples reading the Korān, and had just repeated the verse, "Is not the conquest of the kingdom of Rūm (Anatolia) in my power;" as soon as he perceived me, he compared the circumstance of my arrival, with the moment of pronouncing the above verse, and finding a great accordance between them, he received me with the utmost respect and honour, and seated me opposite himself.

When he finished reading the prescribed portion of the holy book, he said to me, "God hath decreed the downfall of Rūm, and as I perceive in you the signs of royal dignity, perhaps you are to be its destined conqueror;" he further added, "as the final letter of the word (Arz) kingdom, signifies eight hundred, I predict that you will conquer Rūm in the year 800." I was very much encouraged, and rejoiced by this auspicious prediction.

At another visit that I paid the Saint, he bound round my loins his own shawl, put on my head his own cap, and presented me a cornelian, on which was engraved (Rāsty va Rūsty) righteousness and salvation; I considered this also as a fortunate omen, added my own name, and had it made into a seal-ring; and from this time placed my entire confidence and faith in the Shaikh.

[Here the Shaikh entertains him with a story of his having been very ill, and that he had been directed in a vision to visit the tomb of Aly Iben Mūsā, at Tūs, now Mushehed, in Khorasān; that he walked barefooted, and was seven years on the pilgrimage, and got perfectly well as soon as he arrived at the tomb; but the story being very prolix and not interesting, I have passed it over.]

CHAPTER V.

A. D. 1358. During this year, several complaints were received by Amyr Kūrgen, against Melk Hussyn Ghoury, Ruler of Herat,* who had exceeded his authority, and oppressed the people, on which account the principal personages of that city, wrote a petition, requesting the Amyr to come thither, and redress their wrongs. The Prince however thought it better to write a letter of exhortation to Melk Hussyn, commanding him to refrain from oppressing the people of Khorasān, and to alter his conduct, otherwise he should be under the necessity of marching against him, and depriving him of his government and dignity.

But as Melk Hussyn would not take warning, nor alter his conduct, nay for a long time did not acknowledge the receipt of the Prince's letter; the anger of

* Herat, the Aria of the Greeks, long the capital of Khorasān, situated on the Jihun, Lat. 34, N. 50. See Edinburgh Gazetteer.

the Amyr was roused, and he gave orders for assembling the army, with the intention of invading Khorasān; but when he shewed his chiefs the letters from Herat, and asked their advice, they replied, "that they did not consider the persons who had signed the petition as sufficient authority for proceeding to harsh measures, and that it would be better again to ascertain the disposition of the other inhabitants;" this reply vexed the Amyr, he began to hesitate, and asked my opinion, I said frankly to him, "you should not have assembled the army, till you had determined this point, but having done so, you should not now procrastinate, lest the enemy impute it to weakness, but let us manfully attack them, if victorious, we shall gain the object, and at all events fill the bellies of our hungry soldiers, for 'in exertion there is prosperity.'"

Amyr Kūrgen approved of my advice, and instantly gave me the command of a thousand horsemen. I fed these thousand cavaliers daily, and never sat down to a meal without (some of) them; on this account they all became much attached to me: we formed the advanced guard, and marched forward with great confidence; many of the tribes and clans having assembled in hopes of plunder, I induced them also to join me. When I had got my army well equipped and arranged, they were quite unanimous in acknowledging my authority, so that I began to have a prospect of the gate of sovereignty; I wrote a list of the names of the cavaliers, and kept it folded up in my pocket; I also resolved in my own mind, that when I should have dispossessed Melk Hussyn, I would keep the country of Khorasān for myself.

Having thus determined, we moved forward, we crossed the Moorghāb river, and marching by the route of Bashtan, we encamped on the mountains, in the vicinity of Herat.

The next day I mounted and rode to a bleach-green, which was situated on a hill, from whence I determined on the field of battle; I then waited on Amyr Kūrgen, and pointed out the field of battle to him.

Amyr Kūrgen having arranged the army, rode up to the bleach-green, and having minutely examined the field of battle, highly extolled my judgment, as we had our backs to the sun, it was consequently in the face of the enemy; the Prince said, "the rays of the sun will blind our foes, and give us an easy conquest."

Soon after this, the first line of army of Melk Hussyn, which was drawn up behind a low wall, advanced boldly into the plain, but they were unskilfully drawn up. At this time Amyr Kūrgen called me, and said, "my boy, see how ill their army is arranged, we shall soon defeat them;" I replied, "have a little patience till they advance further from the wall;" I then sent orders to our front line to retire gently, upon which the enemy growing bold, advanced further into the field, and drew out in order of battle.

I drew up our line in right wing, left wing, and centre; I then gave orders for the centre to advance; when the two lines met, and were engaged hand to hand, I ordered the wings to charge at full gallop, and pushed on myself; but on the first and second attack, the enemy abandoned the field, and took refuge behind the wall.

At this time Amyr Kūrgen came up, and gave orders that we should dismount, and force the wall, we did so, and were successful; the Prince then divided the troops, and sent a division to erect batteries against each of the gates of the city; he then gave me the command of the attack, and returned to his camp.

The next day he gave orders for the whole army, cavalry and infantry, to attack the city; in consequence of which, we entirely surrounded the place, and cut off all supplies: when the inhabitants of Herat began to be distressed, the principal people assembled, and agreed to make overtures for peace; they then sent to Amyr Kūrgen various curiosities and presents, and promised that if he would withdraw his army, Melk Hussyn should wait upon him at Samerkund, in the course of one month, and pay his devoirs. The Amyr having consulted his chiefs, accepted the tribute, which he divided equally amongst them, agreed to make peace, and returned to Maveralnaher. He however left me at Herat, with a thousand cavalry, and the advanced guard, to intimidate Melk Hussyn, and oblige him to keep his promise of coming to Samerkund in one month.

In consequence of these instructions, I encamped on the esplanade of Herat; but whilst waiting the expiration of the appointed time for Melk Hussyn to fulfil his promise, I proceeded to Bakhter, and took possession of all that part of Khorasān.

I also took this opportunity of again paying my respects to the Kutb al Aktab Shaikh Zyn Addeen Abu Beker, and when admitted to his presence, forgot all my cares and disappointments, and felt the greatest comfort; on the first day the Shaikh received me with the greatest kindness, and clothed me in his own robe; I therefore unburthened my mind to him, respecting my views on the kingdom of Khorasān: he ordered me to be punctual in my prayers, and that whenever any difficulty occurred to me, to offer up my supplications to Muhammed, and to his descendants, so that all my difficulties would be rendered easy.

The second day, the Shaikh said to me, "you will now be supported, the Commander of the faithful (Aly) has ordered one of his agents to attend you, you will not know him at first, but will finally become acquainted with him;" I was much rejoiced by this intelligence, and felt the greatest confidence in the Saint's prediction, and looked forward with patience to the sovereignty and conquest of the whole country of Khorasān. Having taken leave of the Shaikh, I returned to Herat, and encamped in the vicinity; but I shortly after received a confidential message from Melk Hussyn, that his army was in a state of insurrection, had threatened to murder him, and set up Melk Bāker in his place, that if I would advance with my troops towards the city, he would come out and join me, and proceed with me to Amyr Kūrgen: I thought to myself, that if Melk Hussyn spoke the truth, and that his officers were in a state of mutiny, it will be easy for me to get hold of the city of Herat, and to keep possession of it without any associate; I therefore drew out my forces, and having mounted, proceeded towards the city.

Melk Hussyn also mounted his horse, and pretending to his people that he meant to fight with me, came out of the fortress and advanced against me in battle array; as I thought he was deceiving me, I put on my armour, and my officers prepared for an engagement; while we were in this state of suspense, Melk Hussyn, accompanied by his own attendants, came over to me, bringing much of his wealth and property; we met, and embraced each other on horseback; many of his officers also came over, and laid aside all animosity. I then took Melk Hussyn to my own tent, and gave orders for marching immediately.

When the Amyr learned that I was bringing Melk Hussyn to court, he sent his son Abdullah to meet him personally, received him in the most gracious manner, and accepted his presents.

The Amyr also received me in the most flattering manner, kissed my forehead, and offered up prayers for my prosperity (literally, may your face be white.)

The Amyr assigned one of his own special tents for the residence of his guest; but after a few days, the cupidity of the tribes and clans was roused, and they were very anxious to plunder and destroy him; but as the Prince would not give his consent to this measure, he sent for me in the middle of the night, and said, "as you were the means of bringing this hostage here, you must convey him safe home again."

I therefore carried Melk Hussyn (privately) to my own tent, and shut him up close; he was dreadfully frightened, and thought I was going to murder him; seeing him so alarmed, I told him all the circumstances, upon which he offered up prayers both for me and for the Prince.

The next day I (publicly) obtained permission to make a hunting excursion, and as the Prince was very fond of the field sports, he agreed to accompany me with a few of his most confidential servants; and taking Melk Hussyn with us, we went to the banks of the Moorghāb: whilst amusing ourselves in the field, the Prince called his guest to him, and having spoken to him very graciously, they renewed their promises of friendship; on taking leave, Hussyn presented a large ruby armlet, after which, Melk Hussyn and I set off, crossed the river, and encamped on the opposite bank.

Whilst in this situation, intelligence arrived that the chiefs of Ghour, and the army of Khorasān, had raised Melk Bāker to the government, and that he had taken possession of the city of Herat; on receipt of this news, Melk Hussyn was much distressed, and sunk in the whirlpool of consternation.

After some time he asked my advice in this affair, I said to him, "you have no alternative, but to place on your head the helmet of courage, and put on the armour of determination, bind on the sword of resolution, and like an alligator dive at once into the river of blood; if victorious, you will gain renown, if subdued, you need not be ashamed." Melk Hussyn bidding adieu to life, resolved to do his duty, begged me to accompany him, and offered me a year's revenue of the province of Herat; I would not agree to this proposal, but said, "if you and I conjointly recover the province, the city shall be mine;" to this he consented. At this time there was a stewed leg of mutton before us, the bone of which was sticking out; I took it, and having stripped it of all the meat, I resolved within myself to draw from it an omen, whether Melk Hussyn would be successful in his enterprize. I performed the usual ceremonies,* and the result was favourable; I therefore determined to brave the adventure, and after four forced marches, we arrived before daylight at the bleach-green; as we entered the bazar of the suburbs, the day broke, which enabled me to see a cook in his shop taking up a hot dish of broth; when he saw me, he cried out, "welcome, welcome," and brought me a bowl of the soup; I looked upon this as a fortunate omen, and pushed on; when we arrived at the gate of Herat, the guard had just opened it, I gave the horse of Melk Hussyn, a blow with my whip, and we bounded over the planks of the drawbridge, and entered the fortress; I kept possession of the gate, to give entrance to our people, whilst Melk Hussyn proceeded to the apartments of his rival Melk Bāker; the garrison seeing the number of my troops, were confounded, and quietly submitted; thus Melk Hussyn recovered his capital victoriously, and without any loss.

It then entered my mind, that I might as well take possession of the government of Herat myself, but upon further reflecting, that possibly the troops would not support me, I relinquished the idea; and I afterwards found by experience, that I had judged rightly, and that they would not have joined me, which

* The Tartars play with sheep-shanks instead of dice.

convinced me that one sincere friend is better than a thousand pretended friends. In consequence of this reflection, I placed Melk Hussyn on the throne of government, and exacted some promises from him; he very honourably paid me the money he had agreed to give for my assistance; he also sent with me, by the hands of his own agents, numerous presents to Amyr Kūrgen.

When I returned to Samerkund, the Amyr embraced me, and kissed my forehead and cheeks; but when the chiefs of the tribe heard what I had done, they were much irritated, and bound up their loins for my destruction; they also rebelled against Amyr Kūrgen. On this occasion, the Prince again consulted me; I advised him, as it was he who had raised Danishmūndchē Aghlān to the *Khānship*, he should induce the Khān to issue the imperial order, summoning the refractory officers to court, that such of them as obeyed, should be treated with kindness, but those that disobeyed, should have their heads struck off.

In the year 758, I reached twenty-two years of age, and began to put in practice some of my speculations regarding the sovereignty, for several of the chiefs of the tribes and clans being dissatisfied with Amyr Kūrgen, conspired together, and wrote to me, that if I would encourage them, they would be my friends, and would displace both the *Amyr* and the *Khān*, after which we might divide the country between us; but I having reflected that it would be much easier at some future time to dispossess one person, than to have to contend with ten rivals, and recollecting the friendly connection that existed between the Amyr and me, I determined to inform him of the circumstance. A. D. 1359.

But the chiefs having discovered my intentions, wrote to the Amyr, (in the Tūrky language); "be it known to your enlightened mind, that every body "selects some (powerful) personage to be his patron, through whose mediation "he may obtain the object of his desires and wishes; we, in order to obtain our "desires and wishes, have chosen your benevolence and kindness to be our "intermediators; we have taken the liberty of representing this, may your prosperity endure for ever."

When this letter reached the Amyr, as he was a very weak man, he in a kind and friendly manner invited the chiefs to wait on him, and paid no regard to the caution I had given him.

In consequence of this invitation, the chiefs having collected their men, and having put on their armour, came to the palace gate, between the hours of evening prayer and bed time. The Amyr immediately sent for me, when I came to the gate, I spoke to several of the chiefs, and finding that they had armour under their clothes, I suspected that they had evil intentions, bade them good evening, went into the palace and told the Amyr all the circumstances; who, on hearing of the treachery, and the mutinous state of his officers, was seized with a pain in his bowels; he therefore sent them an apology, but gave orders for their being hospitably entertained, and permitted to return to their camp.

He then consulted me, how we were to get rid of them, I advised him to deceive them by presents; he in consequence sent a large sum of money, and desired them to divide it among them according to their rank. As the sum was large, they could not agree on the division, and soon began to quarrel; after which they came singly to ask the Amyr's pardon, and to be again admitted into favour; thus enmity was changed into friendship, and the danger was averted; on this occasion the Amyr again took me in his arms, called me his son, and bestowed on me the district of Shemerghān.

A. D. 1360. In the year 759, I attained my twenty-third year; at this time Amyr Kūrgen being quite absolute in the kingdom of Maveralnaher, resolved to subdue the kingdom of Khuarizm, and in this affair, offered to give me the command of the expedition; I at first agreed, but after deliberation, I thought it advisable that the command should be given to some other person, who might be defeated by the Khuarizmians, after which I would then enter the country and subdue it.

I therefore spoke privately to Amyr Khizer, that he would request Byan Kuly, who was one of the lords of the council, to say to the Prince, that "Khuarizm being an easy conquest, ought to be assigned to his highness's eldest son Abdullah, whose fame would be exalted thereby, and all the credit given to him instead of Timūr."

Byan Kuly having explained these circumstances to Amyr Kūrgen, he approved of the measure, and ordered his eldest son Abdullah from Samerkund, to take command of the army against Khuarizm; Abdullah entered the country, but the Khuarizmians having strengthened their fortresses, kept him at bay, and reduced him to great distress.

The Amyr not knowing what to do, sent for me, and said, "from the first it was my wish to have given the command of the army to you, and still it is my wish that you should take it:" I reflected within myself, that the Amyr wished for my assistance to effect the conquest, but that he meant to keep all the benefit to himself; I therefore thought I might as well make the conquest for myself, and become sovereign of the country. As ambition is a very powerful passion, I resolved no longer to be subservient to any one, but to go and take Khuarizm for myself.

When Amyr Kūrgen had superseded his son, and put under my command a large force, I marched towards Khuarizm, but I ordered that the army of Abdullah should remain stationary till my arrival. As the Khuariznians would not engage us in the field, but shut themselves up in their fortresses, the first thing I did was this, I made overtures to the chiefs of all the wandering tribes and clans that inhabited Khuarizm, and having united them to me, I requested them to intercede with the governors of the forts; they did so, and they (the governors) all agreed to be my servants.

I then divided amongst them the whole of the countries of Khuarizm and Ourkunje; having thus gotten possession of all the fortresses of the kingdom, I appointed a confidential person of my own to be (Kūtwall) superintendant of them, and thus settled the government of the country; I also wished to have raised the standard of sovereignty, but having no dependance on the fealty of my new subjects, I returned with Abdullah to the Amyr, who in return for my successful conduct, gave me the country of Ourkunje.

In the year 760, I attained my twenty-fourth year; about this time, Amyr Kūrgen made a grand hunting party, and came out of Samerkund; whilst we were engaged in the chase, night came on. Kutlug Timūr Khān, the son-in-law of the Prince, having a number of wicked wretches united with him, judged it a favourable opportunity to assassinate the Amyr, seeing that I and the chief huntsman were his only companions; he, therefore, made an attack on him with seven expert swordsmen; at this time it was dark, but I hearing them, called out and threatening them, threw myself between them and the Prince, who immediately alighted from his horse, and drawing his sword, got behind a large stone; the huntsman then joining us, Kutlug Timūr ran off; in reward for saving him from this peril, the Amyr bestowed on me the revenue of Hissar Shadmān. A. D. 1358.

Being now master of the countries of Khuarizm and Shadmān, I divided the revenues with my soldiers; but although I was very kind and liberal to all my servants, they would not support me in my ambitious views.

The eyes of Amyr Kūrgen being now open to the designs of his son-in-law, he left off hunting, and watched an opportunity of seizing him and his companions, with the intention of putting them to death; but Kutlug being aware of his intention, took refuge in the highlands of Maveralnaher, and became a public robber. At length the daughter of the Amyr, who was married to this fellow, pretended to become insane from the absence of her husband.

As the Amyr was a weak and compassionate man, he listened to the deceit of women, and believed that his daughter was really mad, and the other women joining with her led him astray, and prevailed on him to pardon Kutlug Timūr; in consequence of which, an edict was issued for him to return to court.

I opposed this measure, and said to the Amyr, "do not be led away by your women, for God hath said, 'always act contrary to what women advise,' if they have told you not to put him to death, undoubtedly kill him, for according to the orders of God, you should oppose them in every thing, for they are deficient in sense." Although the Amyr knew his son-in-law to be his inveterate enemy, he would not at first follow the advice of the proverb, which I repeated to him, viz. "keep your enemy in your grasp as you would a ruby, till you come to a flinty spot, then knock his head against the stone till you dash it to pieces:" but at length he listened to my opinion, and determined to crush his enemy; he however did not find an opportunity.

In this same year, Amyr Kūrgen one day sent for me, and having repeated his complaints, said, "he was resolved to divorce his daughter and son-in-law;" but his women again rendered him subservient to their orders, and Kutlug Timūr pretending to be sorry for what he had done, the divorce was postponed.

About this time, Amyr Kūrgen took the government of Andijan from Sultān Kūly, the father of his son Abdullah's wife, and gave it to Khuajēh Ayzdy; in consequence of which, the deposed governor bound up the loins of enmity against his master, and conspired with Kutlug Timūr, and agreed to set up the young Abdullah; I frequently cautioned the Amyr against them, and as he had been pleased to adopt me as a son, and had given me a written promise that I should be his successor in the kingdom of Maveralnaher, I watched over him as a child should over a parent, and omitted no part of my duty towards him.*

Till at length the Amyr Kūrgen who was extremely fond of hunting, one day went out (without me) attended only by a few persons without their armour, and having crossed the Oxus, (Jihūn) was deeply engaged in the chase, when Kutlug Timūr and Sultān Kūly attacked and murdered the just Prince.

When I was informed of the circumstance, I was dreadfully affected; I repaired immediately to the spot where the body was lying, and having respectfully taken it up, I transported it to the banks of the river, and there purified it, after which we carried it to Sāly Serai,† and there buried it. Immediately after this event, Kutlug Timūr and Sultān Kūly placed Abdullah, eldest son of the murdered prince, in the government, but took the oath of allegiance to Bian Kūly,

* This accounts for the long rivalship between him and Amyr Hussyn, which only terminated with the death of the latter.

† Sāly Seray was the capital or residence of the Amyr, it is situated on the Jihūn.

the *Khān,* whom the deceased Amyr had set up, and promised to support him in his (nominal) dignity, provided he would employ Abdullah as his Vizier: the whole party then proceeded towards Samerkund, but on their arrival there, they put the innocent and harmless *Khān* to death.

As the Vizier Abdullah was a miser, who took from every one, and gave to nobody, and who had thrown the eyes of cupidity on the wealth of the two murdered personages, (the Amyr and the Khān) the conspirators elevated Timūr Shāh Aghlān, son of Munsūr Timūr, to the *Khānship,* they then attacked the party of Abdullah, and fought three battles with them; but Abdullah having swam his horse across the Jihūn, took refuge in the country of Khutelan and Anderab, where he died.*

CHAPTER VI.

A. D. 1359.

In the year 760, having attained my twenty-fourth year, being much disgusted with the infamous conduct of Kutlug Timūr and Sultān Kūly, and being without any other remedy, I mounted my horse and proceeded to the (Oulus) tribe of Byan Selduz, and implored him to join me in taking revenge on the murderers of the late Amyr and Khān; he agreed to unite with me, and we put on the swords of revenge. Although the fortress of Shadmān belonged to me, yet I divided with Byan Selduz, in a brotherly manner, and gave him possession of it, in order to secure his co-operation, and to prove to mankind that the murderers of Kings should always suffer retaliation.

I also prevailed on Hajy Berlās, a descendant of Kerachār Nuyān, to join us in revenging the death of the *Amyr* and the *Khān;* I therefore drew my troops out of Samerkund, and proceeded towards Kesh; when arrived in its vicinity, I sent to Hajy Berlās, who came and joined me; we then agreed to proceed to Samerkund, and to depose Timūr Khān from the Khānship.

In compliance with this determination, we marched with all our forces to Samerkund, and dethroned Timūr Khān, and took possession of the whole kingdom of Maveralnaher, and we three persons divided it between us; I got possession of Kesh, with its dependencies, and fixed my residence there.

Thus we three persons ruled the country of Maveralnaher like three brothers, and whenever any noble, soldier, or citizen proved disobedient, we united in punishing him: we agreed very well together, and divided the revenues in a

* These countries are situated between the 36th and 38th degrees of northern latitude, and between the 68th and 70th eastern longitude.

brotherly manner, till at length Byan Selduz, from excess of drinking, suddenly bade adieu to this world.

I then said to Hajy Berlās, "shall we divide the portion of Selduz between us, or shall we give it to his son, so that his troops may remain faithful, and things may go on as usual;" but he would not listen to this, and seized on some part of the share of Selduz, in consequence of which violent disputes took place between the followers of Selduz and him.

When this intelligence reached the ears of the surrounding chiefs, each of them exalted the standard of Sovereignty, but I continued to govern my own country quietly and with regularity.

About this time, several disturbances broke out in Maveralnaher, on which occasion both the Nobles and Plebeians of Turan came to me and explained their situation, saying, there is now no King in this country (and the petty Tyrants harass us), we are resolved to abandon the country, till some person is placed on the throne of power (who can protect us). On hearing this, my ambition was rouzed, and I wished to take possession of the whole kingdom, and become absolute Sovereign of it, but I found that I could place no reliance on the support of the people. I therefore thought it better for the present to keep on terms with the different chiefs who had independence, and endeavour to throw the ball of discord among them, so that, by degrees, I might bring each of them under my subjection; but to effect this, I saw that, patience, perseverance, and (divine) aid were requisite.

During this same year, which was A.H. 760, I began to take measures for extirpating these petty princes of Maveralnaher (Mulouk al Tuāef), and I wrote to each of them a separate letter, requesting them to join me, and that we should divide the country in a brotherly manner between us two. They all gave a favourable answer to my letters, but none of them were aware of my correspondence with the others.

Having thus excited the ambition and cupidity of each of them, and having agreed that whatever country should be subdued, was to be equally divided between the parties, they individually bound themselves with the girdle of fealty to me. This was in fact a very important affair, for Elchy Bughā Selduz had raised the Standard of Royalty in Balkh; Amyr Bāyezyd Jelayr had taken possession of Khujend; Khuajeh Ayzdy had established himself in Shumerghānat. The Kings of Badukhshān were contending with each other in the mountains of that province. Hy Khusero and Altaja Berdy had seized upon Khutelan and Arheng, and Khizer Yusury was in possession of all the country from the bridge of Tashkund to the vicinity of Samerkund. Now, to take the kingdom from such chiefs, each of whom vied in splendour with the other, was indeed a difficult undertaking, but I resolved to do it by setting them at loggerheads.

I therefore wrote to Elchy Bughā, that the inhabitants of Badukhshān had complained to me of their rulers, and had requested me to proceed thither to relieve them, that I had determined to do so, and, if he would join me, that country should be annexed to his dominion: otherwise, as it was my duty to administer justice to the oppressed, I should do every thing in my power to assist them. When he received my letter, he immediately drew out his army to attack the Kings of Badukhshān, and they forthwith sought refuge with me, and offered, if I would deliver them from their peril, they would make over the whole country to me, and become my subjects.

I also wrote to Hajy Ayzdy, the Ruler of Shemerghān, that the province of Balkh being now unoccupied, I had sent an army to take possession of it; but that if he had any ambition to partake of the conquest, he might become my partner in this business; this rouzed him, and he immediately invaded Balkh. When this intelligence reached the ears of Selduz, he returned from Badukhshān, and came to Hissar Shadmān and Balkh.

And the Kings of Badukhshān bound the girdle of fealty around their loins, and promised that whenever, or wherever, I should summon them, they would attend me with all their followers.

When Selduz entered the province of Balkh, Hajy Ayzdy of Shemerghān drew out his army and engaged him; but, being defeated, sought refuge with me; having thus made him one of my dependants, I drove out Selduz, and restored Shemerghān to him.

This same year, Amyr Hussyn, the grandson of Amyr Kūrgen, who sought the inheritance of his grandfather, marched from Cābul, with all his tribe and followers, and came towards Maveralnaher; he also wrote me a letter requesting my assistance; as his sister was one of my wives, the sinews of my affection were put in motion.* I therefore encouraged him to advance towards Maveralnaher. This in fact was the greatest error I committed during my whole reign, for I thus admitted into my friendship a person of vile disposition, proud, and miserly, but I being then ignorant of his character, advised him to invade Badukhshān, which he did, and made himself master of that country.

In this year, 760, a son was born to me; as he was my first, I named him Muhammed, after the Prophet, upon whom, and upon his descendants, be the Grace of God; and, as it occurred at a period when I was very successful, I considered it an auspicious omen, and added Jehangyre, (Conqueror of the World). I

* See Note, page 42.

also gave a grand feast, to which all the principal inhabitants of Maveralnaher came, except two of the Nobility; the first was Amyr Bāyezyd Jelayr, the other, Amyr Hajy Berlās.

I however did not shew any displeasure, but acted kindly to all their dependants and followers, which induced them to take my part; in consequence of which the tribe of Berlās, which was under the command of Amyr Hajy, but who were disgusted with his conduct, repaired to me; also his wife's father, ambitious of getting the command of the tribe for his grandson, by which he himself would get the power into his own hands, attempted to assassinate him: but the Amyr having discovered the plot, sent the scoundrel to hell; he then came to consult me whether he should destroy the family; I told him, that to take revenge upon children would be highly improper, and only cause poverty and distress.

In this same year, A. H. 760, Amyr Hussyn got possession of the whole kingdom of Badukhshān, and took prisoners three of the Princes of the country, heirs of the former kings, whom his minister, Mahmud Yusury, very unjustly put to death, but the revenge of their blood seized hold on the skirts of Amyr Hussyn; and their heirs obtained legal retaliation on him, as will be hereafter mentioned.

CHAPTER VII.

When I reached my twenty-fifth year, Tugleck Timūr Khān, the descendant of Jengyz Khān, who was absolute Sovereign of the *Desht Jitteh*, advanced towards Maveralnaher with the intention of subduing it, and encamped on the banks of the Khujend river, from whence he sent me an Imperial edict to summon all the chiefs to his presence.*

Hajy Berlās being much frightened, consulted me what we should do in regard to opposing Tugleck Timūr. I said, "it is advisable that we should wait on him in person, but let us send our tribes and hordes to the south side of the Jihūn, towards Khurasān, that after he has entered Maveralnaher we shall see whether he intends to remain; if he stops there, he will then lay the province waste; but if he does not intend keeping possession, we will attend his court." After much argument it was at length agreed that I should wait on Tugleck Timūr with my own people, and, by my ingenuity, endeavour to preserve the country from being plundered, because "policy is often superior to the sword." It was also determined that Hajy Berlās should proceed towards Khurasān with the Tribes and

* See page 15, printed copy of the Institutes.

Clans, whilst I remained behind to protect, if possible, the country; but, if not, to follow him.

In consequence of this determination, I gave the blessing to Hajy Berlās, and sent him off with all the tribes and hordes, but escorted them two or three day's journey; after which I returned alone, and took up my residence at Kesh.

Amyr Bayezy having explained the order to his Tribe, marched with them to meet Tugleck Timūr.

At this time my Father Teragay was taken very ill: and, in order to attend on him, I was obliged to postpone my visit to Tugleck Timūr; but when the decreed hour had arrived, my honoured parent resigned his life, and bade adieu to the world. I buried him in an honourable manner in the vicinity of Kesh, the burying ground of the Holy men (Aulia). After this event all the principal inhabitants of Maveralnaher waited on me, and by agreement said, "We are twelve thousand Cavaliers, we wish you to accept the Sovereignty: and if you permit, we will read the *Khutbēh* in your name, for it is written in the '*Rules of Government*,' that whoever has twelve thousand Cavaliers true and faithful to him, should he not raise the Standard of Royalty, ought to be reckoned inglorious." As I knew that this proposal of theirs proceeded entirely from fear, (of Tugleck) and that no dependence is to be placed on stipendiaries or needy followers, till tried by experience, I merely contented myself by assuring them there was no danger, and consequently no necessity for this imprudent measure.

At this time I received a second summons from Tugleck Timūr, I therefore explained to the chiefs and principal persons of Maveralnaher, that the coming of Tugleck Timūr was an unexpected calamity, and it would be better, as the Jetes are noted for avarice, to satiate them by presents, and induce them to refrain from murder and rapine.*

Soon after this, the first division of the Jetes, commanded by Mahmūd Yusury, entered Maveralnaher in great force, with the intention of plundering and laying waste the country, and encamped at Heraz, I therefore assembled my own people, and taking with me the principal personages, and a number of curiosities and valuable presents, I proceeded towards the Jete army.

When I arrived at Heraz, I met the general Mahmūd Yusury, and we embraced on horseback; we then proceeded to his tent, where he entertained me; after dinner I presented him a number of valuable articles, and requested that

* These Jetes are not to be confounded with the ancient Getē, they were unconverted Tūrks, and at this time inhabited the country of Jetteh or Deshti Jitteh; Timūr afterwards calls them his countrymen, in fact they were the followers of the descendants of Jengyz Khān. See also printed copy of the Institutes, page 25.

he would halt where he was, while I should proceed to the next division of the army, and visit the other officers; I accordingly marched forward to the *Heravul,* and in the plains of Keshem, I waited on the Commander in Chief (Amyr al Omrā) and other Generals; they all came forward to meet me, and received me in the most gracious manner, and praised me exceedingly; I deceived them also by rich presents, and prevailed on them to halt in the desert till I should have paid my respects to the Khān.

The three generals agreed to my request, considered my visit as an auspicious omen, and wrote in my favour to their master.

At length I paid my respects to Tugleck Timūr, while encamped on the banks of the Khujend, and the chiefs of the tribes and principal persons of the country had the honour of saluting him, (Kūrnish) and of making him their numerous offerings. When the Khān was informed that the generals of the advanced divisions had taken valuable presents from the inhabitants of Maveralnaher, he was incensed, and ordered all the presents to be confiscated, and deposited in his treasury. This order gave great offence to the officers, and they vowed vengeance against him.

At this time, intelligence was brought that the officers of the army in *Jetteh* had raised the standard of rebellion against Tugleck Timūr; he therefore consulted me, saying, "shall I march against the mutineers in person, or shall I send an army to subdue them." I replied, "in going yourself to the desert, there is only one danger to be apprehended, but by sending an army, and not going in person, there are two* to be feared:" the Emperor was much gratified by this advice, and in order to subdue the mutinous officers, returned towards the desert.

And he gave me the command of the (Tumān) tribe of Kerachār, and the government of Maveralnaher, with permission to return; in consequence of which, all the people of that country, both great and small, soldier and citizen, considered themselves under great obligations to me, and offered up thanksgivings and prayers for my success, in recompense for my having (through the grace of God) averted such a calamity from them. Amyr Jelayr, who with his people had also paid their respects to the Khān, came and joined me. Thus I became absolute master of all Maveralnaher; I then compelled all the nomade tribes to conform to my regulations, and I took up my abode in the city of Kesh, called also Sheher Subz or verdant city.†

* First, that his army might be defeated by the mutineers, and second, that they might join them.

† Lat. 39,20 North.

CHAPTER VIII.

About this time, A. H. 762, the Syeds, the prelates, and the learned, and other principal persons of Maveralnaher, waited upon me, and requested that I would permit them to read the (Khutbēh) royal proclamation in my name, but I desired them to postpone doing so, for I reflected within myself, that it was first requisite to clear the country from thieves and robbers, and bring all the nomade tribes into perfect subjection, after which it would be easy to have the Khutbēh read, and have the coin struck in my own name. A. D. 1361.

At this time I received a letter from (the Jete General) Amyr Khizer Yusury, informing me that he was coming with all his tribe to become my subjects; I was much rejoiced that he should thus voluntarily submit to my authority, and was convinced that the standard of my sovereignty was daily rising more and more.

When in this year, I had attained the age of twenty-six, Amyr Hussyn, the grandson of Amyr Kūrgen, whom I had encouraged to the invasion of Badukhshān, attacked the fort of Shadmān, belonging to Myan Selduz, and requested my assistance: in consequence of our family connection, I agreed to assist him; I sent a division of troops, under the command of Khizer Yusury, to join him; a few days afterwards I marched with my own division. When Selduz was informed of my movements, finding himself unequal to contend against such a force, he evacuated the fortress of Shadmān, and fled into Badukhshān; when intelligence of these events reached Behāaddeen, (the legitimate Prince of that country) he fled to the mountains, and Amyr Hussyn with little difficulty got possession of all Badukhshān. A. D. 1361.

Amyr Hussyn was however jealous of my movement, and when I arrived at Shadmān, fearing that "I would take the Lion's share," he wrote me a letter of thanks, stating, "that owing to my assistance, he had gotten possession not only "of the fortress, but also of all the plain country of Badukhshān; he, therefore, "requested that I would not take the trouble of advancing any farther, and that "I would have the goodness to return to my capital; but that I was master, "and might do as I liked; that he should ever consider himself under the "greatest obligations, and reckon Badukhshān as a gift from me."

At this time, Kykubad, brother of Kykhūsrū Khutelāny, who was called the murderer of Kings, for he had put to death the King of Badukhshān, waited on me, and began to flatter me; but as I had no confidence in him, I put him to death.

When I received Amyr Hussyn's letter, I acted in a friendly manner to him, but I appointed Khizer Yusury, whom I esteemed as my right arm, to the command of the fortress of Shadmān, and returned to my capital, which was the city of Subz, and there took up my abode.

Some time after this, I sent an invitation to Khizer Yusury, to come from Shadmān and visit me. After the course of a fortnight, he having previously received valuable presents from Amyr Hussyn, came to me; I received him as my guest, gave him a grand entertainment, and having attached him to me, sent him back to Shadmān.

About this time, an Ambassador came to me, sent by Amyr Hussyn, to represent that he was in great distress, and solicited my assistance, for that Myan Selduz had attacked him, that the people of Badukhshān had deserted him, that he feared every day being seized, and that his only chance of safety was my marching to his aid.

The sinews of my honour being thus touched, I ordered an army to march immediately from Subz towards Badukhshān, and I sent letters to Amyr Bāyezyd and Khizer Yusury, to proceed immediately to the assistance of Amyr Hussyn; the former delayed, but the other very shortly joined him. During this time, I proceeded towards Badukhshān, and when intelligence of my approach, and of Amyr Hussyn's having advanced to meet me, was conveyed to Myan Selduz, he thought it more prudent to flee than to stay; Amyr Hussyn then waited on me, and entertained me hospitably; I having thus delivered him from his enemy, left him in possession of his country, and returned towards my capital.

When I arrived at (Derbund Ahēny) the iron gate, I received information that Hajy Berlās, (Timūr's uncle) who through dread of Tugleck Timūr, had fled to Khurasān, had returned, had visited Bāyezyd Jelayr, (who had disobeyed my orders by not going to the assistance of Amyr Hussyn), and that they had not only agreed to seize upon my city of Kesh, but that he had actually done so.

When he received intelligence of my approach, he drew out his army, and prepared to oppose me: as I always considered Hajy Berlās as one of my own bones, I wrote him a letter;

(Here follows the Tūrky letter ;)

reproaching him for his breach of friendship, and offering to give him the district of Kesh if he would rejoin me: but after the receipt of my letter, he gave orders for my destruction, and drew up his armies in battle-array, at a place called Akyār, so that I could not pass by. Finding them thus determined to annihilate me, I resolved to fight him in a regular engagement, hoping to conquer him by my superior skill in manœuvering.

The following is the arrangement I made for engaging Hajy Berlās: I divided my troops into seven divisions, and ordered each division to attack the enemy in succession, judging that by the time of the seventh charge, his troops would certainly give way. As my opponent still kept possession of Akyār, I drew out my army in the following order; I took the command of the centre (Ghul) myself, the right wing I gave in charge to Khizer Yusury, the left wing I consigned to Jakū Berlās, and divided the troops of Subz into four divisions. The first day was spent in manœuvering, the second day we made frequent charges on their line, and had a good deal of fighting: on the night preceding the third day,* I asked the blessings of the religious personages, and as soon as the day broke, which might be considered as the dawn of my good fortune, I mounted my steed and advanced; but Hajy Berlās being terrified, fled to Samerkund, and took refuge with Bāyezyd Jelayr. After the victory, I made a new arrangement of the troops, and taking some of those of Subz and the Yusurians, under the command of their leader, I went in pursuit of Berlās, and over-ran the country even to the vicinity of Samerkund; but when we had arrived there, a part of the troops of Kesh, notwithstanding I had gained a victory, deserted me, and went and joined Berlās.

I also discovered that all the other troops were disaffected, that even Amyr Jakū, who was descended from my ancestor Kerachār Nuyān, forgetting our family connexion, and Khizer Yusury, whom I esteemed as my right arm, forsaking the path of rectitude, and seduced by the Devil, deserted me, and went and joined my enemies.

After my enemies were assembled, they consulted together, and came to the resolution of making a simultaneous attack, in order to deprive me of the city of Subz; at length they determined to proceed first to Samerkund, and there being joined by Bāyezyd Jelayr, they should then come out and annihilate me.

It is requisite to mention, that when these chiefs paid their compliments to Bāyezyd Jelayr, he received them all in the most gracious manner, entertained them with great hospitality, and endeavoured to ingratiate himself with them; they were however suspicious of his intentions, and fled from Samerkund. On hearing of this circumstance, I immediately wrote a letter to Khizer Yusury, persuading him to return to my service; but as he was afraid of me also, he would not put any confidence in my promises, and said, "the sword must decide our quarrel." When this intelligence was brought me, I drew out my army, resolving at first to stand on the defensive, afterwards to make our attack on him, and if possible, take him prisoner.

* The Muhammedans reckon the commencement of the day from Sun-set.

In consequence of this determination, when Yusury drew out his army at a place named Serūs, I gave orders for my troops to remain on the defensive, till the enemy should have expended their fury, and exhausted their strength, when we should in our turn attack them. The next day I reviewed the troops of Subz, and having given them my own standard, ordered them to advance against the enemy; they accordingly did so, and skirmished with them. When Khizer Yusury saw my standard, he thought I was in the first line, and made a vigorous charge on it; the ground was warmly disputed by both parties, sometimes retreating, sometimes advancing, greatly fatiguing and wounding each other. During this time I was in the rear of the battle, and when I thought that the enemy were sufficiently exhausted, I ordered the trumpets to sound, and with my fresh troops made a vigorous charge, they were not able to withstand this attack, and took to flight.

When intelligence of this event was carried to Bāyezyd Jelayr, the governor of Samerkund, he immediately mounted the throne, and assumed the state of an absolute Prince, and being no longer jealous of me, he wrote me a letter, and again heated the chain of friendship. Hajy Berlās, who was also jealous of Yusury, being now satisfied, went and assumed the command of his own tribe. But notwithstanding all these circumstances, Bāyezyd and Berlās continued to intrigue against me, and entered into a private treaty, stating that as long as Timūr lived, they should consider peace and tranquillity impossible, and that they should therefore do every thing in their power to annihilate him.

In order to carry into effect this treacherous and cunning plan, they wrote me a joint letter, proposing that "we three should divide the kingdom of Maveral-" naher in a brotherly manner; that whatever chief should quietly submit to us, " we should treat him with kindness, but that whoever should oppose us, must " be eradicated:" they also made several other advances to me of pretended friendship, with the intention of deceiving me.

Some time after this, Bāyezyd came out of Samerkund, and having joined Berlās, they encamped in the vicinity of Kesh, and made a great entertainment.

CHAPTER IX.

The scheme which Hajy Berlās and Bāyezyd Jelayr had laid for me was this; that having joined their forces, and encamped in the plains of Kesh, they should give out that they were going to invade Khujend, they were then to inveigle me to the camp, and having murdered me, take possession of the district of Subz.

In consequence of this arrangement, they sent me a letter, stating, "that as "they had resolved to subdue the country of Khujend, if I would join in this "enterprize, it would be very advantageous to all."

As I was not aware of their treacherous intentions, and considered them Muselmāns, I placed confidence in them, and set out to join them. When I reached the plains of Kesh, I saw a great number of handsome tents pitched, and a regular encampment formed.

When I approached the camp, Bāyezyd came out to meet me, and to do me honour, he took my hand and first led me into the public tent (Bargāh); he then said, "as we must have some confidential conversation, and the time is short, we had better go to the private tent," (Khergāh) and he led the way.

When we entered the Khergāh, I saw that the carpet was raised up in a particular part: and when I advanced, it appeared to me, that there was a well there which they had covered over with felt. Suspicion seized my mind! I delayed to sit down, and was convinced that treachery was intended. At this time Bāyezyd sat down on my right hand, and Berlās on my left hand. I then pretended that I was seized with a bleeding of the nose; I drew out my handkerchief, and applied it to my nose, and immediately walked from the private, into the public tent. I proceeded through it, till I was joined by all my Officers, as they were well armed; they sounded the trumpets, and we returned to our own camp.

Bāyezyd was afterwards ashamed of his conduct, and laid all the blame on Berlās.

At this time Myr Syed Aly of Termuz,* who was one of the most learned and devout personages of the age, cursed them both for me, saying, "O Lord, cast down the evil doers to the lowest pit of hell;" his prayer was heard, and God afterwards caused these two scoundrels to quarrel with each other, by which means I was delivered from their malice and treachery.

Immediately after this act of baseness, the camp broke up, the allies marched towards Khujend, and I set out for Termuz. When I arrived at this city, Shykh Aly Jerhyry suspecting that I intended to seize that country, and subdue the Nomade hordes, drew out his forces against me. As Shykh Aly was one of the learned persons, and had formerly been one of my companions, I did not wish to quarrel with him; therefore, when he had assembled all his tribe and connections, and had taken post in Old Termuz, I sent an agent to remind him that he he was under great obligations to me, and that, if he opposed me, the debt of ingratitude would certainly overwhelm him: that we had long been companions:

* Termuz was at this time a celebrated University.

that it was I who raised him to the command of his horde: that he had behaved ungratefully, deserted me, and joined Bāyezyd Jelayr. But my words having no effect on him, and he proving unworthy of his *Salt,* I cursed him, and prepared for battle. Shykh Aly finding that his followers were more numerous than my soldiers, was puffed up with vanity, and advanced with boldness into the field. I formed my troops into three divisions, and made a rapid charge on the enemy; my first division fell among them like a stone among a flock of birds, and they all dispersed. After the flight of the chief, I easily took possession of the horde: whilst the fugitive Aly went and took refuge with Bāyezyd Jelayr; in the end, God caused him to be a wanderer over the earth, till he came and begged my forgiveness. I pardoned him on account of his name (Aly), as it is a saying of the wise, "that when an enemy comes before you as a suppliant, and bends his knees, one should return thanks to God for having reduced him to his dilemma."

CHAPTER X.

In the year A. H. 763, (A. D. 1362) I entered my twenty-seventh year, on which occasion the great and the little, the chiefs of the villages of the hordes and tribes of all Maveralnaher paid their respects to me, and humbly represented that they had no monarch who would redress their wrongs: for, in every district, and every town, there was some tyrant, who unjustly plundered them, and seized on the property of the Muselmāns; their patience was quite exhausted, and that they should certainly abandon the country, unless some Sovereign was placed on the throne, who would protect them. In consequence of this representation, I wrote a letter to Amyr Hussyn (his brother-in-law) who was then in possession of Badukhshān, asking him "if he had the courage to join me in clearing the country of Maveralnaher from all its petty tyrants, and in relieving the wretched servants of God from the hands of their brutal oppressors, that if he would do so, we might then divide the kingdom in a brotherly manner, and thereby gain great fame and celebrity." He promised to do so, but immediately began to enter into treacherous schemes against me, wishing first to over-set me, and then to subdue the other petty Princes. Finding Amyr Hussyn thus bent upon my ruin, and that I had evident proofs of his treachery, I wrote a letter to Tugleck Timūr Khān, (Prince of the Jetes, and a descendant of Jengyz Khān, who was the absolute sovereign of Tartary) stating that "the country of Maveralnaher was now desolate, and only inhabited by kites and crows, but that if he would assist me, I would render it productive."

As soon as my letter reached the Khān, he drew out his forces and marched with an innumerable army towards Maveralnaher; and when he arrived on the bank of the (Sihūn) Khujend river, he sent me a letter, stating, "that he was en-"camped with his innumerable and valiant army on the banks of the Khujend, "that I should join him, but in the mean time inform him what further measures "were advisable." At this time Bāyezyd Jelayr put on the girdle of loyalty, and advanced to pay his respects to his sovereign, but leaving the city of Samerkund under charge of a deputy: as soon as he was presented at Court, the keys of the city were demanded from him, and as he delayed giving them up, the Khān ordered that his head should be struck off; this was immediately carried into execution, and the head was sent to Samerkund. Hajy Berlās, who at first intended to oppose the Khān, was so terrified by the punishment of Bāyezyd, that he took to flight, and sought refuge in the city of Kesh, but sent orders to his horde and his dependants to leave the country. He now repented of his conduct to me, acknowledged his folly, and asked my forgiveness; and then went across the Jihūn.

At this time, Tugleck Timūr Khān detached a part of the army of Jetteh to pursue the horde of Hajy Berlās, and a great battle took place between the contending parties on the banks of the Jihūn: on this occasion, Chughām Berlās, who was one of the Omrahs of that tribe, highly distinguished himself, and so occupied the royal army as to enable the tribe with their cattle, to cross the river in safety, except himself, who while defending the rear guard, was cut down by some of the soldiers of Jetteh. In the mean time, Hajy Berlās crossed the river in safety, and marched the horde towards Khurasān; when he entered that country, he behaved unkindly to the inhabitants, and began to be guilty of oppression and injustice; he also exacted tribute from the wandering tribes of Sebzwār, on which account several skirmishes took place, and the villagers having by surprise seized Aydkū Behader, the brother of Hajy Berlās, put him to death; they also seized the Hajy and put an end to his existence. As I was at that period in possession of Khurasān, I assigned the district of Jaser for the support of the dependants and followers of the Hajy.*

When the letter of Tugleck Timūr, desiring my immediate presence, reached me, it was also reported that Amyr Hamyd, who was the Khān's (chief counsellor) had said to him; "in every town and district of Maveralnaher, there is a separate ruler, they have at least thirty thousand cavalry among them, to oppose whom, we have been obliged to make numerous detachments; it is, therefore, quite requisite that you should prevail on Amyr Timūr to join you, for if he should unite with these petty rulers, they will be too many for us; we must, therefore, hasten his arrival, and as he is a very sensible man, let us consult him on the best measures to be pursued."

* Hajy Berlās was his uncle.

It was in consequence of this advice that the Khān wrote me a brotherlike letter, which induced me to make immediate preparartions for joining him.

The determination that I made on the subject of visiting Tugleck Timūr, was this; I resolved to write letters to all the principal inhabitants, heads of villages, elders of the tribes and hordes of Maveralnaher, stating to them, "that whoever wished to save his life and property from being destroyed and plundered by the armies of Jetteh, should immediately repair to me; but those who declined this offer, ought to quit the country without loss of time." In consequence of this invitation, the greater number of the chiefs and principal inhabitants came to me, bringing with them a number of curiosities and presents; as soon as they were all assembled, I proceeded with them and all my own soldiers and dependants, carrying various presents, and paid my respects to the (Khān) Emperor on the banks of the Khujend river: he received me most graciously, and when he saw the presents, his eyes were satiated; he then consulted me what was requisite to be done, I told him "that I had agreed for so many thousand *Durusts*,* as the revenue of Maveralnaher, and that he had only to appoint collectors to realize the portion of each district, and to punish those who refused payment."

He approved of my advice, and after he had taken possession of the throne of Maveralnaher, he again consulted me, on the best mode of preserving his authority; I said to him, "sovereignty is like a tent, the poles of which should be justice, the ropes equity, and the pins philanthrophy, in order that it may stand firm (against the blasts of adversity);" he was much pleased with this metaphor, and I continued, "you must secure the soldiers of this country in the bonds of kindness, that if they survive the war, you may find them act like men, and if killed, they may die in your service;" I further said, "the *good* of Maveralnaher are very good, and the *bad* are very bad; do you reward the good with goodness, and leave the bad alone, 'for evil shall overtake the wicked.'"

At this time, intelligence was brought, that the Amyr Hussyn had collected a very large army in Badukhshān; on hearing this, the Khān was ashamed of his former conduct to me, asked my pardon, and gave me the entire command of all the country, and all the hordes of Maveralnaher, with the city of Subz, and the Samerghānat, as far as the city of Balkh; he also left me in full possession of all my hereditary rights over my own tribe of Berlās, and other clans.

As it was now certain that Amyr Hussyn was resolved to oppose Tugleck Timūr, and had boldly advanced as far as the river Vahesh for that purpose, the Khān became thoughtful, and asked my advice. I said to him, the state of the case is this, as in addition to the forces of Badukhshān, Amyr Hussyn has been joined

* A gold coin.

by the rulers of Khutelān and Bakelān, he therefore feels bold enough to contend with you, the best plan is this, send the commission of Governor of the fortress of Shadmān and of the district of Khutelān to Ky Khuseru, the chief who commands the first line of Amyr Hussyn." The Khān approved of this advice, sent off the commission by a trusty messenger, and then marched towards the enemy. When he reached the *Iron Gate*, and had pitched his camp, the advance guard of Amyr Hussyn came in sight; the Khān immediately ordered his advance under Beg Chuck, to oppose the enemy; but when the two *Heravuls* met, Ky Khuseru deserted with all his followers, and joined the imperialists.

When Amyr Hussyn saw the state of his first line, he attempted to draw out the remainder of his army, but his right and left wings being panic struck, took to flight; thus Tugleck Timūr gained an easy victory, and the army of Jetteh plundered all the hordes and tribes of those districts, whilst Amyr Hussyn retreated towards Samerkund.* The mind of the Khān being thus at ease with regard to Amyr Hussyn, he returned to Samerkund, and having entered the city, put to death Myan Kūly Selduz; and being now in possession of the whole kingdom of Maveralnaher, all the chiefs of cities, and the heads of all the nomade tribes were obliged to submit to his authority, whilst the rebellious, and all the petty tyrants who reckoned themselves as *Sultāns*, were annihilated: a few of them, who had not been guilty of any gross impropriety, were taken into favour, and ordered to join my army.

When the country of Maveralnaher was thus cleared of all the petty tyrants, I returned thanks to God that what I had wished to do, was thus effected by his decree, and all my adversaries punished.

At this time I deliberated with myself how I should induce Tugleck Timūr to quit the country, and leave me in possession of it. I therefore suggested to him that Khurasān would now be an easy conquest, that in fact he had only to send his army across the river Amū, (Jihūn) and that he would meet with no opposition. He approved much of my advice, and agreed to leave me in charge of Maveralnaher, whilst he should proceed to the conquest of Khurasān.

About this period, news was brought that in consequence of the Divine decree, the chiefs of the Desht Kipchāk had rebelled, and had raised Beishky Aghlān, another descendant of Jengyz to the Khānship. On this occasion the Khān again consulted me; I said to him, " if you set out immediately, and proceed to the Desht before the rebels have gained strength, you may quell them easily, and preserve your authority over all the country, but if you procrastinate, you will

* It has been before stated, that *kund* signifies a town, Samer was one of the ancient heroes of Persia. It is the Maracanda of the Greeks, and is situated in Lat. 39,37 N. Longitude 64,9 E. See Edinburgh Gazetteer.

be overwhelmed in misfortunes and calamities:" as he approved of my advice, he was lavish in his praises of my merit, and gave me the entire management of Maveralnaher, but appointed his son Alyas Khuajē the nominal governor.

When I objected to this proceeding, he shewed me the agreement between our ancestors Kajūly Behader, and Kubel Khān.* In consequence of which, I accepted the office of (Sepah Salar) Commander in Chief, and he gave orders to all the officers of Jetteh, to be obedient to my authority; after which, he set out to quell the mutiny of the troops in the Desht Kipchāk.

As Alyas Khuajē had no talents for government, the troops of Jetteh soon began to exercise cruelty and injustice over the inhabitants of Maveralnaher, murdering and plundering the towns-people and farmers; I therefore lost no time in reporting these circumstances to the Khān, and complained to him of the malconduct of his soldiers: in reply to this, he wrote an imperial edict, "that I "should exercise my authority as Commander in Chief; that I should put his son "under any restraint I liked; that any of the Jetteh officers who were disobe-"dient to me, I should severely punish, and that every person guilty of injustice "should be compelled to make retribution in proportion to his offence." Finding myself thus absolute ruler of all the country of Maveralnaher, as well as of the nomade hordes and tribes, I forbade Alyas Khuajē, or any of his officers from exercising authority over the natives: on this account, the sinews of their enmity were excited against me, and anger converted their hearts into blood; they therefore commenced practising every kind of cruelty and injustice, and carried their tyranny to such a degree, that they carried off four hundred virgins from the city of Samerkund; they also made captives of seventy of the descendants of Muhammed, belonging to Termuz, and converted them into slaves to wait on them.

In consequence of these proceedings, the principal inhabitants of Maveralnaher surrounded me, and said, "is it to be borne by Muselmāns that these Jetes should carry off four hundred of their daughters from Samerkund, and make slaves of them; but if this is not sufficiently disgraceful, how much worse is it to permit them to seize the descendants of the Prophet, (on whom and on his descendants be grace), young men who are firm in their belief, that 'there is no God but God, and that Muhammed is the messenger of God,' without any fault; shall we who daily repeat his holy creed, and hope to be received through his intercession into Paradise, and shall we suffer these scoundrel Jetes to take them away without making any exertion for their delivery?"

On hearing these words, my Muselmān honour was roused, and I first sent

* See printed copy in the Institutes, page 25.

a message to Beg Chuck, who commanded the Jete troops, that he must immediately return all the Syeds, and the children of all the Muselmāns, that had been taken away. As this message had no effect, I spoke to Alyas Khuajē on the subject; but as the Jetes would not pay any attention to his orders, I put them to the proof, by mounting my cavalry, and liberating the seventy Syeds.

In consequence of this pious act, I dreamt that night that I saw the Prophet, who said to me, "in reward for this assistance that you have given to my descendants, the Almighty God will cause seventy of your descendants to occupy the throne of sovereignty." I wrote this circumstance to my *Peer*, who sent me the following answer; "that if the gracious God bestowed on the posterity of "Subuctageen such a reward for his compassion to a deer, you who have assisted "the descendants of the Prophet, how much greater will be your reward even to "the extent of seventy of your descendants:" I was much rejoiced by this answer to my letter, and I daily added to my respect and esteem for the posterity of the Prophet, and I always illuminated my assemblies by the presence of these illustrious personages. For my *Peer* said, "in whatever horde or town there are not any Syeds, and in whatever palace the learned have not free entrance, there exists neither blessings, goodness, piety nor chastity."

As I had exerted myself in repelling the injustice and cruelty of the Jetes, their chiefs bound round them the girdles of fraud and deceit, and they wrote to Tugleck Timūr Khān, "that Timūr had raised the standard of rebellion, and "had taken possession of the whole province of Maveralnaher, and intends to "put your son Alyas Kuajē to death." When the letters of the chiefs, especially that of Beg Chuck, who considered himself the Commander in Chief of the Jetteh forces, reached the Khān, he believed their falsehoods to be truth; he issued an edict for my being put to death; this was the third edict he had issued for my murder.

On receipt of this order, the Jete chiefs consulted together, and laid snares for my destruction; I was quite aware of their intentions, but pretended ignorance, for I could place no reliance on the inhabitants of Maveralnaher, to aid me against my foes; I therefore resolved to consult my *Peer*, and wrote to him on the subject; he replied, in conformity with the holy tradition of Muhammed, "Flee when its not safe to remain:" I then consulted the Korān, and this verse opened, "the sun returns to its resting place, such is the Divine decree of the Omniscient and Omnipotent."

I therefore left Samerkund, and repaired to the mountain of Salan, where I remained eight days; at the end of that time, I received a hint from (the Saint) Amyr Kelāl, that I should go towards the country of Khuarizm.

CHAPTER XI.

At this time, a messenger came from Amyr Hussyn, who was at that period a wanderer in the mountains and deserts, stating that as we were then both emigrants, it would be advisable to unite our efforts; I wrote him a letter appointing to meet him at the well of Sajai (or Sajuch); thither I repaired, and in a few days was joined by him; we then entered into consultation respecting our affairs, and determined that we should go to Tukel Behader of Khyūk, and prevail on him to join us; when we reached Khyūk, that scoundrel pretended to forget our former acquaintance: according to the proverb, " mankind imitate their rulers," and wished to seize us; when I discovered his views, I explained them to Amyr Hussyn, who at first would not believe me, but I gave him such proofs, that he was at length convinced, and we made preparations for going to Khuarizm, intending, when we should get possession of that country, to raise the standard of sovereignty, and endeavour to conquer Maveralnaher.

The plan we laid for invading Khuarizm, was this;* finding that Tukel Behader had behaved in so ungrateful and treacherous a manner, we left Khyūk in the middle of the night, and proceeded with all expedition towards Khuarizm; when we reached Banat (or Bayab), we rested our horses, and resolved to attempt taking the fort of Aurkunj by surprize, which would then lead to the subjection of all Khuarizm: whilst we were deliberating on this matter, we observed a cloud of dust arise in the desert, and could soon discern an advance guard of cavalry coming towards us; we immediately mounted, and I sent off Tughy Berlās to reconnoitre; I then rode to the top of a hill in the desert, and waited there; after a short time, Tughy Berlās returned and informed me, that the foe was Tukel Behader, who had come in pursuit of us, having with him about one thousand cavalry; I immediately sent for Amyr Hussyn, and drew up our forces on the hill, in such a manner as to make them appear more numerous than they were. In fact we had but sixty well mounted troopers with us, these I formed into five sections; the first of these I placed under the command of Tughy Berlās, the second I gave under charge of Syf Addeen, the third to Bulkhy Behader, the fourth consisted of Amyr Hussyn and his followers, and the fifth were my own (Khanēzād) dependants, with whom I took possession of the top of the hill: when I had made this arrangement, I gave each of them a flag to distinguish them.

* Khuarizm is an extensive kingdom, situated on the eastern side of the Caspian Sea, and divided from Maveralnaher by the river Jihūn, which falls into the Aral lake.

At this time, Tukel Behàder having drawn out his thousand cavalry, charged us, but was vigorously opposed by Tughy Berlās and Syf Addeen, so that his leading divisions fell back in astonishment. These two officers pursued their advantage, and fought with such intrepidity, that both their horses were disabled; they however continued to fight on foot, till I sent them two of my own horses, on which they mounted. The horse of Bulkhy Behader, was also knocked down, so that I was obliged to remount him from my own stud. At this period, of the whole number of the enemy, only three hundred remained, the others had been either killed, wounded, or fled. In the mean time, Amyr Hussyn had also drawn the sword of courage, and having charged the centre of the enemy's line approached close to Tukel Behader, but the soldiers of the latter surrounded him; seeing my brother-in-law in this situation, I rushed forward sword in hand, and liberated him.

When the hour of evening prayer arrived, the chiefs of the enemy drew in their reins; at this time they had only one hundred and fifty men remaining, while my strength was reduced to twelve.*

After a short time, Tukel Behader again drew up his men, and charged us; Amyr Hussyn and our remaining companions, devoted ourselves to death, and when they attempted to seize us, I exerted myself in such a manner as to overthrow several of their champions; at this moment, the horse of Amyr Hussyn being wounded by an arrow, threw him; his wife Dil Shād Aghā, however immediately dismounted, and gave him her horse. I remounted Dil Shād Aghā upon the same horse with my wife, the sister of Amyr Hussyn; we then commenced shooting our arrows, not one of which missed its mark, till our quivers were emptied. There now remained of us but seven mounted persons; but the enemy being also very much reduced, they withdrew from the fight, and alighted in the plain: our small party took the opportunity of proceeding on our journey; we were soon followed by our adversaries, but they missed us, and lost their way in the desert. After we had travelled a long way in these extensive plains, we came to a well, and being very hungry and thirsty, we alighted; fortunately for us, the water of the well was delicious.

We remained at the well all night, and in the morning I reckoned our people, and found that they were seven mounted persons, and three foot soldiers of Balkh; we continued by the well all that day, and fortunately for us, a shepherd who was tending his flock in the desert, brought them to drink at the well; as our provisions were exhausted, we bought several goats, parts of them we roasted, and parts of them we dressed between stones, and enjoyed ourselves exceedingly:

* See printed Institutes, page 35.

we remained there another night, during which time, the three footmen of Balkh, ungratefully stole three of our horses, and rode off with them: we were thus reduced to seven persons, with only four horses; but I did not then despond, and even comforted my companions; my respected wife Aljay Tūrkān Aghā, also kept up her spirits, and said, "surely our fortunes are now arrived at the lowest point, (and must rise) that we should be obliged to walk."

What added to our distress was, that none of us knew the road; fortunately we discovered a shepherd, who pointed out a pathway to us, and said, "this path will lead you to the huts of some Tūrkumāns;" I was delighted with this intelligence, and I set out on foot: when we arrived in the vicinity of the huts, we found that the inhabitants had apparently left them, and gone away; we therefore entered and took possession of one of them, but some of the Tūrkumāns who had remained behind, when they saw us, thought we were thieves, and made an attack on us. I placed my wife, the sister of Amyr Hussyn, in one of the huts, and with three or four of my men, we made an appearance of repelling them with bows and arrows, but we were without arrows, (having expended them in the battle); we then drew our swords, but when they came close to us, one of them named Syed Muhammed, who was an old acquaintance, recollected me, came and embraced me, and had compassion on my situation, and when informed of all the circumstances, he forbade the Tūrkumāns to injure us, and said to them, "this is Timūr the Governor of Maveralnaher;" the men being also ashamed of their conduct, came and bent the knee to me; Syed Muhammed took me to his own habitation, and paid me much respect and honour, and shewed us all the attention in his power.

At this time I had on two ruby armlets, one of these I gave to him; in return for which, he procured three horses for me, also some travelling equipage, armour, and arms; for three days he entertained us most hospitably, and gave us an escort of ten troopers, commanded by Fulanchy and Ajerchy.

Of the horses which he provided for me, I gave two to Amyr Hussyn, and being thus well equipped, I determined within myself, that I should go, and remain in the Mahmūdy desert, till my followers gaining intelligence of the circumstance, might come and join me.

I therefore made Fulanchy our guide, and we wandered in the desert for two days and two nights, without water or bread; till at length we reached the village of Mahmūdy, but which we found in a ruinous and deserted state, and void of inhabitants; we however alighted among the ruins, and as we could not find water, we were obliged to dig a well, and remained there for a month.

CHAPTER XII.

At the end of this time, Aly Beg Ghurbāny, chief of the Tūrkumāns, having been informed that Timūr was in the desert, and was endeavouring to collect his followers for the purpose of plundering the Tūrkumāns, was alarmed, and sent a a party to seize me by surprize.

In fact, whilst we were quite off our guard, they made a night attack on us, seized me, and led me to the Tūrkumān cantonment; when arrived there, Aly Beg, without seeing me, ordered me to be confined in a cow-house, swarming with fleas and other vermin, where he kept me and my wife without any other companion than the vermin, for fifty-three days and nights; at this time I made a vow to God, that I would never keep any person, whether guilty or innocent, for any length of time, in prison or in chains.*

At length, encouraged by the predictions of my rising to sovereignty, I resolved either to make my escape from the horrid place, or terminate my existence; I therefore determined to make the attempt, and either to be victorious, or to die manfully: at first I endeavoured to win over my keepers, by promises of reward, but being unsuccessful, I seized the sword of one of the sentinels, and attacked the guard; they fled, and I pursued them even into the presence of their chieftain: when Aly Beg saw my determined bravery and exertion, he was struck with remorse, and repented of his conduct, and sent back all the things that he had plundered from me.

At this time, a letter was delivered to him from his brother Muhammed Beg Ghurbāny, the contents of which were, "it is reported in Khurasān, that you have "seized and imprisoned Amyr Timūr, such conduct is highly unbecoming and "improper; it is requisite that you should immediately apologize to him, that "you treat him with the greatest honour and respect, and that you deliver to "his Highness the curiosities and presents which I have sent." In consequence of this letter, Aly Beg waited on me in a hut, which had been assigned for the purpose, asked my pardon, and gave me some of the presents which his brother had sent, but as he was a mean and avaricious wretch, he purloined many of them.

Having thus escaped from the clutches of Aly Beg, I was enabled to collect twelve horsemen; however, with these I again raised the standard of royalty, and resolved to proceed to the desert of Khuarizm: after two days we reached a village, where I alighted and took possession of a house, but I had no sooner done so, than a party of Tūrkumāns came out of the other houses, and prepared

* See printed Institutes, page 37.

to attack me; I closed the door upon (my wife) the sister of Amyr Hussyn, and attacked them. At this time one of them named Ahmed, recollected me, called out to them to desist, and with his followers, whom he had brought for the purpose of joining me, came and bent their knees, made their salutations, and entered my service. I placed my own turban on his head; in consequence of this honour, he promised to bring me fifty cavalry.

About this time, Mubarik Shāh Sunjery joined me with a hundred cavalry, he also brought me several horses as a present; in short, a number of the Syeds and other people of Khurasān, joined me, and brought numerous presents.

When I had collected about two hundred horse and foot in the desert, Amyr Hussyn, having taken some offence, left me and set off for Gurmsyr and Candahar. At this time, Mubarik Shāh, and some other chiefs, waited upon me, and said, " our remaining here in the desert, will be quite ruinous to our affairs. It is probable that Alyas Khuajē may send a Jete army against us; it is therefore better that we should quit this desert, let us go either to Khuarizm, or the countries of Merve Shāhjehān* or Bādghuish, and subdue one of them." I approved of their advice, but I reflected that it was predicted in my Horoscope, that I should mount the throne of Maveralnaher, the country of my Gūrgān ancestors, and I shewed the Horoscope to Mubarik Shāh, and the other officers, all of whom were pleased with it.

At length we determined that we would take the two hundred soldiers, and canton them in the vicinity of Kesh, where they might remain till wanted, while I should go among the nomade hordes and clans, and endeavour to collect more partizans.

Having repeated the prayer for success, we set out, and having reached the village of Karindān, a dependancy of Bukhārā, I first fixed on cantonments for my officers and soldiers, and I left my wife Aljay Tūrkān Aghā there; being thus alone, I went and passed my time amongst the hordes and tribes.

At this time, Timūr Kujy, who was one of my friends, having heard of my arrival, joined me with forty troopers, and paid me great attention: I therefore let him into my secret, and sent him to remain with my other troops, with orders that as soon as he should hear of my having raised the standard of independence in Samerkund, he should immediately join me. When a number of persons from the hordes, the clans, and the tribes, had agreed to join me, I determined that I would take with me one thousand of my bravest followers, and conceal ourselves in the city of Samerkund, and that another thousand should follow me and take up their abode in the neighbourhood. In consequence of this

* The Antiochia of the Greeks, it is situated on the Mūrghāb river, and is subject to the Khān of Bukhārā. See Edinburgh Gazetteer.

arrangement, I marched in the middle of the night, and proceeded towards the city. The next night, I entered Samerkund about the time of the last prayer, and took up my abode at the house of my eldest sister, Kutlugh Tūrkān Aghā. I passed forty-eight days in the city of Samerkund, but when matters were nearly ready for my breaking out on the troops of Jetteh, and destroying them, some of the inhabitants discovered my plot, and loosed their tongues in divulging my secret; my intentions being thus made known, I was under the necessity of quitting Samerkund; I, therefore, left it in the middle of the night, and repaired to the vicinity of Kesh; but as I found it imprudent to remain there, I proceeded with fifty followers towards Khuarizm; but as several of my people were without horses, and found it extremely uncomfortable to travel on foot, by good luck we discovered a herd of horses which were at pasture in the plains of Ajfer. I sent to inquire to whom they belonged, and having ascertained that they were the property of a tribe of Tūrkumāns, I wrote a royal edict to the proprietors, and seized the herd; having divided the horses among my foot soldiers, and now being well mounted, we galloped on to the banks of the Jihūn, and encamped on the side of the river. After a week, we crossed the river, and having reached the village of Achfy, where the country was composed of hill and dale, and the weather being very warm, we remained under the shade of some trees on the bank of the river Amuvy, for a month, and passed our time in hunting and shooting. At this place, my wife and Mubarik Shāh, with the other officers I had left at Karindān, joined me with their troops.

When my party was augmented to a thousand men, being distressed for provisions, I consulted the officers what we should do, they advised me that we should go and seize upon the country of Badghuish, and having taken possession of it, we might then plunder the territory of Merve Shāhjehān, by which means our followers would be relieved from their distress and want; I said to them, " this is all very well, but it appears to me better that we should go to Bākhter and Kandahār, and if we can take the latter place, we shall then become rulers of Kabulistān, of Sinde, and Moultan;" they all approved of this advice, and agreed to follow it; we then repeated the prayer for success, and prepared to march.

Previous to attempting so bold a measure, I thought it requisite to inspect my forces, and to equip them in the best manner possible; I found that I had just one thousand soldiers of my own, both foot and horse, but as many of them were in a wretched plight, I disposed of various ornaments which I had in store, and divided the amount among them; I then set out at the head of my cavalry; when we reached the banks of the river Hermūn, I entrenched my camp, and gave orders that every person in the army should construct a house or hut for himself. I also determined that I would take possession of Gurmsyr and Kandahār, and raise the standard of royalty. On this principle I sent a summons to Myr Mehedy, the *Kelanter* of Gurmsyr, and followed it in person.

When Myr Mehedy received the summons, and was informed of my approach by the sound of my trumpets; he advanced to meet me with the steps of submission: on his arrival in my presence, I placed my turban on his head, and he brought me many presents; thus I became ruler (Hakim) of Gurmsyr, and subdued it. At this time, Amyr Hussyn, who had chosen to abandon me, came and rejoined me, and I gave over to him half of the revenue of Gurmsyr.

After we had remained for some time in that situation, the ruler (Valy) of Systān sent an Ambassador to me, and laid the foundations of friendship; he also sent me valuable presents worthy of his rank. I made choice of the territory of Gurmsyr for my own residence, and waited a favourable opportunity to take Kandahār out of the hands of the Ghory dynasty, and to erect my own standard.

CHAPTER XIII.

A. D. 1362.

When in the year A. H. 764, I had attained my twenty-eighth year, the Valy of Systān, having entered into a war with some of his enemies, was defeated, lost several of his fortresses, and all his depots were plundered. He therefore wrote to beg my assistance, and " requesting that I would " deliver him from the hands of his oppressors, as he was without any other means " of redress" I soon after received a second letter from him, stating, " his utter " helplessness, but that if I would protect him, he would furnish provisions for " my thousand cavalry." I consulted with Amyr Hussyn on this subject; he was desirous of going alone, hoping that he might thereby get possession of the fortresses for himself; I however consented, and appointed Bihram Jelayr to the command of his advance, but Hussyn had only made one march towards Systān, when Jelayr having no confidence in him, deserted, and went towards Hindūstan; Hussyn considering this as a bad omen, sent a messenger to inform me of the circumstance, and to request that I would join him with my troops, so that we might conjointly subdue the fortresses of Systān.

When we had turned our reins towards Systān, the (Valy) ruler of that province named Jelāl Addeen Mahmūd, performed the ceremony of meeting us, and presented me a number of rarities; on this account Amyr Hussyn was jealous, I therefore sent all the presents to him. The Valy also according to his agreement, furnished the provisions for one thousand cavalry, and made a solemn promise of fealty and attachment; as these promises seemed to be sincere, I resolved to assist him, and having made a suitable disposition of my troops, we commenced our march in regular order.

The mode that I determined on for subduing the fortresses of Systān, was this; the number of the forts which the enemies of the Valy had forcibly taken possession of, were seven. The first of these that we attacked, we took in one night and one day; our troops escaladed the walls and the bastions, and rushed into the citadel: we found a quantity of provisions in the fort, all of which Amyr Hussyn took possession of, and appointed his own governor. The second fort we attacked, the garrison came out and fought with us; as that country produced a quantity of underwood, I ordered our people to make fascines, with which they advanced close to the walls, but the enemy, seeing this, called for quarter, and delivered up the fort; Hussyn again was before hand with me, and immediately appointed his own governor, and divided the plunder among his own people, and did not even give me thanks for my exertions.

When we went against the third fort, we arrived there in the middle of the night; as the fortress was situated in a sandy plain, I ordered the troops to dismount, and prepare their bows and arrows; we then advanced in silence close to the walls, and discovered that all the sentinels, except one, were asleep; my people threw their rope ladders on the battlements, and quickly mounted, and having subdued the garrison, brought them bound to me, and retained possession of the fort; all this took place before Amyr Hussyn arrived with his army.

When the Systān rebels saw our rapid success, they were much alarmed, and made overtures to their ruler, saying, "we have no objection to give up the remaining places to you, but if Timūr is permitted to take them, he will not only retain possession of them, but of the whole country."* The Valy being thus alarmed by this intelligence, marched off without giving me any notice, and having reached his own home, and having been joined by all his other troops advanced against us. I drew out our army in three divisions, Hussyn took the command of the division opposed to the enemy's right, the second division under charge of one of the officers, was opposed to their left, and the third division, consisting of my own troops, formed the first line, (Heravul) I placed the archers in front, and the cavalry with swords drawn in their rear; the archers poured in their arrows, and the cavalry, having made a furious charge, threw the enemy into confusion; I then, accompanied by twelve troopers, dashed in among them; at this time I was wounded by two arrows, one in the arm, the other in the foot, I was so much engaged, that I did not feel them at the time, but continued to

* See printed Institutes, page 47.

fight, till the enemy fled. Having gained the victory, we turned our reins towards Gurmsyr; during the march, I said to Amyr Hussyn, "all this misfortune has been caused by your covetousness," upon which he was much ashamed. I now thought it advisable to proceed to Gurmsyr, and remain there till my wounds should be cured; in the mean time, Amyr Hussyn might invade Bakelān, and subdue it. I therefore selected two hundred horse, and sent them with him, but counselled him to endeavour to make friends of the people of Bakelān, and if the army of the Jetes should oppose him, to avoid fighting them.

When Hussyn entered Bakelān, he conducted himself improperly, and gave no encouragement to the soldiers of that country, who offered to join him; he even disgusted his old servants by his avarice; he also felt so little fear of his enemies, that he began to collect wealth, and to accumulate riches.

At this time, Ajuny Beg, the brother of Beg Chuck, having placed an army of the Jetes in ambuscade, made an unexpected attack on Hussyn, and defeated him, so that he was obliged to flee with only four horsemen, and twelve footmen to the village of Sherkū. I was much vexed and hurt by this misfortune, and wished to go and drive the Jetes out of Maveralnaher, but I was obliged to remain quiet till I had recovered of my wounds: I then commenced arrangements for recovering that province; but at this period, my army was so much reduced, that I had only forty troopers remaining with me.

The first measure I proposed, was to take up my abode either in the valley of Arsuf, or the valley of Kuz, which were situated in the vicinity of Balkh, and having there collected an army, then to make an attack on the troops of Jetteh. In consequence of this resolution, accompanied by Timūr Khuajē Aghlān, who was the commander of my troops, I marched from Gurmsyr: on this occasion, Myr Mehedy, the Kelanter of that district, behaved to me with great attention, by preparing huts for the residence of those I was obliged to leave behind, and by supplying provisions for us all; being now satisfied in my mind, I set off with great celerity.

On examining my forty troopers, I found they were all people of good family, and not an ignoble person amongst them; I, therefore, returned thanks to God, that in my distress, so many persons of illustrious birth still remained attached to my fortunes, and was convinced in my own mind, that Providence intended me for some glorious actions, by having bestowed on me so many noble and disinterested friends.

At this time, Sadyk Berlās,* who was a descendant of Kerachār Nuyān, came out with a party to join me; when they were seen at a distance, my people supposed they were enemies that were come in pursuit of us; I therefore sent Subek

* See printed Institutes, page 49.

Behader, who was the leader of my advance guard, to ascertain who they were; he soon returned and informed me, that it was Sadyk Berlās, who, with one hundred warriors, was come in search of me, I therefore advanced towards him, as he had been one of my intimate companions; as soon as he saw me, he was much affected, I was also much affected, as were all the persons present, and I prayed devoutly to God that he would grant me power to deliver Maveralnaher from the oppressions of the Jetes.

We then left our encampment, and proceeded towards the valley of Arsuf; during our march, a messenger arrived from Amyr Hussyn, requesting me to send some troops to escort him, and that he would rejoin me; I immediately sent off Sadyk Berlās with forty troopers to protect him, and requested that he would meet me at the valley of Arsuf. I then proceeded on my journey, and soon after saw a large party of troops, who had taken post on the top of a hill, and their numbers appeared to be constantly increasing; I therefore drew in my reins, and arranged my people in order of battle, resolving if they were enemies, to attack them; at the same time I sent off the leader of my advance guard with a party, to ascertain who they were; as he was a courageous fellow, he galloped up to the hill, and called out to them, "whose troops are you;" they replied, "we are the servants of Amyr Timūr, and are in search of him;" on this, my officer went and visited the chief, and shortly brought me word, that it was Keranchy Behader, one of my old servants, who with one hundred troopers had deserted from the Jete army, eighteen days ago, and was come to join me. I prostrated myself in gratitude to God for this favour, and gave orders for the chief being admitted. When he approached, I considered his coming as an auspicious omen, I therefore embraced him and placed my own turban on his head, we then proceeded towards the valley of Arsuf.*

During the march, two lions made their appearance, one of them a male, the other a female, I resolved to kill them myself, and having shot them both with arrows, I considered this circumstance as a lucky omen; that night we encamped in a wood abounding with grass and water, and having marched the next day, we arrived at some broken ground in the valley, adjoining to which, was a hill; I took up my quarters on the hill, from whence I could see a great distance all around, and as there was a rivulet running round the bottom of the hill, I ordered the troops to encamp on its bank. In this situation we remained for three days, constantly expecting the arrival of Amyr Hussyn. During this period, my warriors lived upon the game which we killed; at length I sent a party towards Balkh, with orders to search for a flock of sheep, and to bring them with their owners to me.

* Institutes, page 51.

After two days, my people having found several flocks of goats and sheep, brought them with their owners to my encampment. The poor fellows were dreadfully frightened, but I paid them for the animals, with some *Durusts* (a small gold coin) that I had by me, and divided the males among the soldiers, but ordered the females to be kept for their milk and butter, of which I gave a daily portion to each person. When this trait of my justice was made known to the farmers of Balkh, they brought to my encampment, grain and all kinds of provisions, by which my troops were much refreshed.

Whilst we were waiting here in expectation of Amyr Hussyn, my people enjoyed themselves under the shelter of the hill and the bank of the rivulet, whilst I with my confidential friends, had a tent pitched on the top of the hill: on the fourteenth night, when the moon shone bright, I could not sleep, I therefore walked about, and when I returned to the hill, the day was beginning to break; I therefore prostrated myself in prayer, and as I was much affected, I supplicated the Almighty to deliver me from these toils, and render me successful and victorious;* I then employed myself in prayers to the Prophet and his descendants. After this I fell asleep, and dreamt that I heard some person say, "be patient, for victory is at hand;" I was so much rejoiced by this, that I awoke.

Just at this time, I saw from the hill at the distance of an arrow's flight, a number of soldiers, who appeared to be coming from Balkh, and going towards Kumrūd; I feared they were enemies, but resolved I would go alone, and inquire who they were; I therefore mounted my horse, and having approached them, I asked, "whence come ye, and whither are ye going;" they replied, "we are the servants of Amyr Timūr, and have come out in search of him, but cannot find him, although we have heard that he has left Kumrūd, and is come to the valley of Arsuf;" I said, "I am one of the Amyr's servants, if you wish, I will guide you to him:" when they had heard my words, one of them galloped up to the officers, and said to them, "we have found a guide who will lead us to the Amyr." They then drew in their reins, and gave orders for my being brought to them; they consisted of three troops, the first of the officers was Tughluck Khuajē Berlās, the second, Syf Addeen, and the third, Tubuk Behader; when they saw me, they were overwhelmed with joy; they alighted from their horses, bent their knees, and kissed my stirrup; I also came down from my horse, and took each of them in my arms, and I put my turban on the head of Tughluck Khuajē, and my girdle, which was richly embroidered, I bound round the loins of Amyr Syf Addeen, and I clothed Tubuk Behader in my coat, and they wept, and I also wept, and the hour of prayer was arrived, and we prayed with tranquil

* Institutes, pages 53 and 55.

minds; we then mounted, and came to my encampment, where we remained for some time; I assembled my principal people, and gave a feast, and having killed a quantity of game, we had abundance of meat, for which we returned thanks to God.

Having made the valley of Arsuf my head quarters, I sent out detachments on all sides, to gain intelligence, and enjoyed myself in the society of my friends. One day my spies brought information that a party of troops were advancing rapidly from Kumrūd; I immediately ordered my people to draw up in order of battle, and took post myself on the top of the hill, from whence I could clearly see a large party advancing rapidly: I said to myself, "God help us," and having formed my troops into three divisions, I advanced at the head of one of them; presently I saw a horseman coming towards me at full speed, when he drew near, he alighted, and having bent his knee, said, "that the troops were those of Shyr Behrām, one of my old servants, who having left the army with an intention of going to Hindūstan, had repented, was on his return to me, begged pardon for his offence, and requested permission to pay his respects." I accepted the apology, and advanced to meet him; when he came near, he hung down his head through shame, but I embraced him, and placed my own cap on his head, and bound my quiver about his loins; having reached my habitation, we alighted, and I made a great entertainment.

Four days afterwards, intelligence was brought that Sadyk Berlās, whom I had sent to escort Amyr Hussyn, was approaching the camp; I therefore mounted my horse, and went out to meet the Prince, having embraced, I led him to my tent, and we conversed on all the events that had occurred since our separation; after which, I gave him an entertainment: we remained for some time in the valley of Arsuf, and I sent spies to bring me intelligence of the Jete army.

At this time, I determined to seize the fortress of Aulajū, which was commanded by Munguly Bughai Selduz, to deposit my superfluous baggage there, and then make a sudden attack on the army of the Jetes. As Munguly Bughai was an old acquaintance of mine, I sent Shyr Behrām to him, to persuade him to come over to me; when Shyr Behrām came near the fortress, the governor sent a messenger to him to say, "although Amyr Timūr is my old acquaintance, yet as Alyas Khuajē (the Jete Commander) has entrusted me with the command of this fortress, how can I possibly be ungrateful for his Salt, and deliver the place to the Amyr." *

So much good was however effected by this measure, that three hundred men of the tribe of Dulān Jun, who had formerly been in my service, came out and joined me, which induced Munguly to abandon the fort. From this place we

* Institutes, page 57.

marched to the valley of Sūf, and encamped there; at this time Aulum Aly and Mahmūd Shāh Kabuly, with two hundred well mounted cavalry, who were coming from Kandahār, encamped within two *Fersukh* of me; they immediately informed me of their arrival, and of the state of their affairs, in consequence of which, I mounted, and went out to meet them; they also mounted, and came towards me; as soon as they came near, they alighted, and bent their knees, I also alighted and stood till they had made their obeisance, after which, I bestowed a (Jamēh) coat on each of them, and brought them with me to my camp.

After we had remained some days in the valley of Sūf, I resolved to send Amlis Behader with two hundred cavalry to scour the country in the vicinity of Balkh, till my arrival; having despatched him, I sent Temūke Behader with three troopers towards Khūlke, to bring intelligence of the Jete army; that brave fellow attempted to swim his horse across the river at Termuz, but the horse having been drowned, he still effected his purpose, for having joined his relations, he obtained a very particular account of the Jetes, and without staying to visit his children, returned immediately to me in the valley; the information he brought was, that an army of twenty thousand Jetes had plundered all the country about Termuz; when I heard this news, I mustered my army, and found that it only amounted to one thousand cavalry; it therefore appeared to me advisable to go and encamp in the valley of Guz, on the bank of the river Jihūn (Oxus). In consequence of this determination, I marched from Sūf; the first day I encamped at Guz, but the second day I proceeded to the plain of Ilchy Bughā, which is situated on the bank of the Jihūn, and halted there. At this time, Amlis Behader, whom I had sent to plunder the country about Balkh, rejoined me.

At this time, I received letters from the Amyrs Soleyman Berlās, Jakū, Musa, Jelāl Addeen, and Hindukeh, stating, "that upon hearing of my arrival at the "valley of Arsuf, they had quarrelled with the Jete chieftains, and had arrived "with one thousand cavalry at Termuz; that they had sent Tukul Bughā across "the river to obtain information respecting me." On hearing of the junction of these five celebrated officers, my troops were much exhilirated.

During this period, I received intelligence, that Munguly Bughai, who had abandoned the fortress of Aulajū, with Abu Saib, and Hyder Indēkhūdy, had offered the Jete Prince Alyas Khuajē, that if he would detach them from his army, they would come and seize both me and Amyr Hussyn, and bring us bound to his presence; that in consequence Alyas Khuajē had promised each of them the government of a country, and had detached them with six thousand cavalry; that they excited by cupidity, had arrived in the vicinity of Termuz, and had plundered and ravaged the country, thence they had proceeded to Balkh, where they hăd much oppressed the Muselmāns; on this account, all the hordes and tribes of that district had fled and crossed the river Jihūn, and were on their way to take refuge with me.

CHAPTER XIV.

After three days, early in the morning, the three chiefs, with their six thousand cavalry, arrived on the bank of the Jihūn, opposite to our encampment; as the river intervened between us, neither of us had an opportunity of attacking the other; I therefore thought it advisable to send to them Timūr Khuajē, who was a very clever man and good orator, to make them these three proposals. 1st. "As you and I are countrymen and relations, it is highly improper that there should be any enmity between us. 2ndly. It is reported that the object of your coming is to take Amyr Hussyn and me prisoners, and to possess yourselves of the fortress of Shadmān and Balkh, here we are, come take us, and bind us if you can, but remember that in so doing, you will unjustly cause the deaths of thousands. 3rdly. The Jete army will not always remain in these countries, I will shortly send them about their business, then you and I must dwell together in this country." When Timūr Khuajē had delivered my message, the fire of their anger was quenched; the next morning I went to the bank of the river, and requested a conference with the chiefs, when they came, I used such arguments (on the impolicy of their conduct), that they were convinced; I then returned to my tent, and remained all that day in that encampment. The following day the three chiefs disputed among themselves, saying, " we bound on our quivers with a promise of seizing Amyr Hussyn and Timūr, how can we now hold up our heads among the Jete officers, not having even attempted any thing." At length they renewed their threats against me, and marched along the bank of the river in search of a ford, or favourable place for crossing the river, that they might attack me. Hearing of their intentions, I also marched along the bank of the river opposite to them; when they had reached Balkh, they again encamped, I did the same.

On the following day, the three chiefs formed their army into three divisions, and having discovered a ford, crossed the river, and encamped, with a rivulet in their front.

At this time, I mustered my army, and found it amounted only to one thousand five hundred cavalry; but as they were all excellent soldiers, and vastly superior to those of the adversaries, I was not alarmed; I therefore allowed the whole of the enemy to cross the river without moving from my encampment, or shewing any sign of perturbation: when night came on, my chiefs wished to storm the camp of the Jetes; but as my army was so much inferior in numbers, I did not approve of a night attack, but trusting in the Divine aid, I spent the time in prayer.

Early in the morning, the enemy came down in three divisions, with an intention of surrounding me. Amyr Hussyn and I drew up our forces in two divisions, ready to oppose them; whilst in this situation, a horseman came at full speed to inform me that Amyr Soleyman Berlās, and the other chiefs, who were disgusted with the Jetes, had crossed the river higher up, and would join me immediately with one thousand five hundred horse; on hearing of these tidings, I prostrated myself on the ground, and returned thanks to God. I then mounted my horse, and proceeded to meet my allies; when we met, I saluted them in the most friendly terms, and raised their hopes of success. The next day my adversaries seeing that my force was daily increasing, became enraged, and advanced against me with twenty thousand men, drawn up in three divisions.

The arrangement that I made for opposing the Jete army, was this; I divided my three thousand men into six regiments, and having advanced to the brink of the rivulet, took possession of the bridge, and having crossed the bridge, drew up opposite the enemy; I then resolved to attack them in three points.

At this time they were advancing, I therefore ordered the three first regiments to salute them with a shower of arrows; I then sent the fourth regiment to their assistance, and commanded them to charge sword in hand; the flame of battle soon rose between the contending parties; from morning till late in the day, the contest continued with alternate success, and determined obstinacy, neither side giving way; at length both parties being much fatigued, Amyr Hussyn and I ordered our standards to be unfurled, our trumpets to sound, and calling out Allah Yar, (God is with us) charged sword in hand, with our own divisions, from the bank of the rivulet amongst the enemy; on the first and second attack, they began to give way, however their chiefs keeping their ground, actually exchanged some blows with us, but at length took to flight, and gave up the contest, leaving their camp to be plundered by us.*

I advanced into the middle of the plain, when all the chiefs and nobles came up, and congratulated me on our success; I ordered the camp to be pitched and halted there for some days.

When Alyas Khuajē (son of the Khān) heard of the defeat of the three chieftains, he ordered a large force under the command of Aljun Behader, the brother of Beg Chuck, to march against me, whilst I being puffed up with my victory, took no pains to get intelligence of their proceedings.

* See Institutes, page 63.

At this time, I resolved to leave Amyr Hussyn with his troops in the vicinity of Balkh, and to proceed with my own forces towards Kehulkeh.

In consequence of this determination, I marched along the bank of the Jihūn, and having crossed the river in boats at Termuz, encamped on its bank, and sent my advance division towards the fortress of Kehulkeh.

The situation where I encamped, was nearly an island, being surrounded on three sides by water, and I waited there in expectation of the return of my advanced legion; but the advanced party being as negligent as I was, took no precautions for our safety, so that Aljun Behader, with the Jete army, passed them while asleep, and came unexpectedly on me; it was very fortunate that I had taken post in the peninsula, for all the tents that were pitched outside of it, were instantly plundered, and their owners compelled to retreat to the island.

I had luckily secured all the boats, in my rear, and therefore gave orders to send all our baggage and followers across the river, while I kept possession of the island, and annoyed the enemy with our arrows; till at length all the baggage and people having re-crossed the river, I got on board a boat and went over; I first gave orders to sink all the boats, and then encamped on the bank of the river, and remained opposite to the Jete army for a whole month.*

Amyr Hussyn having heard of my retreat, offered again to join me, but I desired him to remain at Khulm, and continued on my guard, while in the vicinity of the enemy. At length they marched off, and I proceeded towards Balkh; when I reached Khulm, Amyr Hussyn drew out his army, and advanced to meet me, and we encamped together in the plains of Khulm, and passed ten days more in feasting and rejoicing.

At this time, we deemed it advisable to unite the Princes of Badukhshān with us, in order to drive the Jetes out of the country; all the chiefs having agreed in opinion with me and Amyr Hussyn, we collected all our troops, and proceeded towards Badukhshān: when we reached the vicinity of the town of Kundez, the chiefs of the horde of Buraltay, came and joined us with one thousand horse; I spoke very kindly to them, and gave each of the chiefs a dress of honour, and considered their coming as a favourable omen.

When intelligence of our approach reached the Princes of Badukhshān, they were much alarmed, and drew out all their forces to oppose us; I at first determined to make a sudden attack on them, and subdue them before they could collect their strength; but when we arrived at Talkhān, we were met by an Ambassador from the Princes, who brought a number of presents, and opened the gates of peace and concord; as the proposals he brought, were founded on

* See Institutes, page 67.

union, not on discord, we consented, provided they would promise to join us in expelling the Jetes from Maveralnaher, for which purpose they should immediately furnish two thousand horse.

When the Badukhshān cavalry had joined us, Amyr Hussyn and I resolved to cross the river at Saly Seray, and enter the country of Khutelān, and compel the people of that place to join us against the enemy.

CHAPTER XV.

A.D. 1363. In the year 765, when I attained my twenty-ninth year, we entered the province of Khutelān, and the Prince of that country immediately came and joined me, as they and all our new allies had shewn a preference to me; this circumstance roused the envy of Amyr Hussyn, but he had no remedy but silence.

When we reached the plain of Kulek, my followers amounted to six thousand: at this time, owing to Amyr Hussyn's parsimony and misconduct, Shyr Behram and Bulad Bughū came and complained to me; soon after this, Amyr Hussyn requested to see me, when we met, he made grievous complaints against these two chiefs; I endeavoured to pacify him, but all in vain; I also exhorted them not to allow any private quarrels to interfere with the common cause; they promised me to meet him, but as soon as they left the assembly, they joined their own hordes. Whilst we were encamped in the plains of Kulek, I sent spies to bring me intelligence of Alyas Khuajē, and the Jete army; after ten or twelve days, the spies returned and reported that Kāch Timūr, son of Beg Chuck, was at the head of the army, which under various chiefs, amounted to twenty thousand horse, and were encamped in a line reaching from the villages of Helany and Seryany, to the stone bridge; that Tugluc Selduz and Ky Khuserū, who had deserted from me, and had now the command of six thousand Jete cavalry, were coming down upon me to take me by surprise.

I immediately ordered a review of my troops, and found that I had only six thousand horse, and that Amyr Hussyn had not that number, as many of his troops had deserted in consequence of his parsimony and improper treatment of them, and had joined my standards.

At this time, I received information, that a body of six thousand of the enemy's cavalry, having preceded the main body, had advanced one day's march from the stone bridge towards us; I therefore resolved to leave Amyr Hussyn in charge of the main body, and with a select corps, make a forced march, take the enemy by surprise, and cut them to pieces.

But reflecting that the army of the Jetes consisted of thirty thousand men, whilst I had only six thousand to oppose them, I sought in the Korān for an omen, and this verse opened to me; "how often has a small army defeated a superior one, by the permission of God:" I was much encouraged by this favourable presage.

The advanced division of the enemy having arrived one day's march on this side of the stone bridge, were informed, that I had retreated with my army towards Khutelān; they therefore called me a coward and run-away, and began to feast and rejoice.

Being hurt at their exultation, I returned from Khutelān, and making a long march with only two thousand cavalry, reached their encampment at the dawn of day, and found them asleep; my advanced guard soon drove in all their picquets, and the *salt of ingratitude* having laid hold of the skirts of Ky Khuserū and Tugluc Selduz, they were seized by my troops, and brought prisoners to me, but I did not punish them. My advanced party having defeated the first line of the enemy, compelled them to fall back on their second line, but before the latter was drawn out, I arrived with the remainder of my division, and after a slight opposition, they all fled towards the stone bridge.

I pursued them, and continued beating them, and capturing their horses till I had forced them across the bridge, when they disappeared, and joined their grand army under the personal command of Alyas Khuajē. I halted that night on the banks of the river, and sent off a messenger with information of my success to my ally, Amyr Hussyn.

The next morning, having said my prayers, I marched along the bank of the river, and having sent out scouts and a strong advanced guard, I encamped in the desert of Khutelān, which was composed of hill and dale, and where my people and their horses rested. I halted there the next day, which gave Amyr Hussyn an opportunity of joining me: I then blocked up all the roads in such a manner, that not even a single animal could pass.

All my troops being now collected, amounting to nine thousand horse, the officers agreed, with all their hearts, to fight the Jete army; it was determined that the first line should consist of six thousand, under my command, and the remainder to form the second line, under charge of Amyr Hussyn.

When the Jete Commander first heard that I had gone to Khutelān, he resolved to send an army in pursuit of me, but his officers calling to mind how I had beaten Tukel Behader in the plain of Khuarizm, with only sixty horse, were afraid, and not one of them would take the command of the detachment.

The determination I came to with respect to fighting the Jete army, commanded by Alyas Khuajē, was this; I said to my officers, "there is no use in our skirmishing, or having drawn battles with the Jetes, we must lay such a scheme that we may have a general engagement, and purify the land of Maveralnaher from the defilement of their oppressions." I then ordered Muvyd Arlāt, Kera Behader, and Amyr Musā to take post, during the night, with five hundred horse at the head of the stone bridge, opposite to Alyas Khuajē, whilst I having crossed the river with five hundred horse, took post on a hill which overlooked the enemy's camp; my tent having been pitched on the skirt of the hill, I entered it, and gave orders to light fires on the sides of the hill; when the Jetes saw the numerous fires, they were much alarmed.*

I spent the whole of that night in my tent, in prayer, and besought the Almighty that he would punish these oppressors. At the dawn of day I fell into a slumber, I was not awake, neither was I asleep, when I heard somebody say, "Timūr, victory and conquest is thine;" I was roused, and looked about, but there was no person in the tent, nor any one on the outside of it; but to be certain, I called aloud, is any one there, I received no answer; I was then convinced it was the voice of an angel, (Hatif Ghayb) I prostrated myself on the ground, and returned thanks to God, and felt strong of heart; when the day broke, I performed the morning prayers with my friends.

At this time I heard the drums of Alyas Khuajē, and as soon as the sun rose, I saw his army going off in troops; my chiefs requested permission to pursue, saying, "we shall have an easy conquest;" but I replied, "this is a stratagem of the enemy to induce us to come down into the plain, that they may attack us to advantage, be patient, till we ascertain what is their real object." When they had marched four *Fersukh*, (twelve miles) finding we did not move from the hill, they encamped; Alyas Khuajē then sent for and abused the chiefs that I had defeated. The next day, Alyas Khuajē finding that I had fortified the hill, drew out his army, and made several attacks on the skirts of the hill, but I kept my post on the top of the declivity, and stationed the troops all around the foot of it.

When the enemy approached us, my people showered down arrows upon them, so that many of them being wounded, they began to take shelter in the crannies, and behind large stones. When the night came on, they relinquished the attack, but continued drawn up in a circle around the hill.

* Institutes, page 79.

About this time, I called a council of my chiefs, and represented to them, that "Amyr Hussyn's force being now separated from us, and as we have neither water nor provisions on the hill, if we remain here, we must be annihilated; let us draw out the troops in four divisions, and before the day breaks, attack the enemy; if we succeed in putting them to flight, we shall gain an easy victory, but if not, we shall open a way to escape from their clutches, and go where we like."

As my advice was approved of by all the chiefs, I put on my armour, and ordered that no noise should be made. At break of day, we marched in silence against four parts of the enemy's camp; as we took them compleatly by surprise, the division which had been ordered against the body commanded by Alyas in person, dispersed his guard, and might have taken him prisoner, but as I approached, I called out, and saluted him, *(Yul Bulshen)** and then forbade his being seized. At this time, as numbers of people had been killed or wounded on both sides, the warriors mutually desisted from fighting.

When Alyas Khuajē heard my voice, he called out to his troops, on which several of his warriors returned and renewed the fight, which was continued with great fury till after sun-rise, without either party gaining any superiority; at length our quivers being empty, my soldiers drew their swords, and charged the enemy, who being much fatigued by the long contest, and many of them wounded, said, "let us flee;" they then set off, and did not halt till they had reached their camp at the distance of four *Fersukh.*

As I did not think proper to pursue them, I remained where I was. When intelligence of my victory reached Amyr Hussyn, he joined and congratulated me on my success.

When the Jete army saw themselves defeated and subdued by such an inferior number, they were much ashamed, they threw their caps on the ground, and said, "*curse on our turbans,* that with such a force, we should have run away from an inferior number." Alyas Khuajē being also ashamed, swore he would never cease fighting till he had taken me prisoner. He then drew up his army, and having marched towards Kesh, encamped at the distance of four Fersukh from that city.

At this time, I distributed sums of money to all the wounded, to pay for their cure, and gave (Yurem) an allowance to the heirs of the killed. I then put on my armour, and having drawn out my army, Amyr Hussyn and I went and took post, in order of battle, opposite the Jete army. When Alyas Khuajē had reconnoitered my army, he forgot his former futile attempts, and having again placed his foot in the stirrup, he advanced a short distance towards us.

* See Institutes, page 83.

At this moment, Alugh Timūr and Amyr Jemshyd arrived express from the *Desht* Kipchāk, with the intelligence that Tugleck Timūr Khān had ceased to exist, and that he had appointed Alyas Khuajē his heir and successor; the two chiefs having delivered their message, bent their knees, and congratulated the Prince on the event; they then took hold of his reins, and led him back to his camp; soon after which, he marched with all his forces towards the *Desht*, leaving me to pursue my own plans. I then consulted with Amyr Hussyn, whether we should pursue the Jetes, and drive them out of the country, but he gave it as his opinion, that it was not policy to pursue a defeated enemy; I said, "they are not a defeated army, for they have not afforded us an opportunity of punishing them, but I fear they will murder the inhabitants, and plunder the country they pass through;" and as all the other chiefs were convinced by my arguments, Hussyn gave up his opinion.

At this time, a report was brought that the Jete army was returning in order to give us battle, after which, they would leave a force to support their governors and other officers in Maveralnaher, and then proceed to the *Desht;* but the fact was only this, that, Alyas Khuajē had sent orders to all his governors to strengthen their posts and remain on the defensive, as he would shortly return.

In consequence of my determination in the council, I drew out my army and marched after the Jetes; having arrived at *Kehulkeh,* I there halted, and reviewed the army; I found that including Amyr Hussyn's division, we had only between seven and eight thousand men, many of whom were wounded; I therefore gave leave of absence to all the wounded, to go away till they were cured; I then new modelled our force, with the resolution of attacking the Jetes; Hussyn's division was commanded by himself, and I retained charge of all my own followers.

Having marched from Kehulkeh, we arrived in the night at Herar, the principal inhabitants of the town came out to meet me, and a great number of people belonging to Kesh, who had served in Alyas Khuajē's army, deserted him and joined me; these people brought me intelligence, that the day before, Alyas Khuajē had sent a force into Kesh, and that he had sent governors and troops into all the strong places of Maveralnaher.

On receiving this information, I detached Amyr Soleyman and Syf Addeen, with a force to drive the Jetes from Kesh, and I commanded these officers, when they should arrive near Kesh, to divide their troops, and to gallop their horses about, so as to raise a great dust. In order to effect this purpose, the aforementioned officers ordered their men to cut down branches of trees, these they fastened to their horses, but dragging on the ground, and as they moved at a quick pace, they raised an immense cloud of dust: this was seen from the town, the Jete governor of which, supposing that a very great force was advancing against him, was much alarmed, preferred flight to remaining, and having assembled his troops, marched away.

The other Jete soldiers, who were dispersed through the district, extended the hands of slaughter and plunder over the unfortunate inhabitants, and made a shew of opposing me; but as soon as my army approached them, they lost their courage and took to flight, my light troops pursued them, and recovered a great deal of the plunder.

After six or seven days, Amyr Soleyman, and the other officers that I had detached, rejoined me, and all the soldiers of Kesh came and joined my standard.

At this time, Shyr Behram, who had left me in the plains of Kulek, and had joined the forces of Khutelān, having been absent forty and three days, came and rejoined me; also Shykh Muhammed, the son of Byan Selduz, came and joined me with seven regiments, (Kushūns) and all the soldiers of Kehulkeh followed their example.

As at this time, I was not satisfied with the conduct of Amyr Hussyn, I therefore carried him to the tomb of the celebrated Saint Khuajē Shums Addeen, where we took the oaths of mutual support and friendship, and I made him add that in case he should break his promise, he wished that I might seize and punish him, which finally occurred.

After taking this precaution for my self-defence, I followed the Jete army, when I approached them, Alyas Khuajē drew out his forces; he gave the command of his right wing to Amyr Jemshyd, the left wing to Tuck Timūr, the advanced line was under charge of Beg Chuck; he had also two flanking parties of horse, commanded by Iskunder and Yusuf; when I found that the Jetes were thus prepared for battle, I sought in the *Korān* for an omen, and this verse opened, "verily we have given you a decisive victory;" I immediately repeated aloud the prayer for victory, and ordered the troops to advance.

When we reached Tash Arighi, I reviewed our army, and directed Amyr Hussyn to halt with his troops, where we then were, and to form the (Kul) second line, and in the event of my being worsted, to support me. I then formed my own troops into seven divisions, and took charge of the (Heravul) first line; when we reached the village of Kupy, the first line of the enemy, commanded by Beg Chuck, came in sight; as I found that the Jete army was very numerous, and were united in solid column, looking formidable as a mountain, I again sought advice from the Korān, and this verse opened, "and we guard them from every devil driven away with stones:" * on this I became strong of heart, and ordered my first line to advance against the division of Beg Chuck; that chief at the same time directed a part of his troops to meet mine; as we approached each other, I commanded the *Chepavul* of the right to charge, then the *Shekavul* † of the left; after these two squadrons had made their attack, I ordered the trumpets to sound, and advanced with the line; when we came near, the right wing *(Juangār)* charged their left wing, *(Berangār)* when the flame of slaughter was thus raging, and the waves of the sea of battle were thus rolling, I saw that my people were worsted, I therefore unfurled my standard, and having caused the royal music to strike up, I made in person, a desperate charge with the centre of my line; all the heroes in every part of the line also behaved most manfully, and made the enemy feel the effects of their sharp swords.

As my opponent Beg Chuck began to recoil, his lieutenants Iskunder, Tuck Timūr, &c. advanced to his support. At this time the horse of Beg Chuck was killed, and I took him prisoner; the Amyrs Jemshyd and Yusuf seeing this, made a violent attack in order to release him, but when Jemshyd came close to me, my groom Aādil, who was on foot, hamstrung his horse; in consequence of which, the general fell to the ground, and was seized: on this Amyr Yusuf spurred his horse with an intention of getting out of the crowd, but losing his stirrup, he fell from his horse, and was also made prisoner.

Immediately after this event, Iskunder with his division, came against me, but being well supported by my body guard, I charged them vigorously, and compelled them to retire, and join their Commander in Chief.

Having thus defeated the enemy's first line, I ordered the trumpets to sound, and halted in the plain; I then commanded that my standard should be held up till all my soldiers who were dispersed over the field of battle, might see and rejoin it.

At this time, Alyas Khuajē roared out to his reserve, to advance; when I saw that he was confounded, I said, (Allah Yar) " God befriend us," and with three hundred and sixteen horse, which were all that were collected near me, I made a furious attack on the enemy's centre, and overturned his standard; when the army of Alyas Khuajē missed the royal standard, they took to flight; at this moment I was very near Alyas Khuajē, but Iskunder Aghlān threw himself between us, he was seized, but his master made his escape.

As soon as the Jete army had turned its face to flight, I ordered several divisions of my troops to pursue them, in consequence of which, they gained much

* See Sale's Translation of the Korān, page 68.

† See Plan of the Army, last page of the Institutes.

plunder of horses and arms; they also killed and wounded a number of the runaways; I then sent off two other divisions to keep in the rear of the enemy, to prevent them encamping or halting, to these I gave orders, not to kill any more of the Jetes, but to seize and bring them into my presence, in order that I might treat them according to circumstances.

I then encamped in the plain of Kupy, and gave orders for a grand entertainment, to be prepared in commemoration of our having defeated the Prince Alyas Khuajē, and thirty thousand Jetes, with only six thousand horse, by which the country of Maveralnaher was purified from the defilement of the tribe of Jete.*

Having halted in the plain of Kupy, which might be called the seat of victory, I commanded that my tents of every description should be pitched, and that a great quantity of soup and meat should be prepared, and invited the chief officers of all the hordes and regiments; the generals having arrived, Amyr Hussyn also came and joined the banquet; during the feast, I ordered all the principal Jete prisoners to be brought forward, I then addressed Beg Chuck, who was the Commander in Chief of the Jetes, and who had made several cuts at me, and said to him, "you have proved yourself grateful for the salt of Alyas Khuajē, in having rejected my overtures, and by standing by him to the last;" I also praised Amyr Hamyd, who was a very brave young man, and I said to Sekunder Aghlān, "you risked your own life to save that of your master, and have therefore behaved in a praise-worthy manner." I then asked them, "how it had happened that I, with so small a force, had defeated their numerous army;" they replied, "your good fortune overwhelmed us, and dispersed the Jete forces; the union of your army was also such, that one thousand swords struck together as one sword; whilst the discord that prevailed amongst us, disunited us, and made us an easy prey to your victorious arms."

I afterwards said to them, "what do you suppose I shall do with you?" They replied, "if you kill us, you will not much decrease the Jete army, but you will thereby raise up thousands of enemies, and all our hordes and clans will seek retaliation for our blood, but if you pardon and let us go, you will thereby confer a great favour on us; our tribes will praise you, and will consider themselves under an obligation to you, and will be your friends; your Highness is the best judge, whether our friendship or our enmity is preferable; with regard to ourselves, we are indifferent whether you kill us or not, for on the day that we bound up our loins, and braced on our swords, we considered our blood as shed, and our bodies decapitated." I was so pleased with their speech, that I endeavoured to prevail on them to enter into my service; but although I made them great offers, they would not consent to remain with me, I therefore conferred on

* This description of the battle differs much from that given by Petis de la Croix, p. 71, and sequel.

them dresses of honour.* I also gave coats to all the other captives, and released them, and I took particular notice of all my own officers and soldiers that had been wounded in the battle. I then despatched the Amyrs Syf Addeen and Jakū to take possession of the city of Samerkund.

Soon after this event, my (Keravulan) scouts brought information that Alyas Khuajē, with the Jete army, had encamped on the (South) bank of the Khujend river, but had postponed crossing; I therefore gave Shyr Behram the command of the (Heravul) first line, and sent him off. I then mounted my horse and proceeded towards them; on hearing of my approach, the enemy immediately crossed, and when I arrived at the river, not a vestige of them was to be seen. I therefore ordered my camp to be pitched on the bank of the river; but as the air was very hot, it disagreed with me, and the wind struck me; but after three days I recovered.

My mind being now at ease with regard to the Jetes, I resolved to amuse my army by a general hunt, and in this manner (hunting and coursing) we reached the vicinity of Samerkund. The inhabitants of Samerkund came out to meet me, and were lavish in their praises, saying, "right has gained its right," and held up their hands in prayers for my prosperity; having thus established myself at Samerkund, I sent an escort to bring (my wife) Aljaÿ Tūrkān Aghā, with the remainder of my followers, from Gurmsyr in Sÿstān.

CHAPTER XVI.

A. D. 1364. In the year 766, I attained my thirtieth year, and having cleared the whole country of Maveralnaher of the Jetes, by the force of my sword, I considered that as there is only one God in the universe, there should only be one monarch in a kingdom, to whom all the inhabitants should be obedient, and by whom sedition should be annihilated.

As at this time, all the leaders of the different hordes and tribes, and the various chieftains, found that the countries of Maveralnaher and Tūrkestān, were freed from the tyranny of the Jetes, each of them trusting to the strength and support of their respective followers, began to assume independence; I therefore deemed it requisite to let them know, that whoever obeyed my orders, should be protected, but that I would severely punish any one who proved refractory.

As the greater number of the hordes and tribes proffered their allegiance to

* Timūr wished to have liberated them, but they were put to death by order of Amyr Hussyn. Sherifaddeen's History.

me, and acknowledged me as their (Kelantur) superior, Amyr Hussyn became jealous, wishing to be himself the Sovereign. He therefore assembled a number of the inferior chiefs, and after consultation, they determined, that as I was not a (*Tureh*) descendant of the imperial family, but only one of the (*Kerachū*) family of the Commander in Chief's progeny, I had no right to assume the superiority.

When I was informed of this circumstance, I sent them the following message; "he who wishes to embrace the bride of royalty, must kiss her across the edge of the sharp sword; I have defeated Alyas Khuajē and the Jete army, without any confederate, and the kingdom is mine." They replied, "our (Kelantur) Sovereign must be a descendant of Jagtay Khān;" and in consequence of this determination, they raised Kabul Shāh Aghlān, a descendant of Jagtay Khān, but who had become a Dervish to the sovereignty or Khānship; and having stripped off his beggars' weeds, clothed him in the robe of state, and supplied him with all the requisites of royalty, and placed him on the throne of sovereignty.

On hearing of this, I called (Kuriltay) an assembly of all the nobles and chieftains of my party, and having marched to Kesh, took up my residence there for the winter; Amyr Hussyn moved at the same time to his former abode of Sali Seray.*

When spring returned, I received intelligence that the Jete army having marched from the Desht Kipchāk, were again about to invade the province of Maveralnaher; as soon as this news reached Amyr Hussyn and the other chieftains, who had raised Kabul Shāh to the sovereignty, they said among themselves, "if we wish again to repel the Jetes, we must make up our quarrel with the Amyr Timūr, and unite him with us, by acknowledging him as the superior, and by being obedient to him, till the Jetes are driven back." In consequence of this determination, they wrote me a joint letter, apologizing for their former conduct, and throwing themselves upon my benevolence and generosity.

When information of this union of all the chiefs was carried to Mulk Behader, the preceptor of the young *Khān*, Kabul Shāh, he very unjustly put the youth to death, and came to congratulate me on having attained the (Kelantury) sovereignty, I abused him and said, "it is not fit that the murderer of a King should live;" I therefore delivered him over to the heirs of the murdered Prince, that they might retaliate on him; and I sent a message to the chiefs, saying, "as you have now acknowledged my superiority, I will march with my own followers to the bank of the Khujend river, and I will defend it in such a manner, that the Jetes shall not be able to pass over."

* It was situated on the northern bank of the Jihūn, near Termuz.

CHAPTER XVII.

The arrangement I made for the third war with the Jetes, was this; when I collected six thousand horse, I formed them into seven divisions, and marched towards the Jetes; when I reached the village of Akyar, I was informed that the enemy were very numerous, and were advancing very rapidly; I therefore halted at Akyar, and sent off an express to hasten Amyr Hussyn; when he drew near, I again marched and crossed the Khujend river, and then fortified its (northern) bank; I also sent out spies for information, these soon returned, and informed me that the Jete army was encamped on the banks of the Badam river; that Shuknūm Behader commanded the right wing, Hajy Beg the left, Alyas Khuajē the centre, and Kipchāk Behader the advanced line.

In consequence of this intelligence, I new modelled my forces; I gave the command of the right, which consisted of Amyr Hussyn's troops, to Belanchy Arlāt; the advanced line was under charge of Melk Behader, and the left, with the Kipchāk tribe, was led by Amyr Sarbuga; I took post with the left, leaving Amyr Jakū and other chiefs with the reserve; I kept a few of my confidential officers about myself; when I had made this arrangement, Amyr Hussyn crossed the river with one thousand horse, and drew up his army.

Every thing being in proper order, I said to Amyr Hussyn, " it is not advantageous that we should make a general engagement, I will advance and attack the enemy with my forces, if you will faithfully promise to protect my rear, or if you choose to lead, I will support you; at this time we were more numerous than the enemy, and our troops were therefore presumptuous; but, according to custom, I consulted the Korān, and this verse opened, " when you are proud of your numbers, you shall be defeated, but God will finally give you the victory;" on which I became strong of heart.

But Amyr Hussyn would not attend to my request of dividing our armies, saying, " do not let us separate, but let us advance in line, and attack the foe;" I again replied, " it is not to our advantage to fight them thus; let us attack them in the *Cossack* manner;" but he would not listen to my advice.

Being without choice, I yielded to his opinion, and he drew out our armies. In a short time, the (Munkelay) skirmishers of the enemy came close to us, and the light troops of both sides charged each other; after which, the advanced lines came to blows, and some squadrons under command of Zindē Khushm, made a furious attack on Amyr Hussyn's right, which fell into disorder, but several of his chiefs kept their ground; Alyas Khuajē then sent a division under charge of Amyr Shumsaddyn, to repeat the attack; this leader approached very near to Hussyn; I, seeing that we were likely to be defeated, made a desperate charge with seventeen squadrons on Shumsaddyn; upon this, fearing to oppose me, he drew in his reins, and turned his face to flight. Having thus routed him, I made a charge on the (Kūl) centre of Alyas Khuajē, and having worsted them, I sent a message by Taban Behader, to Amyr Hussyn, "desiring him to come to me immediately, and the victory would be compleated by the total flight of the enemy."

Amyr Hussyn behaved like a blockhead, abused my messenger, and said, "what, am I a coward, that he thus summons me in front of the army." Again I sent Mulk Mehedy, who was one of his relations, to request that he would come up, as the enemy were just on the point of giving way; Amyr Hussyn was again angry with him, and said, "be patient, till I can unite my broken troops;" Mulk Mehedy replied, "Amyr Timūr has defeated the first line of the enemy, and is now engaged with the reserve which is about to give way; if your reserve will only make its appearance, no doubt the enemy will flee;" on which Amyr Hussyn struck him, and sent him back.

When Mulk Mehedy returned to me, I saw that he was much downcast, but did not tell me that he had been struck, only said, "it is a folly to assist this stupid fellow; the scoundrel wishes that we should uselessly endanger our lives, while he may escape from the vortex of danger." From this hint, I saw that it was Amyr Hussyn's wish to make me a mouthful for the jaws of the enemy. As I had at that time compleatly defeated the right of the adversary, and saw no prospect of assistance from Amyr Hussyn, I desisted from further fighting, and forming my troops in order of battle, I took post on the bank of a rivulet which ran through the plain.

When the enemy saw that I had discontinued the fight, and having collected my men, had taken post in the field, they being much fatigued, were rejoiced, and also took post in the plain.

That night my saddle was my bed, and my officers formed a circle around me; I however sent out scouts on all sides, to bring intelligence; whilst in this situation, a messenger came from Amyr Hussyn, to apologize for his misconduct, to express his sorrow and regret for what had past, and to request that I would recommence the fight; I sent back the messenger to say, "that we had lost the opportunity; that when I had broken the enemy, it would then have been easy to have conquered them; that now they were all collected and formed in order, it would be useless to make any attempt on them."

Having thus passed the night on the field of battle, and the horses having rested, as soon as the morning dawned, we performed our prayers; when the sun rose, the enemy being able to see the situation of my army, beat their drums, and began to practice incantations.*

In consequence, a very heavy rain fell, and the plain became such a slough, that our horses could scarcely move; notwithstanding this, my warriors from their excess of bravery, and sense of honour, beat their drums, drew their swords, spurred on their steeds, and advanced through the mud and slough; I also ordered the trumpets to sound, and dashed forward.

About this time, a (Yedchy) magician was seized by my people; when they struck off his head, the storm ceased:† I then ordered the troops to charge, which they did, and dispersed the enemy; they continued the pursuit, while I halted in the plain, and caused the music of victory to sound.

Whilst in this situation, the (Tugh) flag of Amyr Shumsaddyn, the general of the Jete army, came in sight, followed by all his troops; at this moment I had only two thousand horse with me, I directed one thousand of them to charge the enemy, which they did in so brave a manner, that they broke the first line, and reached the flag, but the second line then came to the assistance of the first, and the battle continued from morning till night; till at length nearly one thousand of my two thousand men were killed; "to God alone belongs power and might."

As the night came on, my troops that were dispersed, rejoined me, and I found that by this calamity, I had lost a thousand warriors; my officers were therefore of opinion, that in consequence of this misfortune, and the want of co-operation by Amyr Hussyn, it was requisite that we should retrogade some marches towards Kesh, where being joined by all my detachments, I might then make head against the Jetes; we therefore set out for Kesh.

From this event, I found by experience, that in whatever army there are two generals, discord must ensue, and I resolved never again to unite with Amyr Hussyn, or to appoint two generals to one army.

When we had reached the vicinity of Kesh, all my troops, that had been dispersed, joined me, and I again formed my army. At this time, Amyr Hussyn came and encamped at the distance of four miles, and being much ashamed of his misconduct, he sent a person to inform me, that it was his opinion we should take all our hordes and tribes with us, and cross the (Oxus) Jihūn,

* See Petis de la Croix's History, page 84. It is remarkable that Timūr does not mention this battle, called the Slough, in his *Designs*.

† In Baber's Memoirs, mention is also made of the powers of the magicians of Tūrkestān, and the wonderful effects of the Stone Jeddy.

and enter Khurasān. I would not see the messenger, but informed him that my honour would not allow me to abandon my country to be trodden down by the savage Jetes, that I would again collect an army, oppose and fight them with all my might, until I should have again driven them out of Maveralnaher.

Amyr Hussyn being disappointed, marched away to his residence at Sali Seray, where having collected his tribe, he crossed the Jihūn, and encamped on the (southern) bank of that river, waiting to see whether the Jetes would come that way, and resolving if they did, to retire towards Hindūstan.

I boldly remained where I was, and fortified the neighbourhood of Kesh, and issued orders for assembling a large army. At length having fortunately collected twelve (Kushūns) regiments, I gave the command of three of these to Timūr Khuajē, Janjy Behader, and Abās Behader; and soon after having heard that the Jete army had reached Kukeng, a town of the district of Samerkund, and had halted there, I detached these three regiments as an advanced guard towards Samerkund; I then appointed Daoud Khuajē, and Hindū Shāh to the command of two other regiments, and sent them after the others; but they all having joined, passed their time in feasting and drinking; at length when they were in a state of intoxication, the former officers said to the latter, "do you know, that it is Amyr Timūr's intention, after he defeats the Jetes, to annihilate you?" these drunken wretches believing what they had heard, took fright, quitted the advance guard, and rode towards the Jete camp.

When I was informed of this circumstance, I cursed the scoundrels; by chance an advance guard of the Jetes fell in with the deserters, who treacherously led the enemy against Timūr Khuajē and Abās Behader; these, after some skirmishing, finding that they were not able to contend with their adversaries, fled.

Being now convinced that wine was the cause of strife, I ordered that whoever should hereafter drink it, should have melted lead poured down his throat, and all his effects confiscated. In consequence of these misfortunes, I felt that the prospect of my good fortune and sovereignty was postponed.

When my broken forces were again collected, I marched with them towards Balkh, and having arrived there, I encamped on the bank of the river Amū, in order to give time for the different hordes that were dispersed, to assemble around me, and in a short time was joined by the tribes of Tumek Khān, and Ilchy Būghā Selduz.

Having learned that the Jetes had arrived in the vicinity of Samerkund, I crossed the Amū, and stationed troops at the different ferries.

At this time, Timūr Khuajē, who by his bad conduct, had been the chief cause of my recent misfortune, came and gave himself up; I at first issued orders for his being put to death, but the other chiefs having bent their knees, and supplicated his pardon, I forgave him.

At this period, letters arrived from the prelates Mūlāzadē Samerkundy, Khurdek Bokhary, Abū Beker, and other principal inhabitants of Samerkund, representing that the Jete army were arrived in the neighbourhood of Samerkund; and although the city had no citadel, they nevertheless had fortified the town, opposed the enemy, and checked their proceedings; that they daily skirmished with them, and requested that I would immediately advance to their aid, when, if it should please God, they would shortly compel the Jetes to retreat.

In consequence of this intelligence, I mustered my army, which consisted of seven thousand horse, and re-crossed the river. I was, however, in two minds whether I should at once advance to the relief of Samerkund, and thereby preserve the property, the honour and lives of the Muselmāns, or whether I should make a night attack on the camp of the Jetes, and in the *Cossack* manner, lay waste the country around them.

Whilst I was thus dubious, I received other letters from the inhabitants of Samerkund, stating that, Providence, as a punishment for the tyranny and oppression of the Jetes, over the Muselmāns, had been pleased to inflict the former with a severe plague, which had destroyed a number of them, and killed all their horses. I therefore drew out my army, and having appointed Abās Behader to the command of the advance, I pushed on towards Samerkund.

When the Jetes heard of my approach, they preferred flight to fight, and tying their armour in bundles on their back, they all set out for the (*Desht*) desert; I sent a force in pursuit of them, with orders to quickly drive these infected wretches out of the province of Maveralnaher: I also followed them, but when I came up with them, I found them in such a deplorable situation, that I had compassion on them; I therefore discontinued the pursuit, and returned to the plains of Bukelān, from whence I detached Amyr Jakū with several other officers, to take possession of Samerkund.

Whilst I remained in the plain of Bukelān, Amyr Hussyn having quitted his winter quarters of Sherkū, came first to Sali Seray, where having left his family and dependants, he came and joined me at Bukelān. As it was then the beginning of winter, we consulted what was most eligible to be done, and it was determined that I should go and take up my residence during the winter, at Ķārshy; and that he should return and remain at Sali Seray. Amyr Hussyn was very jealous that my troops should have got possession of Samerkund, but as he was without remedy, he was obliged to swallow his envy: we therefore parted, and I proceeded to Karshy,* where I remained all that winter; I also permitted my soldiers to go to their homes, and rest themselves during the inclement season, but to rejoin me at the commencement of the spring.

CHAPTER XVIII.

In the year 767, being thirty-one years of age, I prepared for marching to Samerkund, but first gave orders to repair the palace of Kepee Khān, whose name in the Tūrky language, was Kārshy; and I commanded that a fortress should be erected at the gate of the town, and some other buildings constructed. As soon as the morning of spring had dawned, in compliance with my promise to Amyr Hussyn, I proceeded towards Samerkund, and having arrived there, pitched my camp in its vicinity. A. D. 1365.

Amyr Hussyn having preceded me, had taken up his quarters in the city, and the first thing he did, was to cast the eyes of covetousness on the wealth of Amyr Jakū, and my other officers, whom I had sent to take possession of the place; and having determined to plunder them, he appointed collectors over them. As he thus acted in a very shameless manner, I had a great mind to draw the sword of revenge from its scabbard, but recollecting our near connection, and the gratitude due to his family, I restrained my anger, and swallowed all he said or did. As my officers had expended all they had gained, upon the refitment of their men and horses, they had no money: I therefore sent a message to Amyr Hussyn, "that if he wished me to make a brotherly division of the wealth of Samerkund, I would do it;" I therefore sent him several of my own horses and camels; but as his avarice was very great, I further sent him a large sum of money; and his sister (my wife) Aljay Tūrkān Aghā, also sent him some of her jewels: when he saw the ornaments of his sister, he so far forgot his brotherly affection, as to take them all, and even contended for more. In order to stop his further contention, I sent him a second sum of money, but all my officers were incensed by his extortion, and disgusted with his meanness, and thus planted the seeds of enmity against him in their hearts.

The fire of avarice of Amyr Hussyn being thus stirred into a flame, he began to covet also the property of the inhabitants of Samerkund, and he resolved to extort sums of money from them; to effect this, he incited some of the seditious,

* The original name of this place was Nakhsheb, but was changed to Kārshy, in consequence of a palace having been built there by a Moghūl Prince, it is separated from the Jihūn by a desert. Lat. 38.45.

to make a complaint against Mūllā Khurdek and Mūllā Abū Beker, who in order to preserve the city from the Jetes, had collected a sum of money from the inhabitants, and had expended it on the new fortifications. He therefore summoned these respectable persons before him; they in their defence, produced my written order, directing them to use every means in their power to defend the city; that in consequence they had raised a contribution, and had expended it in so proper a manner, that they had succeeded in repelling the enemy; that all the accounts were ready, that he might have them examined, and if he found them guilty of extortion or fraud, he might levy the amount from them: Amyr Hussyn paid no attention to this request, would not examine the account, but ordered them to pay him the whole amount; this unjust demand not being complied with, he punished several of the Mūllā Zādēs (learned men) with his own hands. In consequence of this misconduct, and the excessive avarice of Amyr Hussyn, all the people were disgusted with him, and sought his ruin.

It was in consequence of this conduct, that his enemies caused a breach between him and me, and although I swore that my only feeling towards him was that of friendship, he would not believe me, but persevered in his enmity and hatred.

At length the party who wished for his destruction, deserted him and came over to me: I however comforted them, and requested them to return, and wrote to Amyr Hussyn, "begging him to be reconciled to his officers, and to treat "them with kindness;" but in his usual passionate manner, he would not listen to my advice; till at length Amyr Musā, Aly Derveish, and Ferhad Behader, all of whom were brothers of Amyr Hussyn's women, rose up in enmity against him, and resolved to destroy him. To effect their purpose, they determined to widen the breach between Amyr Hussyn and me; they therefore in conjunction with the Princess Audu, a relation of his, wrote him a fictitious letter couched in these words; "O blockhead, rouse yourself from your sleep, the Amyr Timūr is your "avowed enemy, he has bound round him the girdle of animosity; in a short "period, in union with your chiefs, he will overwhelm you, and make you his "prisoner, like the King at Chess." When this false letter reached Hussyn, he bound round him the girdle of hatred and aversion to me, and sent me the letter.

In consequence of which, I summoned the Amyrs Musā, Aly Derveish, and Ferhad to my presence; but they being sensible of their treachery, were ashamed, and fled to Khujend; although their flight was a clear proof of their falsehood, the wound still rankled in the liver of Hussyn, and encreased his enmity towards me; in consequence of which, he devised schemes for my destruction.

In order to avert this misfortune, I consulted with Shyr Behram Jelayr, by what means I might satisfy the mind of Amyr Hussyn; as Shyr Behram was at enmity with the Prince, he did not conceal it from me, but openly said, " Hussyn is not only your avowed enemy, but mine, and whenever he finds an opportunity, will certainly destroy us both, I have, therefore, no confidence in him whatever."

On hearing this discourse of Behram, I began to be alarmed, but did not say any thing on that subject; I merely replied, " that as there had been a long friendship and near connection between Hussyn and me, how can I possibly oppose him, or raise the standard of enmity against him; I will not believe your accusation, unless you can give me some proof of his treachery:" Behram said, " if you do not believe me, try him; let me write him a letter, begging his forgiveness, if he bears no malice against me, he will pardon me, otherwise he will refuse to do so." I consented, and he wrote the letter, but Amyr Hussyn immediately tore it to pieces, got into a passion, and sent him a message, " that he hoped shortly to annihilate him."

When informed of this circumstance, I was convinced that Amyr Hussyn was now my implacable enemy, I therefore assembled my army, and I sent Shyr Behram into Khutelān, that he might collect his forces there; I also sent with him Aādil Behader, but made the former leave his son Tash Khuajē with me, as security for his behaviour.

Shyr Behram having reached Khutelān, collected a number of troops, possessed himself of the fortress of *Pelak Suturg*, and raised the standard of rebellion against Hussyn; the latter however thought it proper to dissemble, contrived to deceive him, and brought him over to his party.

He then induced him to forget all his promises and oaths of allegiance to me; I therefore wrote to Shyr Behram, a sharp letter, reproaching him for his ingratitude and want of fidelity, and ended by saying that, " as it was he that had blown up the flame of discord between Amyr Hussyn and me, I prayed to God that the same flame might consume him, and that he might have cause to repent of his treachery." After some time it all came to pass, as had been reflected on the tablet of my mind; and he was overwhelmed with misfortunes.

Finding that Amyr Hussyn was now my determined enemy, and that it was requisite to attend to my personal safety; I therefore sent Behram Jelayr, Amyr Jakū, and several other officers, by way of Khujend, to secure the horde of Jelayr, and to effect some other business of importance. Behram succeeded in dispossessing his cousin, and in getting the command of the tribe of Jelayr; but being doubtful whether the enmity between me and Amyr Hussyn would last, and that he might be involved in difficulties, between the two parties, he procrastinated his return.

CHAPTER XIX.

A.D. 1366. In the year 768, I entered, the thirty-second year of my age, and was busily employed in getting my army into proper order; when that was effected, I marched with all my troops from Kārshy, with an intention of going to Samerkund, in order to increase my forces: at the end of the first days' march, Amyr Soleyman and Javerchy, who were the chief instigators of the quarrel between my brother-in-law and me, deserted and went over to Amyr Hussyn; but just at this time, the commander of the *Yusury* tribe having died, was succeeded by his brothers Aly Derveish, Alyas Khuajē, and Hajy Mahmūd, who all came and joined me with the whole tribe of *Yusury*, and entered into my service. Also Amyr Jakū and Abās, whom I had sent with Behram Jelayr to Khujend, rejoined me with their divisions.

My army being thus considerably reinforced, I proceeded towards Samerkund; when I had nearly reached that place, the principal inhabitants of the city came out to meet me, and requested that I would appoint (Hakim) a governor over them; I in consequence did appoint Kera Hindūke Berlās, to be governor of Samerkund, and I returned towards my cantonments at Kārshy; but when I had made two marches towards home, that *Hindū* like character quitted the government of Samerkund, and went over to Amyr Hussyn.

At this place, I received intelligence that (my wife) the illustrious Aljay Tūrkān Aghā, whom I had left very ill, had departed this life; on hearing this, I said, "verily we belong to God, and to him shall we return."

When the news reached Amyr Hussyn, that his sister was dead, he was very much afflicted, and was sensible that the bond which had hitherto united us, was now broken, and our connection dissolved. He was nevertheless very violent against me, and made preparation for war; I also assembled my troops, and did not relax in my precautions. In the first place, I sent Amyr Syf Addyn with the troops of my victorious army, towards Chughtayān, where Amyr Hussyn was encamped, to gain intelligence. He soon sent me word that Amyr Hussyn was determined on war, but that he wished to carry it on by intrigue and artifice, and recommended me to be on my guard.

When Amyr Hussyn heard that I had left Kārshy, and had sent a detachment towards his camp, he despatched his son Abdallah with a letter, and a deceitful message. In the letter it was stated, "that his overtures proceeded from the "heart, not from the tongue; that he had the most sincere friendship for me, and "that I might place the most implicit confidence on this promise."

When Abdallah reached my encampment, which was at Kehulkeh, he delivered his message, and presented the letter; I refused to read the letter, and paid no attention to the message; my reason for which, was this, that most of my chiefs were persons who had deserted from Amyr Hussyn, and had come over to me; they were, therefore, alarmed, lest if peace should take place between us, they might fall a sacrifice to our reconciliation, and as I suspected that this was the motive which induced Amyr Hussyn's overtures, I sent for the heads of the Yusury clan, and said to them, "Amyr Hussyn has knocked at the door of friendship, and I know that his object is to cause discord between you and me; but, between him and me, the only thing that now remains is the sword." On hearing this, the chiefs, who were hesitating how they should act, finding that I was determined to continue the war, became strong of heart: thus I reconciled all the Yusurians, and afterwards conferred favours on them.

When Amyr Hussyn found that I would not enter into any treaty with him, he refrained from hostilities, and I also returned towards Kārshy; he however soon after assembled his army, and having appointed Shyr Behram to the command of his advance, came towards Kārshy, wishing by fraud and stratagem, to seize me. While I was encamped at Herar, he sent his treasurer Kezer to me with a *Korān*, on which he pretended to have taken his oath, that he had no animosity against me, and prayed that if he should be guilty of a breach of his oath, that the holy book would bring down destruction on him; but in order to confirm our friendship, he stated it was requisite that we should have a meeting, and therefore proposed that we should meet at the pass of Chuckchuck, and renew our amicable engagements, in such a manner, that hereafter no seditious scoundrel might be able to excite strife between us; notwithstanding these protestations, I discovered that he had sent detachments to both ends of the pass, with orders to conceal themselves, and that when I entered it, they should close up in front and rear, and seize me. I nevertheless listened to the proposal of his messenger, which was, "that I should leave my army where it was, and that Amyr Hussyn should also have his troops at Chuganian, and we should both advance with one hundred men each, to a delightful spot in the pass, abounding with water and verdure, where we might enjoy the society of each other, renew our vows of friendship, and divide the province of Maveralnaher between us in a fraternal manner." *

Having heard this deceitful message of Amyr Hussyn, I privately gave orders for part of my forces to march at night, and take post on the road, in front of the pass, and the other part to take a strong position in the rear of it. I then

* See Institutes, page 101.

proceeded with three hundred horse towards the appointed place, and Amyr Hussyn advanced with one thousand cavalry.

When I arrived at the place where Amyr Hussyn had concealed his first division, I halted, but the enemy immediately rushed upon me; at the same time, my troops, who were concealed, charged them, and a severe contest took place; at first my people were worsted, but I reinforced them, and we soon put the enemy to the route, killed many, and took a number of them prisoners.

During this time, Amyr Hussyn, who had remained on one side of the pass, waiting in expectation of seeing me brought bound to him, was surprised to see his defeated army running in all directions, he was, therefore, much disappointed and ashamed;* but being convinced the veil of his deceit was now rent, he suspected Shyr Behram, who had deserted me, and had been employed confidentially by him, of having given me intelligence; he therefore commanded him to be put to death, which circumstance realized my prediction, when Shyr Behram quitted my service, as formerly related. In consequence of this victory, I returned exulting towards Kārshy, and encamped in its vicinity.

CHAPTER XX.

Being now thoroughly convinced of Amyr Hussyn's implacable enmity, I earnestly set about refitting and strengthening my army; to effect this, I sent for each of my chiefs separately, and made them promise and swear fidelity to me; I said to them, "whoever remains with me, I will treat as a brother, whatever I now possess, I will divide with you, and whatever I may in future obtain, shall be also divided; whoever is averse to my service, let him leave me this very day, I shall refer his retribution to the Omnipotent." They individually declared their attachment to me, wrote their names in the muster roll, took an oath, and signed the following written promise; "we call God to witness, that if we shall be guilty of a breach of our promise, or desert the Amyr Timūr, we hope we may be overwhelmed with the Divine anger." Being now at ease with respect to my army, I deemed it most advisable to march to Mākhān, and bring over to my party, the tribe of Sunjury, who resided in that neighbourhood, then to proceed against Amyr Hussyn, and wait for whatever might be concealed behind the curtain of futurity.

At this time, I received information that Amyr Hussyn had collected a large

* This account is different from Petis de la Croix's History.

army, and that he had despatched Amyr Musā and Melk Behader, with twelve thousand horse against Kārshy, and to oppose me. When this news arrived, my officers began to despond, I therefore summoned the chiefs, and again demanded their promise. After some hesitation, they replied, "if you will give us some strong place to secure our families and provisions, then we will devote our lives to your service:" I therefore sent edicts to the chiefs of the tribe of Sunjury, who were under great obligations to me, and stated the case; they proved themselves grateful for my favours, sent me one thousand men, and promised to take the families of the whole tribe of Berlās, with their effects, into their fortresses.

My officers being now at ease with regard to their families and stores, agreed to march with me, but I did not place much confidence in them, which they having heard, came to me with the Korān (on which they had sworn) in their hands, and their swords suspended round their necks, and said, "here are the Korāns, and here are our swords, if we have broken our oaths, kill us." The first of these was Amyr Jakū, the others were Ayk Timūr, Sarbugā Jelayr, the Amyrs Daoud, Muvyd, Syf Addeen, &c. &c. When I saw them in this state, I wept, and they wept; they then vowed they would devote their lives to my service, and I praised and lauded them; and with a tranquil mind, I mounted my horse, with the full intention of fighting Amyr Hussyn, but I thought it proper first to go to the tribe of Sunjury, and leave all the heavy baggage with them; I therefore quitted Kārshy, and proceeded towards Makhān.*

Amyr Musā and Amyr Hindūkē, the generals of Amyr Hussyn, having heard of my departure from Kārshy, were rejoiced, advanced against that fortress, and finding it without any garrison, took easy possession of it; they then wrote to their master that they had defeated me, compelled me to flee to Khurasān, and that they had taken the fort of Kārshy: when their boasting was communicated to me, the sinews of my honour were irritated, and I resolved to return to Kārshy, and seize them. I therefore caused it to be reported that I was gone on to Khurasān, and having sent the families of all my people to the protection of the Sunjury tribe, I selected a few of my best soldiers, and having marched to Isāck's well in the desert, halted there several days, to give time for all my followers to join; then turning to the south, I advanced on the road to Makhān, and having arrived at the Amū or Jihūn, and encamped on its bank, and crossed over during the night. When the intelligence of my having crossed the Jihūn, was brought to Amyr Musā and his colleagues, they were delighted, and began to enjoy their tranquillity. I halted two days on the south bank of the river, till all my people had crossed; I then sent off a letter to the Prince of Herat, and

* Latitude 37,30, Longitude 85, East.

another to Muhammed Khān Ghorbany. I also sent intelligent persons into Khurasān, to ascertain the disposition of the people towards me.

As I had no reliance on the people of Khurasān, I quitted the banks of the river, and marched into the (Jul) desert, and encamped near a well of brackish water, and I remained for two months in the desert; but as it abounded with wild animals, we caught a number of them, which served us for food. At the end of this time, the dromedaries that I had sent to the Prince of Herat and Muhammed Khān Ghorbany, returned, and brought me letters replete with professions of friendship; each of them sent me presents, also a number of arms, consisting of bows, swords, and quivers, of these I kept one bow and one sword, the remainder I gave to the officers and soldiers.

At this time, I received information that a caravan from Khurasān, carrying goods to Kārshy, was approaching,* I therefore marched towards them on the Herat road; when the people of the caravan saw my army, they were afraid; some of them however advanced to meet me, and presented me their offerings, whilst seated on my horse; I asked them a number of questions respecting the news of Herat, and what were the reports about me in Khurasān, they replied, "we heard that your highness was coming into Khurasān, at the invitation of the Prince of Herat, and that you had crossed the Amū; the people would not believe the report, but we are now convinced of its truth by our own eyes." I replied, "as the tyranny of Amyr Hussyn has been excessive, and he has even led an army against me; I have been under the necessity of abandoning my country, and proceeding towards Khurasān."

The people of the caravan blessed me, and requested I would give them a guard to protect them against my followers, and to escort them through the dangerous places. I then made two more marches on the road to Khurasān; when the caravan arrived at Kārshy, Amyr Musā, the governor of the fortress, sent for the leaders of the caravan, and asked them about me, they replied, "we saw the Amyr Timūr in the desert, with his whole army; he was going on to Herat, at the invitation of the Prince of that country, and he was making long marches in order to arrive there quickly." When the governor heard this intelligence, he immediately came out of the fort with seven thousand horse, pitched his tents in the plain of Bimragh, and commenced feasting and carousing; before leaving the fort, Amyr Musā appointed his son Muhammed Beg to the command of it, and strengthened the fortifications. He also sent off an express to Amyr Hussyn with the good news; previous to this time, the Amyr had sent a reinforcement to Kārshy, of five thousand horse, but the commander of these troops being also off his guard, halted at the village of Ghashūn.

* See Institutes, page 95.

CHAPTER XXI.

As soon as I had obtained information of the state of Kārshy, honour instigated me to draw the sword of revenge from its scabbard, and to go and subdue the fortress; at this time my spies informed me, that the garrison consisted of only two thousand men, but that the other ten thousand were encamped in two divisions in the vicinity. I therefore summoned all my chiefs, and asked their advice, whether we should proceed to Khurasān, or return and endeavour to take Kārshy; they replied, " if we go to Khurasān, we shall all be made prisoners, and our people will be dispersed; let us call on God to assist us, and return towards Kārshy, please God we shall be victorious:" as this advice appeared to me good, I determined to make the attempt.

But when my soldiers heard that there were twelve thousand of Amyr Hussyn's troops, in or near the fort, they were afraid: I therefore determined to select three hundred and forty warriors, whose courage I had often experienced,* and with them to make a forced march against the fortress, whether successful or not. On this subject I sought an omen in the Korān, and the following verse opened; " he assists whom he pleases, for he (God) is all powerful and all wise;" from this verse I derived hopes of success; I therefore made the requisite arrangement of my troops, and at night, placing my trust in Providence, commenced my march with three hundred and forty warriors.

At this time, Amyr Muvyd Arlāt, who was married to one of my sisters, Tuvukkel Behader, Jakū Berlās, Surugtumush Aghlān, Dilavur Behader, who was married to another of my sisters, and the other officers came and made their salutations: as Muvyd Arlāt was the first who bent the knee, I considered his name (the Strengthened) as auspicious, and as Tuvukkel (Hope) was the second, I also considered his name as a good omen.

I however again consulted the Korān, and this verse came forth; " whoever places his faith in God, shall obtain his wishes:" from this verse I felt confident, and continued my march.

I crossed the river Amū (Jihūn) that same night, and halted at the village of Akhshēb, and before day, I sent off an advance party to shut up the road to Kārshy, by seizing and detaining all travellers and passengers; that day I halted at a spot that was far from any inhabited place: when night came on, we again mounted, and arrived at Berdalygh, and immediately seized and confined all Amyr Musā's people, who were in that place; we then went to rest, very early

* In the Institutes, only forty men are mentioned.

in the morning we were again on our horses, and when we stopt to rest, I sent on the (Keravulan) light troops to detain all passengers. When night arrived, we again mounted, and having reached Shyrkund, I wished to have gone further, but Amyr Jakū came and bent the knee, and represented to me, that in consequence of the length and rapidity of our march, many of our warriors were fallen behind; "your Highness had better halt a little to give them time to come up; what we have undertaken is of great importance, let us avoid any risk of failure by impatience."*

In consequence of this advice, I drew in my reins, and it then occurred to me, that while we were waiting for the men to come up, we might employ the time in making ladders and fascines from the trees which were growing on the side of the road; we therefore procured some cord and ropes, and began to make ladders.

During this time, it entered my mind that I would go myself and examine the state of the fortress; I therefore proceeded with only forty men, and in the course of the night, arrived near Kārshy; it happened that the night was extremely dark, but as soon as we could distinguish the walls, I ordered the men to halt, and taking only Abdallah, who was born in my house, with me, we came to the bank of the ditch; I found that the ditch was full of water, and having examined several places of it, at length I discovered a plank thrown across it; I therefore alighted from my horse, and gave him in charge to Abdallah; I then buckled on my sword, and crossed the plank, and reached the *fause bray*; I continued to walk round the walls till I came to the gate, I struck the knocker of the gate, but no one answered, I was therefore convinced that the guards were asleep. I then proceeded round the wall, and examined it attentively; after some time I perceived a breach in the wall, very favourable for applying ropes or ladders; I therefore returned very coolly by the way I had come, and having received my horse from Abdallah, I mounted. Soon after this time, my people, being well armed and carrying the ladders, arrived, I informed them of all the circumstances that has been related, and when they heard, that I had alone inspected the fortress, their courage became ten-fold; they were astonished at my courage and bravery, and bit their fingers with amazement; some of them found fault with my rashness, others devoted themselves for my safety; I then repeated the prayer for victory, and proceeded.

I left forty persons in charge of the horses, and with three hundred and thirteen dismounted men, with drawn swords, myself on horseback, advanced till we came to the ditch, here I also alighted, and we crossed the plank singly, and

* See Institutes, page 97.

reached the *fause bray* in safety; I then led my warriors to the low part of the wall, where they carefully fixed the ladders; I then commanded them to mount, and when forty of them had got up, I also mounted the ladder, and took possession of one of the bastions, after which all my people climbed up the wall; fortunately for us, not a sentinel awoke during all this time.

I then ordered a party to go and seize the gate-way, when they reached the gate, they found the guard fast asleep, and bound the most of them; but those who attempted resistance, were put to death, they then broke open the gate; when the inhabitants heard the uproar, they began to tremble, and lost the use of their hands and feet.

At this time, I ordered the trumpets to sound, and when the inhabitants heard the sound of the trumpets, they in great perturbation mounted the flat roofs of their houses. Muhammed Beg, the son of Amyr Musā, who was left as governor of the fort, mounted the roof of his house with a party of his followers, and began to fight; but when the day broke, and he saw my troops, he retreated to an upper roomed house, and barred the doors and windows; my troops surrounded the house, and threw fire into it, on which the family of Amyr Musā called out for quarter, and sought my protection.

When Muhammed Beg, who was then very young, was brought into my presence, I praised him for his courage, and I called him my son; then both the soldiers and citizens came and begged for quarter, I forgave them, and ordered them to keep every thing in order in the fort, to secure all the provisions, and to collect all the arms, whether arrows, bows, swords, or quivers, all these I divided among my troops.

I then made arrangements for the defence of the fort; I gave one of the gates in charge of Amyr Sarbugā, Syf Addeen, and Muvyd Arlāt, the other gate I gave over to Surugtumush Aghlān, Amyr Abās, and Hussyn Behader; I appointed the other chiefs to take care of the different bastions; I afterwards ordered Muvyd Arlāt to take post with forty troopers, outside of the walls; having made these arrangements, I treated kindly the family of Amyr Musā, and sent them to him.

When the intelligence of my having taken Kārshy by surprise, was communicated to Amyr Musā, he in conjunction with Melk Behader, immediately mounted, and with their twelve thousand horse, surrounded the fortress, and laid siege to it; my men who were dispersed, on hearing the news, collected together, but were afraid to approach the fort.

Having taken post with my three hundred and thirteen men, within the walls, I gave orders that all the gates should be thrown open, and with such an inferior force, contended with my twelve thousand adversaries; but during the latter part of the night, I sent out two detachments of forty troopers each, under the command of Muvyd Arlāt and Balkhy Bughā, to beat up the enemy's encampment; and these brave fellows having dashed on, about the dawn of day reached the tents of Amyr Musā, killed a number of his people, and took others prisoners; some of my soldiers were also killed and wounded.

Of the chiefs that were taken, the principal was Shādruān Behader; when brought into my presence, I treated him very kindly, and with much respect, and gave him the choice either of remaining with me, or of going back; as he was much affected by my condescension, he agreed to enter my service.

The next day, having recalled my detachments, I the following night sent out Ak Bughā and Shādruān Behader, with two hundred horse, and they returned with sixty horses taken from the enemy. That day, a party consisting of two hundred of the enemy's cavalry, got close under the walls of the fort, and blockaded the gates; for two days I did not molest them, but on the third day, I ordered the draw-bridge to be let down, and sent out Balkhy Bughā and Ak Timūr Behader with sixty warriors, who having taken the enemy by surprise, cut the greater part of them to pieces; but at this time, a large party of the troops of Amyr Hussyn came to their assistance, on which the flame of slaughter and combat again blazed: I then sent out a reinforcement of twenty other warriors; a severe contest took place between the enemy's general, and Ak Timūr Behader, in which the former was thrown down: during this scene of confusion, a young (Auzbek) Usbek in the service of Amyr Musā, who was celebrated for his strength and courage, advanced with a battle-axe in his hand; one of my bravest chiefs, named Ghuzān Bughā, opposed him, and when the Usbek raised his arm to fell my champion to the ground, the latter seized him by the two arms, and dragged him into the fort, where he was killed. When the enemy's soldiers saw this circumstance, they exclaimed, "this realizes the stories of *Rustem* and *Isfundiar*,"* and being terrified, they covered their heads with their shields, then fled, and took refuge in the ditch.

At this time, I sent out another reinforcement to my people, who having well beaten the enemy, drove them out of the ditch, and compelled them to seek for shelter in the lanes of the suburbs.

When Amyr Musā and his confederates saw this circumstance, they mounted their steeds, and having collected all their forces, advanced towards the fortress; they then sent troops to support those in the suburbs, who after a long and arduous struggle, compelled my people to retreat; I then rushed out of the fort, and ordered my trumpets to sound: when my soldiers who were dispersed,

* Two heroes of the *Shāh Nameh.*

saw my flag, they became strong of heart, and renewed their attacks on the enemy.

At this period, I called out to Balkhy Bughā and Behram Behader, and pointed out to them the adversary's general, Tuvukkel; they immediately advanced towards him, but he took shelter under the wall, on which Balkhy got on the top of the rampart, but not being able to reach him, thrust his sword through a hole in the wall, which compelled Tuvukkel to run away; Behram Behader pursued him, but one of my Khurasān officers, supposing that the latter belonged to the enemy, killed him by a single blow of his sword.

When Amyr Musā beheld the bravery of my troops, and saw me coming out of the fort with my retinue, he sent off his confederate, Melk Behader, to endeavour to force the other gate, which leads to Khezar; on observing this, I sent orders to Sar Bughā and Syf Addeen, to shut the gate; these brave officers having secured the gate, came out and boldly repulsed the five thousand horse of the enemy. At the same time that Musā sent off his confederate to the other side of the fort, he advanced in person with four thousand horse against me; I also directed one hundred of my warriors to meet him: when my party had extricated themselves from the lanes of the suburbs, and appeared in sight of Musā, he looked at them with ineffable contempt, and spurring on his steed, expected to have instantly made them the food of his scymetar; but at this moment, I having also come out of the town, urged on my horse, and being nobly supported by my body guard, a severe conflict ensued in the plain; at length, by the decree of God, an arrow struck Amyr Musā in the forehead, upon which he turned tail, and fled with his seven thousand horse to his camp; my chiefs wished to have pursued him, but I would not permit them. At this time, a messenger arrived from my officers on the other side of the fort, stating that they had also repulsed Melk Behader, and his five thousand horse, and that if I could come to their assistance, they had no doubt of our gaining a complete victory.

Having thus totally defeated Amyr Musā, and being quite satisfied with my success, I returned to the fort, and having posted guards all round the interior, I proceeded to the Khezar gate, and found that Melk Behader had driven my troops into the suburb, and had compelled them to take refuge under the walls of the fort, where they were warmly engaged: on seeing this, I marched with all the cavalry and foot soldiers that were with me, out of the fortress; and when I came near the enemy, I called out with a loud voice, "the Lord is on our side." When Melk Behader saw my suite, he knew that it was me, and convinced that I was come to seek revenge, he advanced to meet me, on which the nerves of my courage and rivalship being roused, I made a charge on him with forty troopers; he opposed me with sixty horsemen, and endeavoured to turn my right, but having failed, and seeing my standard advancing, he turned round and fled, with the intention of joining his principal; but having learned that he had also been defeated, he continued his flight towards his camp, which was at Kenbud-luly. I immediately sent off Amyr Jakū and Syf Addeen, with a party to pursue him, whilst I followed them closely; I also sent another party to show themselves in the vicinity of Musā's encampment.

When the enemy's general saw the dust raised by my party, he was alarmed, saddled his horses, and galloped off; I ordered Amyr Dāud to pursue him, and to seize as many of his horses, and as much plunder as he could lay hands on. When this brave officer had nearly come up with the enemy, the rear guard (Chundavul) faced about, and made a charge on Amyr Dāud, and a severe conflict took place; as soon as I came up, I also engaged them, but when our hands reached their collars, they could not contend with us, and took to flight; in consequence of which, a number of their led horses were seized by my people, and by my auspicious fortune the standards of the enemy's pride were overturned.

During this time, the officers and chiefs of the enemy being quite discomfited, were retreating towards Khezar, and it so happened that Arzū Melk Aghā, the daughter of Amyr Jelayr, and the wife of Amyr Musā, who in the confusion of the defeat, had been left behind, having joined the runaways, was overtaken; when I saw her, I instantly sent to her my (Shadruān) canopy to conceal her from public view, and gave her in charge of Dūlet Shāh, the pay-master, who was a (Hery Maimur) eunuch, or pilgrim; and what was very extraordinary, the lady being big with child, was safely delivered of a daughter in that desert.* I pursued the enemy as far as the village of Feriltay, and spent the night in that place.

As soon as the morning dawned, the whole of the enemy were driven from the vicinity of Kārshy; and my Amyrs Jakū and Syf Addeen, having followed the runaways as far as the village of Jugerlyk, returned, and congratulated me on victory.

As the winter was now approaching, I deemed it advisable to take up my quarters at Kārshy, during the inclement season; but some of the chiefs advised my making Bokharā my winter quarters; I said, " although Amyr Hussyn's army has been defeated, his jealousy will be roused when he hears that I have in person, taken possession of Bokharā, and will endeavour to annoy me; besides it is a ruinous place, and provisions are very scarce, it will be better to fix our winter quarters at Kārshy: I will send Mahmūd Shāh to Bokharā, that he may repair and render it populous, and he may remit the amount of the collections to

* The latter subsequently became his wife.

my treasury; I will also invite Beg Shāh, who is now an emigrant in Khurasān, and give him charge of the country; I will further write to Aly Beg Yusury, who is now a wanderer in the desert, to join his son-in-law, Mahmūd Shāh, at Bokharā; but we will in the mean time remain at Kārshy, and repair the losses we have sustained, during the late campaign; my people also will collect their families, and refresh their animals." After the council was concluded, I returned towards Kārshy, and encamped on the plain of victory, and there enjoyed myself.

CHAPTER XXII.

The arrangement that I made for renewing the war with Amyr Hussyn, was this; when the defeated generals of Amyr Hussyn presented themselves before him at Sali Seray, they threw their caps on the ground, and made some excuses; he abused them for their negligence, in the first place, for having permitted me to surprise Kārshy; and secondly, for allowing themselves with twelve thousand horse, to be defeated by three hundred and thirteen men.

After having given vent to his rage, Amyr Hussyn resolved to make a vigorous attack on me before I should get settled in my quarters; he in consequence quitted Sali Seray, and gave orders for all his forces to join him. He appointed the defeated Amyr Musā to the principal command, which consisted of ten thousand select horse, with a number of his best officers.

Amyr Musā having seized the sword of revenge in his teeth, advanced with his army towards Kārshy. When I was informed of the proceedings of Amyr Hussyn, and that the Amyr Musā, with ten thousand horse, had advanced as far as the fort of Kehulkeh, and had encamped near Checkichec; I resolved to make a night attack on them; I therefore marched by the road of *Belghun Bāgh*, which lay to the left of the enemy, and having arrived there, passed the night in that grove: I then sent one of my scouts, named Termunay, to observe the situation of their encampment, to examine the roads of ingress and egress of it, and to send me intelligence as soon as they should pass the straits of Checkichec. He went, and having seized one of the enemy's soldiers, examined him, and sent me the information that Amyr Musā, with his ten thousand horse, had passed the straits of Checkichec, and were to encamp that night at Chekdalyk.

I therefore passed that day in the desert, and when night came on, I mounted my horse; but when I arrived near the enemy's camp, found I was attended only by three hundred horse; I however gave the (Tekbyr) war cry, and having entered their camp by the left, came out of it by the right: this unexpected night attack, threw them into great confusion; but having recovered from their fright, they mounted their horses. At this time, the day began to dawn, and Amyr Musā having drawn out his army in line, stood looking at my party; but without molesting us. I therefore alighted in the plain of Chekdalyk, and having performed the morning prayers, again mounted, and retreated by the way of Kūrdenk.

I now resolved to return to Kārshy, and having strengthened it, to proceed to Bokharā, and on being joined by my other troops in that city, then to turn about and oppose Amyr Hussyn's army. When I reached Kārshy, having made all the requisite arrangements, I marched towards Bokharā; when I drew near the city, Mahmūd Shāh, whom I had appointed governor of the place, came out some distance to meet me, accompanied by Aly Yusury, and they both professed their allegiance.

When I had halted in Bokharā, Amyr Jakū, who was not on friendly terms with the governor, and had no confidence in his professions, privately requested leave of absence to go to Khurasān; I said, "I will consider of it, and do whatever shall appear advisable;" I then summoned the governor, and all the principal officers, and entered into consultation on the state of affairs; I said to them, "although we are much inferior to the army of Amyr Hussyn, which is approaching, nevertheless, if you will all unite firmly with me, we will go and meet it, give them battle, and let the conqueror take the bride of the kingdom by the hand." My brave generals approved of this opinion; but the governor and Aly Yusury being heartless, advised that we should fortify Bokharā, and that I should, with a light army, in the *Cossack* manner, annoy the enemy, and that no doubt we should prove successful.

Finding that Mahmūd Shāh and Aly Yusury were afraid, and that Amyr Jakū was doubtful, I gave him leave to go to Khurasān; and I also sent off Abās Behader and Syf Addeen to Makhān, to levy troops along the banks of the river Amū;* I appointed the Prince Pyr Muhammed, to escort the baggage and followers, and intrusted the charge of the city to Mahmūd Shāh and Aly Yusury, and advised them, if they found themselves unequal to stand a siege, to abandon the place.

After this arrangement, I quitted Bokharā, with my three hundred *Cossacks*, and advanced towards the enemy; when we approached their encampment, we seized a number of their horses and camels that were grazing, and I gave them to my people; I then proceeded towards Khurasān, and during the night crossed the river Amū; I then passed over the desert, and having reached Makhān, joined the heavy baggage, and the remainder of my victorious troops.

* In the vicinity of the city of Amū, the Sihūn is called the Amū.

I amused myself for some time in hunting in the plains of Makhān, waiting for intelligence from Mahmūd Shāh, and news from Bokharā; at length a letter arrived from him, representing that he had fortified the city, that Amyr Hussyn had come with his large army, and laid siege to it; that for some days he had resisted, but the inhabitants had proved treacherous, and had taken part with my enemy; that Amyr Hussyn had gone to the tomb of Shykh Syf Addeen, and there taken an oath, that the inhabitants of Bokharā had nothing to fear from him; in consequence of which, the citizens had rebelled, had taken possession of several of the bastions, and had fortified them; that although he had taken much pains to reconcile them, they had turned their backs on him; that being without remedy, he had armed his cavalry, and taken the field as Cossacks.

I was much distressed by this intelligence, and sent off spies to learn whether Amyr Hussyn still remained in Bokharā, or had returned to Sali Seray. About this time, Mahmūd Shāh and Aly Yusury, having made long journeys through the desert, arrived, and had the honour of kissing my carpet; as they had lost several of their horses, and much property, I recompensed them, and waited for the return of my spies.

At length the spies came back, and informed me that Amyr Hussyn had left a large army under the command of Amyr Khelyl, in Bokharā, and had gone back to Sali Seray.

On receipt of this intelligence, I deliberated whether I should go to Melk Hussyn, Prince of Herat, and enter into a confederacy with him against my enemies. I had formerly rescued this Prince from the hands of the officers of Amyr Kurghen, had carried him to Herat, and there placed him on the throne; on which account, he was under great obligations to me. But as I had no great dependence on his gratitude, fearing that he might have been gained over by Amyr Hussyn, and might prove an enemy, I wavered in my opinion.

I soon after received information, that Melk Hussyn had arrived at Serkhush, with the intention of visiting me; I therefore sent off Amyr Jakū as my ambassador, to meet him, and instructed the latter, that he was to discover the bottom of Melk Hussyn's heart, and to ascertain whether he was sincere, or inimical; if the former, he was to endeavour to strengthen the chain of friendship, and to return immediately.

In a short time, Amyr Jakū came back, and brought me a letter from Melk Hussyn, replete with affection and friendship; as his kindness and sincerity made a great impression on me, I therefore opened my mind, and wrote him, "that as the chiefs of Bokharā, and all Maveralnaher, had entreated me to

" return to them, in compliance with their request, I meant to do so, but with his " permission, would leave my son Muhammed Jehangyz, and all my family, in " the vicinity of Makhān, under the protection of his kindness and friendship."

CHAPTER XXIII.

My plan of proceeding from my cantonment, at Makhān, towards Maveralnaher and Khurasān, was this: my spies having brought me intelligence, a second time, that all the chiefs of Maveralnaher were very negligent and inattentive to my proceedings, but that they still retained numerous followers; I therefore took a review of my troops, and found that they did not exceed one thousand horse, and in an auspicious hour sought in the Korān for an omen, this verse opened, " God is all sufficient for those who place their faith on him." As I ever placed my confidence on the Almighty, I committed my son Jehangyr to to his protection, and having appointed Mubarik Sunjury to be his preceptor, left them at Makhān: I marched to the banks of the Jihūn, and when all my followers had joined, I crossed the river in the night, and having left the high road on the left, I halted in the fields of canes near the river: I remained concealed there during that day, and deliberated whether I should, by a forced march, endeavour to surprise the city of Bokharā, and then proceed towards Samerkund, or whether I should first attack the different chiefs of Maveralnaher, and subdue them, before they could form a junction with each other; and having thus cleared the country of them, then take possession of one of these cities, as the seat of my government.

At this time, I was informed that Amyr Musā was encamped in the neighbourhood of Kārshy, I therefore consulted the Korān whether I should attack him, or Hindū Shāh first; this verse opened, " the fire of Moses was like lightning;" I took this for an auspicious omen, and remained in the lanes by the side of the river the whole day in ambuscade. When night came on, I made a forced march against the army of Amyr Musā, and having taken him by surprise, I I took two of his generals prisoners, and dispersed all his soldiers.

It happened that in the town of Kārshy, there were some merchants from Bokharā, whom my people seized, and brought to me, with all their camels and goods; but I immediately ordered Shykh Aly Behader to escort them with all their merchandize, to a place of safety, which raised my fame through the country.

When information of my having defeated the army of Amyr Musā, reached the other chiefs, they immediately assembled, and with the troops that I had dispersed, amounting in all to five thousand horse, took possession of a strong post called Kūzy. It therefore appeared to me advisable to make a sudden attack on them before they should learn the small number of my forces, or be aware of my intention. In consequence of this determination, I formed my small army into seven divisions, six of which I gave in charge to several officers, and took post myself with the seventh. At this time, news arrived that the enemy having arranged their troops, were advancing. I immediately mounted and drew up my army, and called out to the chiefs, "before we shall have made the seven attacks, our adversaries will be annihilated;" and it turned out exactly as I said.

In a short period, the enemy's army made its appearance in the plain of Kūzy, and I soon learned that Hindū Shāh commanded their advanced line. I immediately advanced with my staff officers, and took the command of our advanced division; I then examined, with the eye of experience, the mode of attack and retreat, and I observed that the enemy's divisions were much separated; but at this moment, Aly Khān Behader, who commanded the right wing of my first line, being terrified by the appearance of the foe, ran away; I instantly ordered Amyr Jakū, who had the command of the left wing of the first line, to charge, and the right wing of the second line to advance, and take up the ground in the first line: during this manœuvre, Amyr Jakū having defeated his opponents, had a fall from his horse, and was for a short time bewildered, but he again mounted and halted; as soon as I heard of the accident, I sent him some (Mumia) medicine, which I had about me, and he recovered.

At this time, the right wing of the enemy made a violent charge, on which I called out to my left wing, to do the same, and spurring on my horse, charged in person. We were warmly engaged from breakfast time, till noon-day prayer; but when the sun became vertical, the enemy gave way, and dispersed; at that moment I had alighted on the field of battle, and was saying my prayers, to which I then added my thanks for the victory.

My warriors pursued the enemy as far as Chekdalyk, and having taken a number of their chiefs and officers, brought them as prisoners to me. Among the prisoners that were brought in was, Aljaytū Sultān, governor of Talkhān; when brought into my presence, I was doubtful whether I should give orders for killing him or not; but as soon as his sight fell on me, he said, "O Commander, I have been grateful for the salt I have eaten of my master, and I have bravely fought against his enemy, you may either slay me, or liberate me."

(Here follows a Tūrkish verse.)

I said to my nobles, "he speaks the truth, he has been a loyal subject, for I have frequently endeavoured to entice him into my service, his constant reply has been, 'as long as I can eat the salt of Amyr Hussyn, I will not turn my face towards any other person:'" the prisoner then said, "if I shall ever eat of your salt, I will devote my life in exchange for it." As I felt inclined to favour him, some of the persons present said, "there is no reliance to be placed on this man;" I replied, "there is no doubt of his manliness, he may lose his head, but his promise will endure; if he once eats my salt, I am convinced he will prove as faithful to me, as he has shewn himself to Amyr Hussyn; in retaining him in my service, there are several advantages, and in killing him, several disadvantages, of his present or future worth, you are no judges; I, at all events, shall gain his father, whom I have respected for thirty years, and I shall obtain the present services of this young man;" I therefore encouraged him, and released him: he ever afterwards attended my stirrup, fought many battles with me; and at the time when Shāh Munsūr attacked me in person, he protected and saved me; upon that event, I said to my nobles, "one should endeavour to know the worth and value of a man, whether friend or foe;" they assented, bent their knees, and prayed for my prosperity.

As soon as the army of Amyr Hussyn had fled, and repassed the straits of Checkichec, I called a council of all my chiefs, and proposed that we should pursue and annihilate the remainder of the enemy, at the head of whom, was Khizer Behader, but who had shut himself up in the city of Samerkund. In consequence of this determination, we marched to Kesh, of which place I appointed Tughy Shāh, governor, and Turmajūk to be collector of the district, and realize the revenue due to government; I then proceeded with my victorious army toward Samerkund.

When we arrived near Samerkund, I encamped in the vicinity of the city, and sent a summons to the governor, Khizer Behader, offering him the choice of my favour, or my revenge; he wrote me this answer, "if I should come over to your "highness, the salt and kindness of Amyr Hussyn would seize me, and the world "would call me an ungrateful wretch, and a scoundrel, for being guilty of trea-"chery in giving up a place confided to me by a Muselmān;* such conduct is "inconsistent with the duties of a person professing the Muhammedan religion, "if I should be base enough to commit this act of villainy, neither your High-

* The followers of the Arabian Prophet never call themselves Muhammedans, but Muselmāns, (resigned) or Muminān̤s, (believers) they consider it disrespectful, and making too free with his name; for a similar reason, they do not call us Christians, but (Nessāra) Nazareens.

" ness nor your officers would ever place any confidence or reliance on me; if I " shall be killed bravely doing my duty, it will be better in every respect than " to be guilty of dishonesty." I praised him for his fidelity, but drew out my army, and advanced close to the city, and my warriors were about to attack it, when the governor attempted to make his escape; Ak Timūr Behader met him near the gate, and seized him by the belt of his quiver, but the belt broke, and the governor with difficulty again got inside the gate, and saved himself. Ak Behader brought the quiver to me, as a proof of his zeal, in recompense for which, I promoted him; I then drew off from the town, and encamped at the village of Retin, from thence I marched to the village of Shāh Rūkh, where the water and air was very good, and rested there for some time.

At this place, I obtained intelligence that Amyr Hussyn had detached Aljaytū Bughā with an army to relieve Samerkund, and that they were approaching: I also received a letter from Tughy Shāh, my governor of Kesh, stating that, a party of the enemy had suddenly entered the district, and had seized my collector Termajūk.

On receipt of this bad news, I was much dispirited, and formed to myself three plans; 1st. That I should turn *Cossack*, and never pass twenty-four hours in one place, and plunder all that came to hand. 2nd. That I should make a forced march to meet Amyr Hussyn, surprise his camp, and annihilate his army. 3rd. That I should leave the country, and proceed to Khujend; being still undecided, I placed my foot in the stirrup, and having crossed the river Yam, I encamped on its bank.

At this time, my whole force consisted of one thousand horse; when I mentioned the three plans to my chiefs, they all agreed that the one of retreating to Khujend, was the best; we then quitted the river Yam, and after three or four marches, reached the bank of the Khujend, (Sihūn) where we encamped.

At this place, I received letters from Ky Khuserū and Behram Jelayr, who were formerly in my service, but who had quitted it for that of Amyr Hussyn, stating, that being in danger of their lives from Hussyn, they had therefore deserted in the night, and had taken refuge at Khānchyn; they further represented that the Amyr had killed their brothers, and plundered their tribes, in revenge for which, they had collected seven thousand horse, and were waiting at Tashkund, ready to join me whenever I should order them.*

In consequence of this intelligence, I resolved to march to Tashkund; when I reached that country, Ky Khuserū being delighted, advanced to meet me; he carried me to his own residence, and made a great feast on the occasion. As

* Khujend and Tashkund are both cities on the banks of the Sihūn.

the Emperor Tugleck Timūr Khān had given his daughter in marriage to Ky Khuserū, by whom he had a daughter, now arrived at the age of puberty; we agreed to betroth her to my eldest son Jehangyr, to which measure, Behram Jelayr, who was her relation, also gave his consent. In consequence of this ceremony, I passed a whole month in luxury and every delight at Tashkund. It must be explained that this Behram Jelayr had been brought up by me, that I had promoted him, that he became proud, but being reduced to low circumstances, had asked my pardon; in consequence of which, I forgave and restored him to his former rank, and afterwards further promoted him.

CHAPTER XXIV.

At this time, I received intelligence that Amyr Hussyn, with a large army, had passed by Kesh, and was encamped at Saryelāk; I therefore resolved to march with Ky Khuserū, towards him, and make a sudden attack on his army. In consequence of this resolution, Ky Khuserū and I repeated the prayer for success, and set out, leaving Behram Jelayr in the rear to support us.

About this time, I obtained further information that Amyr Hussyn had detached Amyr Musā, with several other chiefs, and twelve thousand horse from Saryelāk, that they had passed Samerkund with the intention of fighting me, that the main body was encamped on the banks of the river Belenghūr, that their advanced division, consisting of three thousand men, were encamped in the plain of Surengerān, under Melk Behader, and that another division of four thousand men, under the command of Jehān Shāh, had been sent to Rebāt Mulk.

At this time, I deliberated on two plans, the first was to leave the road on the left, and proceed to attack Amyr Hussyn, while separated from his principal officers; the second, to march against the several divisions, and cut them off in detail.

Having in conjunction with Ky Khuserū, taken a muster of our forces, we found that we had in all only three thousand horse; I therefore resolved to attack the detached parties, and having proceeded with my own troops, amounting only to one thousand horse, I attacked Jehān Shāh, dispersed his army, and seized a great quantity of plunder before my confederate came up; when he arrived with his division, we halted at the village of Azuk, that our men and horses might be refreshed; when night came on, we agreed to march against the other division of the enemy, commanded by Melk Behader, at Surengerān; I then formed the army into three divisions, I took command of the advanced one, and left Ky

Khuserū in charge of the rear one, as a covering party. I then put my foot in the stirrup, and placing my trust in God, advanced towards the enemy; I ordered the *Moghul* standard to be raised, and gave out that the Moghul army was arrived.

When my three divisions were seen from the vicinity of Surengerān, the peasants informed Melk Behader, that the whole Moghul army was coming, and that Amyr Timūr commanded the advance, and he himself seeing the Moghul standards and colours, had no doubt of the fact; but feeling himself unequal to the contest, gave orders for a retreat, on which his whole army ran off, and during the night, reached Amyr Hussyn's camp; I pursued them for a considerable distance, and returned victorious to my camp; I then sent intelligence to Ky Khuserū, that I had defeated Amyr Hussyn's detachments, and that if he would now advance with his Jete forces, we might take Hussyn prisoner; he replied by my messenger, "that the Jetes were not fond of fighting, that they only loved plunder, that it would not be fitting in us as followers of Muhammed, to permit these infidels to plunder and murder the Muselmāns who were in Hussyn's camp, as it would in the first place be sacrilegious, and secondly it would induce them to desert with the plunder to their own country." I was satisfied with this hint, and turned my reins toward Rebat Mulk; Ky Khuserū came out to meet me, and we passed the day there in feasting.

Having heard that some of the Jetes had collected a quantity of plunder, and had set off towards home, I sent a party to force them back; I then halted to wait for intelligence respecting the conduct of Amyr Hussyn, after he should have heard of the defeat of his detachments. In a very short period, some of my spies returned and informed me that when the defeated chiefs appeared before Amyr Hussyn, he abused them, and the fire of anger being lighted up, he had severely scolded them, that he had vowed vengeance against me, and that having assembled all his warriors, he was advancing towards me.

On hearing this news, Ky Khuserū and I drew out our troops and advanced towards the enemy: when we arrived at the village of Barsyn, we obtained information that Amyr Hussyn, with a select division of his army, had arrived at Ak Kutel, and was advancing; I immediately ordered the trumpets to be sounded, and my troops to mount. At this time it began to snow, and as the army of Amyr Hussyn had nothing to eat or cover them, but the snow, they were therefore greatly harassed, and could neither advance nor retreat: after some time, not being able to procure shelter, and afraid of being buried in the snow, they dispersed, and made towards their home.

Ky Khuserū and I, with our troops, passed that day in the houses of Barsyn, and the next morning we mounted our horses, and marched towards Tashkund:* at this time I was informed that Behram Jelayr, whom I had left to cover our retreat, (if necessary) had gone back to Tashkund with his Jete followers.

In a short time we were met by my family and dependants that I had left behind, and having entered the city, I took up my winter quarters there. It happened that this winter was so very severe, that even the very birds of the forest came into the town, and entered into the houses; I however enjoyed it extremely, as Timūr Beg, the (Kud Khoda) superintendant of one of the quarters of the city, sent me daily forty eggs, and a large tureen of (Joghrāt) soup; I ever remembered this obligation as a debt of gratitude.

Having now taken up my winter quarters in Tashkund, I sent letters of congratulation to my son Muhammed Jehangyr, whom I had left at Makhān, and to the other persons of my family that I had left at Merve, in Khurasān, and administered comfort to them all.

As the enmity of Amyr Hussyn to me was excessive, in order to avert its evil consequences, I resolved to send an embassy to the Khān of Jetteh, to request assistance, and having mentioned my intention to my chiefs, they all approved of the measure; I therefore dispatched Shumsaddyn with three other officers to carry a number of presents to the Khān, and to solicit his aid.

About this period, news arrived that Amyr Hussyn had fortified the city of Samerkund, had appointed Pulād Bughā to be governor, and had then proceeded to Arheng Seray. I continued tranquilly at Tashkund, waiting for intelligence from my ambassadors, at length Ak Bughā arrived with the information, that the Khān of Jetteh had sent ten thousand horse with the ambassadors to my assistance, and that they would shortly arrive.

When this news reached Amyr Hussyn, he was greatly alarmed, and immediately sent by the hands of his generalissimo, Amyr Musā, a copy of the Korān, addressed to the prelates and learned body of Tashkund, Khujend, and Andijan, imploring them to wait on me, and endeavour by all means in their power, to conciliate me, and stating that Amyr Musā and Mulānā Aālum would bear testimony of his having sworn on the Korān, that he would henceforth be my friend. In consequence of this measure, early in the spring, all the prelates and learned bodies of the three cities having assembled in council on this important business, waited on me, and laid before me the sacred book, on which Amyr Hussyn had taken the oath of reconciliation, and entreated my forgiveness; I replied that the Amyr had frequently before sent Korāns, on which he had taken the oaths of amity, and afterwards forgetting his vows to God, had broken his promises, I

* It is situated on the N. E. bank of the Sihūn, Lat. 42,40, N. Lon. 64,48, E.

therefore had no confidence in his oaths or promises. After the learned body had used many entreaties, Mulānā Aālum proposed that we should consult the Korān; he did so, and this verse came forth, "when two parties of Muselmāns quarrel, do ye make peace between them:" the prelates then said, "in conformity with the orders of God, you must make peace." * In compliance with this request, I agreed to a reconciliation, but said, "I will first send some confidential persons to Amyr Hussyn, that he may confirm his promises, after which, I will meet him at any place that may be agreed on:" Amyr Musā and the prelates replied, "that they would attend me to Samerkund, and would see the treaty confirmed." I therefore placed my foot in the stirrup, and accompanied by all the learned body, I crossed the Sihūn, and arrived in the vicinity of Samerkund.

About this time, in order to discover my real intentions, Amyr Hussyn had caused a report to be spread, that he was dead, but this was only one of his stratagems to try me, because if I should impatiently enter Samerkund, it would render me suspected, and would be injurious to my character.

I therefore paid no attention to the report of his death, but while seated on my horse, I resolved to proceed towards the fortress of Shadmān; in consequence of this determination, I turned my face (without alighting) towards the plain of Shadmān, attended by all the prelates. I then sent a letter by the hands of Bukhtē Behader, to Amyr Hussyn, at Sali Seray, to ascertain whether he was dead or alive; in the mean time, I proceeded, and did not draw in my reins till I entered Shadmān, where I waited the return of my messenger, but Amyr Musā stopped at Samerkund.

During this period, a detachment of the army of Amyr Hussyn approached us, and fearlessly began to murder my people; I therefore mounted a rising ground, in the middle of the plain, with a party of my troops, and sent out two other divisions to oppose them; these divisions turned their flanks, while I advanced in their front, and compelled them to make a speedy retreat; we however took some of them, whom I abused and liberated. I then resolved to cross the Kumek river, accompanied by the prelates, and to halt at a fortress in that vicinity, till I could procure further intelligence.

Soon after this affair, Bukhtē Behader returned from Sali Seray, and informed me that Amyr Hussyn was alive and well, that he was much rejoiced on hearing of my approach, and was anxiously looking for my arrival, in order that he might relinquish all animosity, and repeat his oaths of friendship; my messenger

* The ten thousand Jetes that were coming to his assistance, were Idolaters, and would have done much injury to the Muselmāns.

further stated, " that while he was in Amyr Hussyn's presence, his general, Amyr Musā, had arrived, and informed his master, that he had accompanied me as far as Samerkund, where I had heard the dreadful report of his death; that I had in consequence marched to the fortress of Shadmān, while he had gone into Samerkund, to inquire into the grounds of the report." On receiving the information from Musā, that I had gone towards the fort of Shadmān, Amyr Hussyn became much alarmed, and had despatched a confidential person to me, named Turān Shāh, who would shortly arrive, in order to confirm the amicable promises he had made.

When Turān Shāh came into my presence, and had repeated all that has been related, I was satisfied, and conferred an honorary (Khelāt) dress on him; he however requested that I would again send a confidential person with him to hear Amyr Hussyn repeat his promises, I therefore sent Abās Behader, who was one of my most confidential servants, with instructions, that if he should think Amyr Hussyn was sincere in his protestations, he might then propose we should meet at the tomb of Atā Aly, " blessed be his remains," and there repeat our promises of perpetual friendship.

When Abās Behader delivered this message to Amyr Hussyn, he sent two of his most confidential generals, viz. Amyr Musā and Aljaitū, to meet me; at the time that these officers were coming into my presence, some of my chiefs represented to me, that these two persons were the main pillars of Hussyn's power, that we had better bind them, and make a sudden attack on that Prince; I replied, " it is beneath my dignity to be guilty of a breach of promise, or to rebel against God and his holy book;" this silenced them.

When Mūsā and Aljaitū were introduced, they made a speech on the part of their master: after this, they returned, and having persuaded Amyr Hussyn to mount, he went, attended by several thousand horse, to the tomb of Atā Aly, where I met him, and we sat down to confer; he said, " we will not talk of what has past;" I replied, " a repetition of grievances, would only be the cause of mutual dissatisfaction." He then said, " if you and I are united, we need not fear the power of any stranger;" this he said as an allusion to some person, (probably the Jetes); I answered, " if the stranger is a friend, he is welcome, and if he is an enemy, he may still remain a stranger." He then laid his hand on the Korān, and repeated his oath of friendship, I trembling, placed my hand on the sacred volume, and said, " if Amyr Hussyn does not break his promise, I will faithfully preserve mine, but if he shall ever attempt to kill, or imprison, or injure me, I will not be deficient in the preservation of my life, my property, and my honour;" being thus reconciled, we mounted, and sitting on our horses, we bade each other farewell.* After this ceremony, Amyr Hussyn returned to Sali Seray, and I proceeded to Kesh.

CHAPTER XXV.

Upon my arrival at Kesh, I sent orders to my son Muhammed Jehangyr to leave Makhān, and bring all my family with him to Kesh: I soon after received a letter from Amyr Hussyn, informing me that the Princes of Badukhshān had raised the standard of rebellion, and that it was incumbent on him to proceed against them. I immediately wrote and sent him an answer, wishing him success, I then took up my abode, and enjoyed myself for some time in the city of Kesh.

At length I received information that Melk Hussyn, the (Valy) ruler of Herat, had invaded the territory of Balkh, and plundered the inhabitants of the country. I therefore placed my foot in the stirrup, and having crossed the river at Termuz, I made forced marches, and having come up with the marauders, took from them all their plunder, and restored it to the owners, and wrote to Amyr Hussyn all the particulars: he immediately requested that I would proceed to his assistance in Badukhshān.

Having restored all the plunder to the people of Balkh, I set out for Badukhshān; but when I arrived at Kundez, the Princes having made their apologies to Amyr Hussyn, he was on his return home, and we met at Kundez; we embraced each other on horseback, we thence proceeded to the plain of Askemush, where we encamped; I entered his tent, and all the jealousy and enmity which had existed in our minds during our separation, was entirely removed.

Soon after this time, Amyr Hussyn was informed that Ak Bughā and Pulād Bughā having strengthened the fortress of Cabūl, had raised the standard of rebellion; on receipt of this intelligence, he came to my tent, and entreated that I would accompany him to Cabūl, and that he would divide that country in a brotherly manner with me, and he wrote with his own hand the following agreement; "if it shall please God that we may subdue the country of Cabūl, it shall be divided in a brotherly manner with the friends of Timūr:" having folded this letter, he placed it before me; confiding in his written promise, I made arrangements for subduing Cabulistān, which much gratified Amyr Hussyn.

This Pulād Bughā, and his brother Ak Bughā, had formerly been two of Amyr Hussyn's most confidential servants; he had appointed them to the

* This passage differs from Sherif Addeen's History, who says, the ceremony was performed by deputies. Petis de la Croix's History, page 159.

command of the province of Cabūl; this elevation turned their heads, and they raised the standard of independence in that region. In order to subdue them, I took the command of the advanced line of our army, while Amyr Hussyn led on the main body; we departed unexpectedly from Arheng Seray, and crossed the Hindū Kūsh mountains,* and by rapid marches, entered the Cabūl territory. When this news reached Ak Bughā, being puffed up with pride, he advanced with an army to meet me; I formed my troops into three divisions, the advance guard was commanded by Jughtai Behader, the second by Shykh Aly Behader, and I in person, brought up the rear; I then gave orders to the advanced division to attack the rebels with vigour, when Jughtai and Ak Bughā met, they exchanged three cuts of the sword, on the fourth cut, Jughtai was wounded, at the fifth cut, Aly Behader joined with his division, and the two armies fought hand to hand; after some hard work, my people began to lose ground, but at this time I came up, and when my warriors saw me, although many of them were severely wounded, they returned to the charge; I then called out to an officer who was standing near me, to take a party and block up the road to the fort, and thereby cut off the retreat of the rebels. At the seventh cut of the sword, Ak Bughā was wounded on the head, which confounded his brain, and he was taken prisoner; his brother Pulād Bughā effected his retreat to the fort, but I encouraged my men to break open the gate with sledges and hammers, which being effected, we entered the citadel, took Pulād prisoner, and I gave quarter to the garrison.

Two days after this event, Amyr Hussyn arrived, and I went out of the fort to meet him; he alighted from his horse, took me in his arms, and congratulated me on my success. As I was greatly incensed against these two rebels, I should have died of vexation if I had not succeeded, I therefore as soon as I was seated in the fort, had ordered them to be brought into my presence, they were brought before me bound; when I saw them, I was convinced by experience, that a Prince should never promote a servant so as to turn his brains, but ought always to keep him between fear and hope, and should appoint a (Kutel) successor as a spy to watch over him. It also came into my mind that no legitimately born person would have acted in the infamous manner these two scoundrels had done; I therefore addressed Bughā, and said to him, "may your face be black, if your mother had been a virtuous woman, you never would have been guilty of such ingratitude to your benefactor, the Amyr Hussyn, who raised you from a low situation to an important command; it has been truly said that 'a bastard never quits this world till he has injured his patron,' you are the son of a whore, as you have clearly proved."

* This name (Slayer of the Hindūs) was given to these mountains, in consequence of a Hindū army having suffered severely from the cold in these regions; Hindū signifies black.

Soon after Amyr Hussyn's arrival at Cabūl, he appointed agents to all the public offices, quite forgot my services, and never even thanked me; I was ashamed to produce the written agreement he had given me, and when I saw his total want of kindness, I left the retaliation to Providence; but I quitted the fort, mounted my horse, and encamped in the plain.

Amyr Hussyn having made all the requisite arrangements respecting Cabūl, prepared for his departure and while we were seated on horseback, consulted me whether he should make the city of Balkh,* the residence of his government; I told him by no means to think of it; but as the evil star of his destiny was then in the ascendant, he would not listen to advice, but went to Balkh, and having arrived there, he repaired the fort of Hindūan, and compelled the inhabitants of the city to remove thither, I returned to my residence of Kesh, and continued there.

CHAPTER XXVI.

In the year 769, I entered my thirty-third year, and being of a restless disposition, I was much inclined to invade some of the neighbouring countries; but at this time my spies came and informed me that the Jete army was approaching, I considered this a fortunate circumstance, and employed myself in equipping my army; soon after I had received this intelligence, a messenger arrived from Amyr Hussyn, who stated, "that the Jete army, resembling a dark cloud, were advancing, and that a sun-like Timūr, was requisite to disperse it," and made use of many other flattering expressions. In reply to these fulsome compliments, I produced to the messenger, the agreement written by Amyr Hussyn, for the division of the country of Cabūl, and said, "after having conquered that place, your master did not even thank me for my assistance, much less fulfil his promise of giving it to me." A.D. 1367.

When Amyr Hussyn received my message, he immediately sent his general, Musā, to me to say, "that the whole of the country of Cabūl was at my service," but I did not credit this speech, and replied, "if it shall please God, I will retake the country from the Jetes, without being under any obligation to your master." I then resolved to allow the Jete army to enter the country.

At this time, Amyr Hussyn sent an order to Musā, to cross the river Sihūn, with all his forces; Musā complied, and having crossed the river, came in sight of the Jetes, who immediately marched from their cantonment, near Tashkund, and made a rapid charge on the army of Musā, the latter being defeated,

* The Bactria of the Greeks, Lat. 36,28, N. Lon. 65,16, E. See Bulkh; Edinburgh Gazetteer.

recrossed the river. When this news reached Amyr Hussyn, he marched from Balkh, and halted in the plains of Kesh: during this time, the Jetes being puffed up by success, continued to advance; on which Amyr Hussyn being greatly alarmed, came to my habitation, and having entered, said to me, "when our enemies the Jetes shall have destroyed me, what do you mean to do;" I replied, "whatever God shall please, I will do;" the Amyr was much affected by my speech, and said, "God grant that you with a strong heart, may mount and take command of the advanced army, and march against the enemy, while I protect the rear, for I see that Providence has written the signs of victory and success on your forehead;" on hearing this, my chiefs were very much incensed, and said, "how long are we to fight the battles, and be killed and wounded in the service of another, and wear the clothes, and eat the morsels of a stranger."

In the public assembly, Amyr Hussyn wrote out and offered to me an agreement, that Samerkund should be mine as formerly; I replied, "I will not accept Samerkund from you, but if it shall please God, I will take it from the enemy by the power of my sword."

When Amyr Hussyn saw my magnanimity, and that I would not accept of Samerkund from him, he put on a melancholy countenance, told me of the defeat of his forces, and of the power of the Jetes; although he was apparently sincere in his desire to make friends, the real fact was, that he wished me to be defeated, as Amyr Musā had been, and compelled to retreat.

But I placing my confidence in the aid of the Prophet, and his illustrious companions, determined to fight the Jetes, and having assembled two thousand horse, marched from the plain of Kesh, towards the bank of the river Sihūn. As we went on, it entered my mind, that as there was a great jealousy existed between Kummer Addyn and Hajy Beg, the enemy's two generals, if I could foment a quarrel between them, I might soon settle the business of the Jetes. It so happened as I had wished, for they openly quarrelled, in consequence of which, one half of the army took the part of Kummer Addyn, and the other half, the part of Hajy Beg, and a regular battle took place between them. When I received this news, I immediately marched to attack the Jete forces; when I approached them, they were alarmed, and fled towards their cantonments; thus by the Almighty aid, I returned victorious and successful. When intelligence of this event reached Amyr Hussyn, he came to meet me, took me in his arms, ordered the carpet of pleasure to be spread, and made great rejoicings.

While thus employed, information was brought that the Princes of Badukhshān had placed their feet on the path of transgression, and had plundered the city of Kundez; this intelligence caused Amyr Hussyn much anxiety, and he turned the face of entreaty towards me, for such was the practice of that Prince, that whenever any misfortune occurred, he cried like a woman, but when successful, he boasted as if he had been a hero: another of his bad qualities was, that he was very envious, in so much, that he envied his own servants, whom he had promoted, whenever they were fortunate, and by his bad conduct to them and folly, caused them to rebel. Thus whenever he had appointed a new governor to a district, he wished to take from the preceding one, every thing he had made, and never allowed any governor to remain more than a year in any country, so that they never had an opportunity of realizing their expences.

It was in this manner he treated the Princes of Badukhshān, who had been very submissive to him, and paid him a large tribute, which this year he had encreased far beyond their power of liquidating, and had even taken Kundez from them, contrary to agreement. In consequence of this oppression, they were incensed, and plundered part of Hussyn's territory; the Amyr sent an army against them, which was defeated, for the fact was, that many of his officers were so disgusted with his empty professions and conduct, that they united with the Princes of Badukhshān, in a determination to depose Hussyn, and even wrote letters to me on the subject, with complaints against him. When intelligence of these circumstances were communicated to the Amyr, he came during the night to me, and with much supplication, begged that I would preserve him and his government: I shewed him the letters I had received, on reading them, he was astonished and bewildered; I therefore comforted him, and said, "I will bring over the Princes to you, either by war, or by peace; but there are two of your generals who have been always hypocrites, my advice is this, do not trust to them, but let me arrange the army; I will advance against the Princes of Badukhshān, and do you keep one days' march in the rear:" he having agreed to this measure, we repeated the prayer for success; I then made long marches, and crossed the Jihūn, and encamped in the desert of Keshem, which is part of the territory of Badukhshān.

At this time, I received a letter from Amyr Hussyn, informing me that he had sent his son Jehān Mulk, to join me; I also was informed that the Princes of Badukhshān had taken possession of the summits and passes of the mountains of Hindū Kūsh, and had blocked them up; I therefore sent Jehān Mulk, who by this time had arrived, to force the passes, and clear the country, and then wait for my arrival.

Jehān Mulk immediately marched, and entered the passes of the mountain, and began to ravage and plunder the country; but the Princes of Badukhshān having dismounted their troops, closed up the ends of the passes, and opposed him valiantly; at length, the young man finding himself unable to contend with them, commenced his retreat, losing not only the plunder he had collected, but all his own effects; beside which, four hundred of his father's soldiers were taken prisoners; in consequence of this misfortune, Jehān Mulk lost all self confidence, and retreated to me for safety.

I now placed my foot in the stirrup, and having arrived near the summit of the mountain, at the first charge I gained possession of the pass, cleared it of the Badukhshians, and took some of them prisoners. The remainder of them continued their retreat to the summit of Jerm, where they took post, and resolved to oppose me; I again mounted my horse, and having ordered the trumpets to sound, proceeded towards the enemy; when they saw my standards, and knew that I was advancing against them in person, they were terrified, and sent an ambassador to beg for mercy.

The next day a number of the respectable inhabitants and prelates of the city of Badukhshān, came and supplicated that I would spare the country, and requested that I would come and take up my abode with them. I therefore had compassion on their feelings, sent them back, and followed them to the city of Badukhshān.

At this place, the great men and officers of the army, and some of the Princes, waited on me, and brought me a number of presents, and returned all the plunder and cattle that had been taken from Jehān Mulk.

In consequence of their conduct, I resolved to remain in the city till I could ratify a peace between the Princes of Badukhshān and Amyr Hussyn. But the Amyr being dissatisfied at my delay, suspected that I was confederating with the Princes against him, he therefore sent an officer to inform me that Shykh Muhammed, son of Byān Seldūz, and Ky Khuserū, had assembled all their clans, had raised the standard of rebellion, and that he being satisfied with the reduction of Badukhshān, was on his return to Sali Seray. On receiving this information, I immediately put my foot in the stirrup, and followed the Amyr.

When I arrived at Sali Seray, which was his capital, I discovered the cause of the enmity of Shykh Muhammed and Ky Khuserū, for when I reached my own cantonment, I received letters from them, *(written in the Tūrky language)* saying, " we are afraid of the severity and stratagems of Amyr Hussyn, and " are convinced that your Highness being an unsuspicious character, will shortly " fall a prey to his deceit and fraud; we speak with the frankness of Tūrks, and " have repeated with our tongues whatever was in our hearts."

At the same time, I learned that these two chiefs had written letters to Amyr Hussyn; I therefore shewed him the letters I had received, hoping that he would with the same openness and friendship, shew me those addressed to him, but he kept whatever was in his mind concealed, although I guessed that the contents of the two letters were nearly the same, in order to foment a quarrel between us; but Amyr Hussyn still believed that I was inimical to him, and meant to play him some trick; I further learned that the Amyr had said in a council of his confidential people, " as long as Timūr lives, my sovereignty and dominion is in danger, and that he was resolved to seize me:" I replied to my informant, " it is impossible, for Hussyn has taken his oath on the Korān, and promised never to attempt any thing against me, if he is no longer a Muselmān, the holy book should be taken away from him.

About this time, I also received a letter from Aādil Sultān, whom Amyr Hussyn, supposing him to be a descendant of Jengyz, had raised to the dignity of Khān, informing me that Hussyn certainly planned treachery against me: when I had read this letter, I was convinced that Hussyn having forgotten God, had some evil intentions against me. I however remained quite tranquil, and continued in appearance my friendship towards him, till the quarrel between him and the two before-mentioned chiefs, arose to extremes.

When Hussyn was convinced that Muhammed, son of Seldūz, and Ky Khuserū, were in an actual state of rebellion, he was much alarmed, and placing his foot in the stirrup, we both marched to the bank of the river Jihūn, and encamped there; the next day he directed his generalissimo, Amyr Musā, to cross the river with his troops, and attack the rebels, but the general refused, saying, " he was unequal to the task;" upon which, the Prince being helpless, came to my tent, and said, " I am well convinced that nothing can be effected without your assistance, I therefore entreat that you will take measures for quelling these rebels;" I immediately acquiesced, and having repeated the prayer for success, crossed the river. When the rebel chiefs were informed of this circumstance, they drew up their forces in order of battle. I did not delay an instant, but without giving them time to wait, advanced against them; when I arrived near them, Ky Khuserū said, " Timūr is too fortunate a personage for us to contend with, there is no utility in our drawing the sword against him, it will be better for us to separate, do you go to Khujend, and I will go to Alay," and they accordingly set off.

When I received intelligence of their motions, I pursued them, but not being able to overtake either, I turned my reins towards Tashkund, and having written a report of all the circumstances, sent it to Amyr Hussyn: on the receipt of my letter, Hussyn being well satisfied, returned to Sali Seray: I amused myself some time in hunting, and then came back to my residence at Kesh.

Soon after this time, I received a lêtter from Amyr Hussyn, informing that he intended leaving Arheng Seray, and going to reside at Balkh, and asked me to accompany him, saying, "that after we are conjointly seated on the throne of dominion, we will take possession of all Khurasān, and then divide the countries of Turān and Khurasān between us, in a brotherly manner." At the same time, a friend of mine, who was one of his council, wrote to me, advising me to say, "that I was quite satisfied with my residence at Kesh, and did not wish to change it;" he further cautioned me to be on my guard against Hussyn's stratagems. From this hint, I was convinced that the Amyr had designs either to kill or confine me, I therefore refused to go to Balkh. This circumstance encreased the animosity between us, and he devised several plans for my destruction, and used many stratagems to get me in his power, but finding he could not succeed, he then endeavoured to disperse my followers, and send my Kushūn and horde into the desert. As his avarice and envy exceeded all bounds, he forgot all his solemn promises and oaths to me, and sent Pulād Bughā and Amyr Khēlyl, who were nearly connected with him, to expel my tribe out of the country, and compel them to remove to the district of Balkh.

The enmity of Amyr Hussyn being thus evident, I delivered him to the vengeance of the holy book, but my twelve chiefs came to me in a body, and having made their salutations, said, "if your Highness wishes to keep the command of your horde and clan, exert yourself; if not, let us go, that we may do the best we can for ourselves; till this day we have worn the sword of manliness, and have often used it in your service; now Pulād Bughā and Khēlyl are come, and wish to treat us as peasants, to tie us hand and neck, and oblige us to remove to Balkh." Although I endeavoured to comfort them, they would not be satisfied, till I took an oath that I would not do any thing without their advice and concurrence: when I had thus tranquillized them, I said to them, "Amyr Hussyn has sworn on the Korān never to injure me, if he should break his promise, be assured that the sacred volume will throw him into my power;" and it turned out exactly as I said.

When the violence of Amyr Hussyn rose to the extreme, his disposition totally changed, and he became proud, haughty, and arrogant, and did every thing he could to annihilate me; it therefore became requisite to take measures for averting the danger, and of living in safety. I in consequence arranged my army, and placing the foot of courage in the stirrup of resolution, I ordered Pulād Bughā and Amyr Khēlyl, although the agents of, and supported by Amyr Hussyn, to be brought before me, I addressed them as follows; "what has Amyr Hussyn become a renegado, and turned Christian, that he forgets his oath taken on the holy Korān, and has bound round him the sword of vengeance against me, and against my horde and clan? He shall not do so with impunity; three times has he sworn by the sacred volume, and given me solemn promises, and now breaks his vows, and has beaten the drum of enmity, and seeks my life; I have therefore made my preparations, and will shortly pay him a visit."

I then summoned all the (Oulemā) learned body, and having explained to them all the circumstances above related, demanded their (Futwā) decision, they replied, " as he has been the first to break his promise, and has dared to forswear himself, doubtless he will fall into your Highness's power." When Pulād Bughā and Khēlyl heard these words, they trembled, I therefore sent them away that they might inform their master of what they had seen and heard. As soon as this intelligence was communicated to Amyr Hussyn, he beat the drum of discord, and sought an opportunity of seizing me by intrigue, but I placing the foot of determination in the plain of sincerity, boldly declared whatever came into my mind, and said, " as long as Hussyn chose to be my friend, I was his friend, but now that he has chosen to be my enemy, he shall find me an enemy, and placing my trust in the favour of God, I loudly proclaimed, that up to this time, I have been amicably inclined towards him, but he, having broken his oath and promises, seeks to destroy me, I will therefore do every thing in my power to avert his evil designs:" on hearing this speech, my chiefs were all delighted, bound on the sword of unanimity, and prepared their clans for war.

CHAPTER XXVII.

The plan that I proposed for encountering Amyr Hussyn, was this, seeing that my chiefs were unanimous in their determination to oppose Amyr Hussyn, and that they were firmly attached to me. In a fortunate hour I sought for an omen in the Korān, and this verse came forth; " you cannot better testify your gratitude to him, (Muhammed) than by doing good to his relations;" the (Oulemā) prelates said, " the meaning of this verse is, that you should consider the descendants of the Prophet as of your own tribe and friends, and in obedience to this order it is incumbent on your Highness to come forth, for from this expedition, much benefit will arise to the descendants of his holiness." This prediction of theirs was verified, when, during the war with Hussyn, I took possession of Termūz; the very illustrious and venerable prelate, Abū al Berkāt, who was the chief Syed of that city, came out to meet me, and presented me the drum and standard of Amyr Hussyn, saying, " by the command of the Prophet, whom I have seen in a dream, I have brought you this drum and standard:" I was much pleased by the arrival of Syed Abū al Berkāt, considering it a most auspicious event, and therefore conferred great favours and honours on all the posterity of the Prophet, who dwelt in the city. I made him sit by me, consulted him on all occasions, and did not deviate in the smallest degree from his instructions; nay, I even considered him, as one of the many favours received from Providence, reposed all my confidence in him, both spiritual and temporal, and made him my constant companion, either while marching or halting, and whenever any difficulty occurred, I referred the business to him, and he solved the difficulty.

When he brought me the drum and standard of Amyr Hussyn, which were the insignia of his royalty, the news soon spread through the country, in consequence of which, several of Hussyn's enemies joined me; the first of these was Shykh Muhammed Seldūz, who having deserted from Amyr Hussyn, was wandering about the desert; when he heard of my opposition to that Prince, he came over to me with all his horde, but as the smoke of vanity had mounted into his brain, he conceived himself one of the greatest of my nobles, and when he was joined by all his horde and partizans, his pride became excessive, he was in short a light-headed man, and a great talker. On the very day that he joined me, he asked me to give him the district of Khutelān, and I gave it to him: but at this time, Amyr Ky Khuserū Khutelāny, whose brother had been put to death by Hussyn, in consequence of which he had deserted, and for some time wandered about the country, at length entered and took possession of Khutelān, and having collected a great number of followers, wrote to me, "if you are determined in your opposition to Hussyn, I will join you:" I sent him an answer,* in which I recapitulated every circumstance of Hussyn's unprincipled conduct towards me, and concluded by saying, "that I had taken the field with a firm resolution of defeating his projects, and trusted that the Korān by which he had sworn, would avenge his perfidy."

When Ky Khuserū received my letter, he was much delighted, and joined me with all his troops; when he came into my presence, I took him in my arms, and assured him of my support. I then ordered the drum of march to be beaten, and leaving Termūz, I kept along the bank of the river till I came to Hissarabād, where I halted. At this place, Aljaitū, who was governor of Kundūz, on the part of Hussyn, came and joined me with his troops, and said, "I trust that by the good fortune of your Highness, I shall be delivered for ever from the grasp of this tyrant."

* The letter is given in the text, but it is merely a repetition of what has been stated.

At this time, I also received a letter from Muhammed Shāh, the (Valy) ruler of Badukhshān, replete with complaints against Amyr Hussyn; I sent him an answer, in which I stated, "that my injuries from Amyr Hussyn, far exceeded "his, that I now considered that tyrant as an unbeliever, and that I was deter-"mined to ruin him, therefore if he would join me, (please God) his complaints "should soon be converted into thanksgivings."

As soon as Muhammed Shāh received my letter, he marched from Badukhshān with a large force, and paid his respects to me.

The people of Badukhshān, and the hordes of Maveralnaher, also sent me petitions full of complaints against Hussyn, and entreating me to send some person to take the the command of them. In compliance with their request, I sent Amyr Jakū to them, and every person who was discontented with Hussyn, assembled round my officer.

When all these valiant chiefs had joined my standard, I considered this assistance as sent to me by the Prince of Prophets, Muhammed, (on whom be blessings) and exulting in the presence of the holy Syed Abū al Berkāt, I sought in the Korān for an omen, and this verse opened, "verily God intends to take away impurity from your house, and to render you pure," which the learned expounded to me, as relating to the family of the Prophet, whose spirits were purified from the defilement of associating with idolaters and unbelievers, the instant they quitted the body. And that it was applicable to my situation, as I should soon be freed from the impurity of my enemies and adversaries; this circumstance encreased my affection and friendship for the posterity of Muhammed, and I considered the arrival of the holy Syed Abū al Berkāt, as one of the greatest blessings of Providence, and resolved in future, that the Korān and the Syed should be my constant companions, so that in every important transaction, I might consult with them, and ever regulate my conduct by the commands and prohibitions of God.

When I found myself surrounded by a numerous army, consisting of natives of various countries, and by different tribes, I summoned the principal chiefs to council, and laid before them my apprehension that Amyr Hussyn would doubtless endeavour to escape from this desert of difficulties, by some of his innumerable artifices and intrigues, and that I was distrustful of the people of the hordes as being easily alarmed or deceived, and instanced to them the case of Amyr Musā, who from some apprehension, deserted and went back to Samerkund; that it was therefore advisable to summon a general assembly, and let us conjointly take the oath of animosity to Amyr Hussyn, and confirm it on the Korān; the measure was agreed to, and all the chiefs of the hordes and clans, being collected, again took the oath required of them.

The whole of the chiefs of the tribes and hordes having thus bound round them the girdle of fealty to me, the first thing I did was to send off Shykh Behader Aly with a number of warriors, as an advance guard, for at this time I received information that Amyr Hussyn had despatched an army, under the command of Chubān Serbedal, to oppose my progress.

My advanced guard soon fell in with the enemy, and in the first charge, broke and put them to flight, I therefore beat the drum of march, and having crossed the skirts of the mountain of Shadmān, and keeping close to the river, entered the valley of Guz, and encamped near the fort of Azburg.

At this place, I was informed that Amyr Hussyn had sent letters to various of my chiefs, to excite them to mutiny, saying to them, "that they had deviated from the custom and manners of the Tūrks, and of the ancient chiefs of the hordes, clans, and tribes, by paying obedience to any person but their legitimate Sovereign, and according to the Tūrkish canons, our lawful monarch (Khān) must be a descendant of Kubūl and Jengyz Khān, this conduct of yours is an act of injustice to the posterity of these Princes." When I heard of this circumstance, I immediately summoned all the chiefs, and said to them, "my only object in engaging in a war with Amyr Hussyn, is for the ease and comfort of the Muselmāns, and my other subjects, who are all dissatisfied with him; and with respect to the canons and rules of the Turks, have we not the Prince Syurghumtumush as our Khān, therefore how can any person venture to say that we have deviated from the laws and customs of our ancestors." I then issued the orders for immediately marching against Amyr Hussyn, in order to put a stop to his attempts of seducing my people.

About this time, Shykh Behader Aly, to whom I had given the charge of my advanced guard, brought bound neck and hand to me, Chubān Serbedāl, the commander of Hussyn's advance guard, whom he had taken prisoner. I was also joined by Muhammed Khuajē with his troops. I then resolved to move rapidly and attack the city of Balkh, so that if Amyr Hussyn should come out and meet me in the plain, I could not wish for any thing better, but if he should fortify the place and stand a siege, God would soon render it an easy business, in consequence of his breaking of his oath on the Korān.

Soon after this time, I received information that Amyr Hussyn had come out of the fort into the plain; I therefore ordered my chiefs to advance rapidly, and attack his army; I also sent my son Omer Shaikh (then only sixteen years of age) to assault the walls of the town, he advanced so close to the place, that an arrow pierced his foot, and entered the side of his horse; notwithstanding this severe wound, the Prince continued the attack, till Hussyn being alarmed, took refuge in the citadel, and ordered the gates to be barred. My courageous son, in spite of his wound, rode up to the gate of the fort, struck it with an axe, and returned exultingly; the warriors were all delighted with this proof of his courage, and devoted their lives to him.

The next morning I placed my foot in the stirrup, and having drawn out my army, made an attack on the walls of the town; Amyr Hussyn came to the top of the citadel, and displayed his standard, he then resolved to oppose me, and sent out a body of troops to engage me; a severe contest took place, and many brave men were killed on both sides; but Hussyn kept himself like the stone of a ring safe within his enclosure, and beheld from a distance, his defeat and disgrace; he however continued the battle till night, but as soon as it was dark, he sent me the following letter; "from the day that I bound round my loins the "girdle of enmity to thee, I have never enjoyed a moment of happiness, and I "am convinced that all opposition to thee will only increase my misfortunes; "experience has proved that you are aided by Providence, and that good fortune "and prosperity attend you, while calamity and misfortune have seized me by "the neck, and drag me towards you, forgive me, and let me quit this country, "to go on a pilgrimage to Mecca."

I consented to his request, and wrote to him to send one of his sons, who might enable me to satisfy the minds of all the chiefs of the hordes and tribes that he had injured and disgusted, and that I might exact a promise from them not to injure or molest him. He did send out his eldest son, and I promised the young man, in the presence of all the chiefs, that if Hussyn would come out of the fort, and depart for the sacred territory, I would furnish him with every thing requisite for the journey, and protect him by a guard.

Hussyn would not listen to my advice or promise, but having tied his most valuable jewels in his girdle, he resolved to escape from the fortress in the dress of a (Kulender) pilgrim, and try to reach some place of safety. He therefore, without acquainting his family, changed his dress, and unknown to his servants, came out: at this time the morning dawned, and being afraid of detection, he entered a mosque, and concealed himself in the cupola of the minaret; soon after the (Muazin) crier mounted the minaret, in order to call the people to the first prayers, and as soon as his eyes fell on the Prince, he recognized him; Hussyn offered the Muazin a string of pearls if he would not divulge his secret: the crier being afraid of scandal or suspicion, came to my tent and proclaimed the (Azin) hour of prayer; I ordered him to be brought before me, when he entered, he told me all the circumstances, and shewed me the string of pearls which had been offered to him as a bribe to keep the secret:* I desired the crier to return to

* This differs from Sherif Addeen's History.

Amyr Hussyn, and tell him to conceal himself in the best manner he could, till he might find an opportunity of going away wherever he chose. Hussyn fearing for his life, came down and hid himself in a room under the tower, but his enemies having heard of his retreat, surrounded the mosque, and having found him, brought him to the (Dyvan Khanē) council chamber; I then gave orders that they should deliver him over in charge to *Aādil Tuajy,** until the chiefs of all the tribes and hordes should be assembled; that whoever had any complaints against him, might have the affair inquired into.

Trial by (Berghūy) sound of trumpet on Amyr Hussyn.

When I delivered Amyr Hussyn to the charge of the gaoler, I sent him a message, saying, "that as there is a solemn compact between us, and as we have "placed our respective hands on the Korān, vowing never to attempt each other's "lives, I will not now break my promise, but this calamity which is fallen on "thy head, does not proceed from enmity to thee, it is the vengeance of the "Korān that has overtaken you; I have nothing to do with the business, but I "cannot liberate you from the hands of the chiefs, who are thirsty of your blood, "in retaliation for the injuries they have received."

When he received my message, he began to entreat and supplicate for mercy, and I endeavoured to comfort him; I therefore ordered all the chiefs to be summoned, and when they were collected, we formed a council; I then sent for Amyr Hussyn, and when he arrived, I addressed him; "Hussyn, it has been the want of good faith, and disrespect to the word of God, which has brought thee into this deplorable situation, and such is ever the consequence of a breach of promise, and the guilt of falsehood." Syed Abū al Berkāt then quoted the proverb, "a strict regard of truth never injures a man, fidelity to his promise is better than faith."

I then said aloud in the presence of all the assembled chiefs, "I have given Amyr Hussyn my promise of safety;" but he with that pride and haughtiness, which was habitual to him, said in the Tūrky language, "if I had been in your place, I would not have done so;" I replied, "I thank God that I am not like you, who cannot forgive, and can be guilty of perjury, and dare to offend both God and the Prophet."

At this moment, Ky Khuserū bent the knee, and demanded vengeance for the blood of his brother, who had been killed by Hussyn; I endeavoured to mitigate his anger, and sent for Shykh Muhammed and the other Cazies and Judges; before their entrance, Muhammed, the ruler of Badukhshān, said in a tremulous voice, "Amyr Hussyn has been the cause of the ruin of my family, and has

* I doubt whether this is a proper name, or signifies an officer of the court of justice.

embittered all the days of my life, by murdering several of the pious Princes of Badukhshān;" Muhammed, the son of Byan Seldūz, also called out, "thousands of the families of my tribe are wandering about the deserts in consequence of Hussyn's injustice, and he has plundered the greater part of our cattle and property: many others of the chiefs were also very clamorous that he should be put to death. But in consequence of my near connection with him, I found my blood begin to boil, and melancholy rushed on my heart, but I was helpless, because the clamour was universal, and the hearts of the people were turned from him. I then asked the judges, what do you say in respect of putting Amyr Hussyn to death; they replied, "if the heirs of the persons whom Hussyn has murdered, forgive him, it is well, otherwise, by the law of retaliation, he must suffer death." When the words of the judges had reached the ears of the complainants, one of them who had been in the service of Hussyn, said, "O Prince, this Hussyn has much injured and oppressed mankind, and has been guilty of great violence, and through covetousness, confined and imprisoned one thousand seven hundred men and women, who were liberated on the day you came here;" I said, "perhaps they were kept in confinement till then, that they might not complain against him." One of the learned body said, "I have read in the heavenly books, that it is more incumbent to destroy a wretch who oppresses or injures mankind, than it is to kill a snake or a scorpion, for the former plots mischief deliberately to the ruin of another, whilst the noxious reptile only stings, when he is afraid of personal injury, and to save himself." When these words were heard by all the persons in the Assembly, viz. that it was proper to put to death an oppressor or bad man, and the Amyr Aljaitū who had been (Sepah Salār,) Commander in Chief of the army of Hussyn, seeing my melancholy, and that I would not consent to the execution of the Prince, remonstrated with me; I replied, "Amyr Hussyn is my prisoner, he shall not be put to death;" I then rose to leave the Assembly.

The Chiefs immediately called out, Amyr Hussyn has been found guilty by the law, and worthy of death, it is therefore improper that Timūr should delay his punishment. I however requested that they would permit me to postpone it, in hopes that I might by some means save his life.

But as it did not please Providence to permit the continuance of Hussyn's existence, Amyr Ky Khuserū who sought retaliation for the murder of his brother, with Aljaitū and Muhammed Shāh assaulted the unfortunate Hussyn, and he, washing his hands of life, struck at them with his fists, got out of the Assembly and fled as far as the tomb of Khuajē Akāshā, there these three Chiefs overtook and put him to death, and having returned from thence, they murdered his two sons Khān Saiid and Nurūz Sultān, two other sons named Jehān Mulk and Khelyl Sultān made their escape and fled towards India. I was much affected by this melancholy catastrophe, and went to see his body, repeated the funeral prayers over it and ordered it to be buried with all due respect.

Having then taken possession of all Amyr Hussyn's treasure, which he had accumulated by so much covetousness and avarice, I divided it among the Chiefs. The next day I called a general assembly, and gave orders for all his followers and attendants to be taken care of, and directed that his women and children should be sent to Samerkund.* It happened that one of the persons who attended the Assembly was cloathed in black. I asked him why he was so, he replied, " I have lost a friend, but it was I who killed him, and for grief have put on mourning." One of the learned said, " if it had not been his fate to have been killed, how could you kill him, therefore why do you grieve."

I then addressed the learned body and asked them, " what is the very worst thing in this world," some of them said one thing, some another. I then continued, " the *best* thing in this world is a good man, that is a person endued with excellent qualities, consequently the *worst* thing in this world, must be a bad man, imbued with every vice, who like Amyr Hussyn is a tyrant, miserly, covetous, and ignorant, and who fears not God." The whole Assembly praised my definition and offered up prayers for my prosperity.

* In Sherif Addeen's History, it is stated, that he took four of the ladies himself and divided the others among his Chiefs.

MEMOIRS OF TIMŪR.

BOOK V.

CHAPTER I.

Account of my mounting the throne of the Sovereignty in the city of Balkh.

WHEN I had thus cleansed the region of Turān from the evil machinations of Amyr Hussyn, there were three other claimants to the succession, each of whom being puffed up with pride in consequence of being the Chief of a great clan, and having numerous followers, was desirous of raising the standard of royalty. The first of these was Shah Muhammed, of Badukhshān, who considered himself as one of the Princes of that country. The second Amyr Ky Khuserū, who called himself son-in-law to the Khān of the Desht Kipchac and was governor of Khutelān. The third Muhammed the son of Byān Seldūz, who was the chief of several thousand families of the horde of Seldūz, when I heard of their various pretensions I clothed myself with patience.

When this news was brought to Syed Abū al Berkāt (the father of blessings), he invited several of the (Khānē Zadehs) young syeds of Termuz, Abū al Mualy and Aly Akber to join him; he then summoned all the claimants to a general council, and when the Assembly was arranged in proper order, he addressed them, "Praise be to God that the whole land of Turān is now cleansed of all disturbers of its tranquillity. If you unite and elect one person as an *elder brother*, your union will insure prosperity, but if you divide and form different kingdoms, the infidel Jetes will very shortly overwhelm you; whatever is the opinion of each of you, be so good as to state it." Muhammed Shah who was the head of the Princes of Badukhshān said, "let us divide the country into four portions in a brotherly manner, each ruling his own province, but let us unite in opposing every enemy that dares to invade or oppose us." Abu al Berkāt replied, "a variety of rulers always occasions quarrels and dissentions, if it were intended by Providence, that there should have been two Monarchs in the same kingdom, there would have been two Gods, one to govern the Heavens, the other the earth; but as there is only one God who is the Lord of all, there must only be one Monarch in the same country, that the proof of unity may be evident and certain." Muhammed Seldūz said, "it is contrary to our code of laws, that any of us should fill the throne of the Khān, or that the people should be subservient to us; the Prince Syurughtumush Aghlān, is of the posterity of Jengyz, place him on the throne of sovereignty, and let the Amyr Timūr be his deputy and Commander in Chief, and we will be obedient to him."

Abū al Berkāt replied, " it is contrary to the religion of Muhammed, that his followers should be subservient to you who are infidels; Jengyz was an inhabitant of the desert, who by violence and the force of his sword formerly gained a superiority over the Muselmāns, at present the sword of the Amyr Timūr is not inferior to what Jengyz Khān's sword was; When you all fled from Hussyn, and concealed yourselves in the desert; it was not till Timūr advanced alone against him, that any of you dared to quit your hiding corners; he did not want your assistance to subdue his enemy, nor does he now want it;" after a long discourse he thus concluded, " I have hitherto spoken to you as Tūrks, but I know that you are Musselmāns and believe in the religion of Muhammed, now it is evident to all the followers of the Prophet, on whom be the grace of God, that he conquered the world from the unbelievers, from Polytheists, from Jews, and from Christians, by the force of his victorious sword, therefore he (Muhammed) became sole proprietor of the terrestrial globe, after him the succession fell to the illustrious Khalifs, who with their followers spread the religion of Islam over the face of the earth, after them the property descended to the posterity of the Prophet, who having legally obtained the inheritance, may appoint whomever they choose for their deputy. I, who am the lineal descendant of Hussyn, the Grandson of Muhammed, in conjunction with all the Syeds of Mecca and Medina, do consider and esteem Amyr Timūr as the deputy of the illustrious Khalifs. We therefore do appoint him to be Ruler over all the Muselmāns in the territory of Turān."

When the Assembly heard that the Muselmāns were unanimous and agreed in their choice, and that the people were inclined to me, Amyr Ky Khuseru said, " let us draw lots for the sovereignty, and let us solemnly promise that we will be obedient on whomsoever the lot shall fall;" in consequence of this proposal, Abū al Berkāt wrote my name, and the name of the other three competitors (on slips of paper) and placed them under the (Musella) carpet for prayer, he then said to them, " thrust your hands under the carpet and take out the lots," they did so three times, and the lot of sovereignty came forth in my name: they were all ashamed, but they could not deny their agreement.

The next day all the Chiefs of the hordes and tribes came in a body to my tent, and the three competitors also entered and made their obeisance to me, after them came the Amyrs Aljaitū, Sar Bughā and Daoud, and bent their knees; when these illustrious Chiefs had paid their respects, the Assembly congratulated me, and Abū al Berkāt, with the syeds of Termuz offered up prayers for my prosperity. Then the abovementioned chieftains with the twelve chiefs of the hordes stood up and formed half circles to the right and left of my seat; after which Abū al Berkāt thus addressed the Assembly; "O Assembly of Muselmāns, the Prophet hath said, I bequeath to my people two illustrious things; first, the sacred volume; secondly, my descendants; now these bequests are in the hands of the Amyr Timūr, those who obey him shall be fortunate in this world, and happy in the next; but those who disobey him will be unfortunate in this world, and miserable in futurity." He then took up the Korān which was lying before me, and placed it on the head of each person, saying, "let those who choose to enter (into this covenant) come, and those who choose to fall off, let them fall;" each person replied, "we have heard and do obey;" thus they all agreed to my sovereignty, and inaugurated me."

CHAPTER II.

In the year 771, I entered my thirty-fifth year of age, on which occasion four of the most revered Syeds, viz. Abū al Berkāt, Abū al Muāly, Zynaddyn, and Aly Akber, having chosen a fortunate hour, took me by the arms, and placed me on the throne of sovereignty: after I was seated on the throne, I opened the Korān, which was my constant companion, to search for an omen whether my government would endure, and this verse came forth, "Say, God is the master of the world, he gives the kingdom to whom he chooses, and takes it away from those he chooses." The learned body who were standing at the foot of my throne, wrote the interpretation of this verse, and read prayers for the perpetuity of my dominion. In the same manner all the people, both great and low, held up their hands in prayer for my prosperity; after which all the nobles bent their knees and congratulated me; then all the chiefs and officers of the hordes payed their respects; then all the people, whether soldiers or citizens, called out, "may your good fortune endure."

A.D. 1369.

Previous to the day of my coronation I had formed regulations for my courts; I assigned to the Syeds, to the prelates and learned body a place on my right hand, to my sons and relations and nobles, that they should be seated in a half circle round my throne, the (Kurjyans) life guards were to be placed behind the throne, the commanders of divisions to be in front, facing me, the twelve (Yusuval) aides de camp or orderlies, were to stand three in front, three on each side, and three behind the Kūr,* and the other officers and soldiers to be seated

* The *Kūr* is a railing which surrounds the throne.

according to their respective ranks. After forming the court in this manner I sent for all the treasure and valuables that I possessed and distributed them amongst the nobles, the officers and soldiers, according to their respective ranks, and I then gave away to the persons assembled, all my ready money, my horses, swords, caps; so that all that remained were the clothes on my back and two horses in my stable; and even of these Amyr Jakū asked for one, which I gave him, by which means all I kept to myself was one horse, one sword, one shield, one spear, one quiver with its bow and arrows.

When the nobles of the hordes and tribes witnessed my liberality and generosity they came and bent their knees, and said, you are well entitled to the throne and sovereignty. At this time one of my confidential servants said to me, "there is not a single article left in your store." I replied, "if I am a King all the wealth of the world is mine; whatever property my subjects possess is mine, they are merely my repositories; and if I am not a King, whatever I may now have will not remain."

I then commanded a proclamation to be made, that "all people whether great or low, Tūrks or Persians, Noble or Mean, Officer or Soldier, were in perfect security from me, and I issued edicts through all parts of my dominion, stating that I had pardoned all guilty persons of every description; that all those who had drawn their swords against me, done evil to me, or had excited enmity against me, I now considered as my friends, and that I had eradicated from my bosom all animosity or revenge, that they might feel confident and happy, and whatever property of mine had been stolen or plundered during the disturbances, I freely gave to the possessor; that I forgave all the followers of Amyr Hussyn, and that they might remain secure wherever they were dispersed, and keep whatever property of his they had."

I then issued orders to all the Chieftains on the boundaries and the Governors of the fortresses of Shadmān, Kunduz, Badukhshān, Andijān, Tūrkistān, Kabulistan, Ḳāshghur, Tashkund, Khujend and the confines of the Desht Kipchāk and Khuarizm, confirming them in their governments and commands and assuring them that they need not harbour an idea of any change.

When the (Eid) festival of the month of Ramzān arrived, I went to the great Mosque of Balkh and performed my prayers. The Muselmāns invited me to commence the service. I replied that I did not consider myself worthy of acting as (Imam) president. They said we consider your Highness as the successor of the illustrious Khalifs and the (Muruvij) Patron of the Muhammedan religion, the Guardian of the holy land, the Protector of the servants of God, the Respecter of his Saints, it is therefore proper that you should preside.

The (Khētyb) Preacher then mounted the pulpit, and after offering up glory and thanksgiving to God and the Prophet, and praise of the illustrious Khalifs (Khūlfā Rāshidyn*) may Paradise be their dwelling, he commenced the *Khutbeh*† in my name, in these words, " O Lord, assist the Muselmān armies and camps wherever they are, or wherever they may be, whether in the East or in the West, by the good fortune of the just *Sultan*, the illustrious *Khākān*, (title of the Tūrkish Sovereign) the renowned Emperor, the exalted Prince, the Khākān son of the Khākān Amyr Timūr Gūrghān, may God Almighty perpetuate his dominion and government, and extend his beneficence and justice to all Muselmāns." After the conclusion of this speech all the Nobles and principal persons of Jagtay and the Chiefs of the tribes and hordes came up and congratulated me.

When I quitted the Mosque I placed my foot in the stirrup, and attended by all the Commanders and Officers I proceeded to the (Kytūl) palace, I then politely took leave of them, sent each of them a feast on account of the *Eid*, and dismissed them to their respective homes.

Some days after I appointed Murād Behader, son of Chūghān Berlās, to be governor of Balkh, and gave him a written code of regulations for his guidance, pointing out to him how he was to behave himself, both to soldiers and subjects and in what style he should live and conduct himself on all occasions.

On the 2d day of the month of Shū,āl, A. H. 771, being then thirty-five years of age, having selected a fortunate moment, I marched from Balkh and proceeded towards the capital, Samerkund; the first day I encamped on the banks of the Jihūn, which was seven *Fersukh* (twenty-one miles) from Balkh, and enjoyed myself there, till my family and all the heavy baggage of the army came up.

At one of the assemblies Shykh Hussyn Sūfy‡ who had arrived from Khuarizm, came and joined me: I asked him, " how will the Almighty reproach tyrants in the day of Judgment?" he replied, " God hath said to them (by his Prophets) ' don't think of me; if you do so, I will curse you;' this is a sufficient indication of their lot, the tyrant shall be seized both in this world and the next by his injustice." He then added, " the punishment of an infidel King, provided he is just, shall be less than that of a Muselmān Monarch who is a tyrant; also the torments of a generous unbeliever shall be fewer than those of an avaricious believer." On hearing these words I determined as long as I lived to make justice and liberality my constant practice.

* The four first Khalifs. † Resembles the prayer read in cathedrals before the sermon.

‡ This was the celebrated saint mentioned in the Appendix, No. 7. See also Sufy, Richardson's Persian Dictionary.

All my people having now joined the camp, I crossed the river Jihūn and encamped in the plains of Kesh, where I halted for some time and was waited upon by all the Nobles and principal inhabitants of the towns, and by all the Chiefs of the hordes and tribes: whether formerly friends or enemies all came and claimed my protection. From thence I marched to the vicinity of Samerkund and was there met by all the Nobles and persons of note, by all the prelātes and learned body of that city, who congratulated me and made offerings (Nesār) for my prosperity.

That very day being *Friday*, I went to the great Mosque and said my prayers with a very numerous congregation, after which the *Khutbeh* was read for my success from the pulpit of Samerkund, being now the capital of my empire. But Khuajē Abyd Allah, who was the most celebrated theologist of the age, refused to join in the blessing. *Here follows the anecdote related in page* 12 *of the Omens, &c.*

In consequence of this manifestation of the Prophet's regard, I ordered that another large mosque should be built in Samerkund, also a monastery, and houses for the Dervishes and pious Muselmāns.

CHAPTER III.

After I had mounted the throne in my capital of Samerkund, I formed a council and drew up a code of regulations for my goverment, I then ordered a general proclamation to be made, that whoever had any claims on me should come forward and make them known; and every person that I had been intimate with from the days of my childhood to the present time, I called by his name, and conferred favours on him; and with whomsoever I had been acquainted either as friend or enemy, I acted in a uniform manner to all, and bound them in the ties of gratitude.

I gave injunctions to all my servants, that they were never on any account to change or alter the orders that I should issue; and that if any minister or officer should be guilty of deviation from this rule, he should be punished; because one of the rights of Princes is, that their words and orders should be the *law* of the land.

I ordered that a code of regulations should be formed for the payment of the officers and soldiers and their allowance of provisions; also rules for conferring titles and the high offices of generals and ministers, which were to be considered as a standing order and guidance of their conduct. In the same manner I directed that regulations* should be written for the holding of public assemblies in peace, and for manœuvring armies in the field during war, and for the conduct of my soldiers towards their fellow subjects.

In the first council I fixed the (Syurghelāt) permanent grants of land for charitable purposes, and I appointed Syed Abd Allah to be the (Sudder) superintendant of this institution, and to be chief magistrate of the Syeds, and I nominated Syed Abd al Rehmān to be the (Shykh al Islam) head of religious affairs, and Syed Zya Addeen, to be the chief judge; and I ordered that on all occasions of ceremony, the Syeds and the (Mushykh and Oulemā) prelates and learned body, should be seated on my right hand.

But there arose a great controversy between them, the Syeds and learned body for precedency, or which should be the nearest to the throne, as the arguments on both sides were very long and noisy, I was much amused with the disputation; I however took care that the Syeds were never to be treated with contempt or abused, and forbade their ever being bound or put to death, and if any person injured them, he was to be severely punished.† One of the holy and learned Syeds named Abū al Muālу, who had frequently opposed my ambition, and had done every thing to injure me, I treated with the greatest respect, which made him ashamed of his past conduct and desirous of my pardon; I therefore for the sake of the Prophet forgave him.

While I was seated in the Assembly, an ambassador (from Syed Aly) the (Valy), ruler of Mazinderan was introduced, and delivered a message from his master; after he had been seated some time, Syed Abū al Berkāt asked who his master was, and of what family; the ambassador immediately traced the Valy's genealogy to Aly the son-in-law of the Prophet, and acknowledged that he had been sent to learn my character and disposition. I said to him, " well, what do you think of me," he replied, " I find that you prefer justice to violence, truth to falsehood, virtue to vice, and that you honour and respect the descendants of Muhammed, which is a clear proof that victory and fortune will be the constant attendants of your Highness's Stirrup, as the supporter of the Muselmān religion."

I praised the ambassador for his ability and ingenuity, Syed Abū al Berkāt was also lavish in his praise, and pronounced that as long as I persevered in such conduct, I should be triumphant and successful; ignorance, irreligion, vice and tyranny being ever the cause of the ruin of a government.

At this council I gave the government of Samerkund to Amyr Daoud, and conferred the insignia of the standard and kettle drum on Amyr Jakū and several

* See Davy's Institutes, page 231 and Sequel. Also page 305.

† Here, as in some former instances, the royal author leaves us in doubt of the result.

other Chiefs; I made Hussyn Berlās, President of the Council. I gave charge of the large seal to Ayk Timūr, and disposed of all the other appointments among my friends. I also ordered that no revenue or taxes should be collected from the inhabitants of Samerkund, Bokhara, or their dependencies, and issued a public edict that they were to be exempt from all claims.

CHAPTER IV.

The first disagreeable circumstance which occurred in the commencement of my reign, was the rebellion of the chief Zindē Khushm, and which required all my exertion to quell. It has been before mentioned, that when Amyr Hussyn was killed, I confirmed all his governors in their posts, one of the most important of these situations, was the government of Shyrghān, held by Zindē Khushm; but as he was suspected by my ministers to be unworthy of confidence, they had advised me to remove him; I replied, " I have promised safety and security for three years to every person, whether friend or enemy, provided they behave properly;" but Zindē Khushm soon raised the standard of opposition by taking under his protection Amyr Musā, formerly Hussyn's Commander-in-Chief, who had come over to my party; and when I marched against Balkh, had accompanied me the first day's journey, but had again deserted at the second stage, and fled towards Tūrkistān; but hearing of the death of Amyr Hussyn, he had sent me an apology for his conduct, and solicited my forgiveness, in consequence of which, I sent him an assurance of safety; but as he was a deceitful fellow, and suspicious of others, notwithstanding he had suffered much in wandering about the deserts, and had been frequently routed by my troops, still he had the impudence to refuse the edict I sent him, accompanied by a promise of safety, and his heart not being clean, he again made battle, but being a second time defeated, he fled on foot with his family, and took refuge with Zindē Khushm, who at his instigation, now raised the standard of rebellion, and began to act improperly.

On being informed of this circumstance, I did not take any notice of it, and pretended such ignorance, that I never mentioned either of their names, or said good or bad on the subject. At length my nobles said to me, " it is quite requisite to go and subdue these two rebels;" I replied, " if I proceed against them in person, it will make them of too much importance in the eyes of my subjects; for if they venture to contend with me, and I shall prove victorious, what fame shall I gain, it will be merely said, that I have punished two of Amyr Hussyn's servants; no, I will summon them to come to court, if they obey it will be all well, if not, they will be guilty of disobedience, and evince their hostility, I shall then find no difficulty in punishing them."

In consequence of this resolution, I sent an invitation to Zindē Khushm, by the hands of Amyr Aljaitū: on the receipt of my edict, he treated my messenger with great respect, made use of many flattering expressions, and promised immediately to wait on me. Aljaitū therefore returned and informed me of his success, but I told him I feared he had been deceived, which proved to be the case.

Shortly after this circumstance, it happened that Byram Shāh Arlāt, who had deserted from Amyr Hussyn, and had gone into Khurasān, having heard of the death of his late master, and my having mounted the throne, was on his way to pay his respects to me, but Zindē Khushm intercepted him, and under pretence of hospitality, seized and confined him.*

On hearing of this event, I sent another summons to Zindē Khushm, by the hands of Taban Behader, but that impudent scoundrel imprisoned my messenger, on which the fire of my anger being stirred, I ordered that my tents should be pitched on the route to Shyrghān; when Zindē Khushm was informed of this circumstance, he was much alarmed, and shut himself up in the white fort of Shyrghān, but wrote to Amyr Aljaitū to beg for my forgiveness, and sent him a shroud and scymitar to lay before me as emblems of his forlorn condition, and after a few days, he sent his younger brother, Islām and Amyr Musā, (both of whom had behaved treacherously towards me) bound neck and hand to Samerkund.

I immediately pardoned Amyr Musā, and gave him the command of his own tribe, but my ministers remonstrated that it was improper to confer such an honour on a treacherous scoundrel, I replied, "that in consequence of this act of kindness, many of the disaffected and rebellious chiefs would be induced to come in;" in fact the sending Amyr Musā in the manner described, was a stratagem of Zindē Khushm's to ascertain my disposition, whether it was of a forgiving or revengeful nature; I therefore put confidence in his protestations, and remained quietly in my capital.

The second disturbance that took place in the commencement of my reign was this: notwithstanding my having pardoned the crimes of Zindē Khushm, and drawn the pen of forgiveness over his evil actions, he at the instigation of the disciples and scholars of the prelate Abū al Muāly of Termuz, again placed his foot on the path of insurrection, and endeavoured to excite commotions against my government; he therefore collected an army, and plundered the hordes who resided in the vicinity of Balkh and Termuz.

* It appears by Sherif Addeen's History, that he killed him.

On hearing of this event, I gave orders to those chiefs who were in attendance, to march immediately with their troops, and without halting on any pretence, to attack Zindē Khushm, and compel him to restore all the plunder he had taken; I also sent off two other detachments to the right and left, to surround him, my victorious army having marched with great expedition, came up with the rear of Zindē Khushm's troops as they were crossing the Jihūn over a bridge of boats, and caused a number of them to be drowned in the river, and of those, who had crossed and were drawn up on the opposite bank, many were killed or wounded, and all the cattle were retaken.

After this event, Zindē Khushm fled, and was pursued by Arghūn Shāh, nearly as far as Shyrghān; but the rebel having secured himself in the fort, began to fortify it: my general wrote and informed me that he had surrounded the fortress, and requested reinforcements, assuring me that he would soon bring the rebel bound hand and foot to my presence. On receipt of this intelligence, I presented Amyr Jakū with a scymitar, a dress of honour, and a horse, and sent him off with a considerable reinforcement.

Amyr Jakū marched with great expedition, and laid siege to Shyrghān, but as the winter had just set in, he could only blockade the place for three months; at the expiration of this period, the garrison being much in want of provisions, Zindē Khushm requested Amyr Jakū to intercede with me for pardon, and trusting to my mercy, came out of the fort and proceeded to Samerkund; when he approached the city, I ordered all my chiefs to go out and meet him, and to pay him much respect and honour.

When brought to my presence with the sword hung about his neck, he was much downcast, and expected that I would command his being put to death; I however said to him, "Zindē Khushm, I have it now in my power either to kill you, or to keep you in perpetual confinement, but as I consider you a brave young man, I will generously forgive you, provided that contrary to your past behaviour, you will not in future transgress, nor allow yourself to be led away by insidious people, but go to your own tribe and bring them all into subjection to me:" he replied with great warmth, "I will in future devote my life as an offering to your Highness;" I therefore conferred a dress of honour on him, and admitted him into my service. He immediately went across the Sihūn, and in a short period persuaded the horde of Timūr to submit to my authority, and brought their (Kelanters) head men to my court, in reward for which, I again conferred on him the government of Shyrghān,* and gave the command of the horde of Timūr to Kepek Timūr.†

* It is situated 36 degrees, 45 minutes, N. L.

† This account differs from the History; See Petis de la Croix, page 219.

The third disturbance which took place in the commencement of my reign, was the rebellion of Kepek Timūr: this was a person that I had raised from a very low situation, but when he found himself in authority, he soon betrayed the baseness of his origin, and evinced his ingratitude; he even erected the standard of rebellion, and collected a considerable army. I therefore promoted Behram Jelayr, (who had been for some time in disgrace for misconduct at Tashkund, but who had offered to go and bring Kepek Timūr bound hand and neck into my presence) and sent him with Shykh Aly Khetay Behader, and other officers to punish Kepek Timūr.

It so happened that a party of Jelayr's own tribe were dissatisfied with him, and watched an opportunity to assassinate him, but he having discovered their intentions, was obliged to take refuge with Shykh Aly. About this time the two armies came in sight, but were separated by the river Aishē Khātun: when the royal army had reached the bank of the river, Khetay Behader having taken offence at his superior officer for some imputation against his courage, drew his sword, plunged his horse into the stream, and having crossed alone, pushed on towards Kepek Timūr's standard, but was immediately surrounded by the soldiers of the rebel, Shykh Aly, and his troops having by this time crossed the river engaged the enemy, who alarmed by the vigour of the attack, were shortly broken, and during the night, fled in every direction. Shykh Aly then made peace with Kepek, and having severely punished the mutineers of Behram Jelayr's division, returned to me.

The fourth disturbance that occurred was, the invasion of the Jetes: it appeared that during the insurrection of Zindē Khushm and Amyr Musā, they had written to the Khān of the Jetes, that if he would advance with an army into Maveralnaher, they would seize me, and deliver up the country to him; in consequence of which, the stupid Khān collected an army, and advanced towards Maveralnaher: as soon as I received intelligence of this event, I resolved to be before hand with him, I therefore marched from Samerkund, and advanced rapidly as far as Nekah, to meet the Jetes, but when they heard of my advance, they deemed it prudent to retreat.

At this time, four of my chiefs, viz. Zindē Khushm, Amyr Musā, Abūlys, and Abūal Mualy, of Termuz, all of whom were under great obligations to me, entered into a confederacy to assassinate me whilst I was enjoying the amusement of hawking or hunting. Thus one day while I was amusing myself, and had a Falcon on my hand, these four cavaliers attacked my attendants; I immediately placed the small drum I held in my hand, on my head as a helmet, loosed the bird, drew my sword, and called out to them with all my might; when they heard my voice, they were terrified, and attempted to run away, but my attendants seized them: I then gave orders to confine them, and continued my sport.

When I returned to my capital at Samerkund, I summoned a general assembly of all the chiefs, and the learned body, and the Syeds; I then ordered the four prisoners to be brought before the assembly, when they were brought into the court, I addressed the judges and said, "what is the punishment due to a party of confederates who conspire against the life of a Muselmān;" they replied, "the punishment of the law is retaliation, but forgiveness is better, for the first offence." I then said to Abū Muāly, "you know that I am a Muselmān, and that I am obedient to the law of the Prophet, how is it possible that you who call yourself a descendant of the Prophet, and who have received so many favours from me, should dare to make an attempt against my life? but I pardon you for the sake of his holiness the Prophet."

I then said to Abūlys, "I also forgive you, because you are a Shykh, (Arabian descent)" and I dismissed him. To Amyr Musā, I said, "you and I are connexions, (by marriage) * and I have made a vow never to destroy any of my relations, I therefore pardon you." With respect to Zindē Khushm, I conferred his government of Shyrghān upon Myan Timūr, and gave the prisoner into his charge to do as he pleased with him.

The fifth disturbance that took place in my government, was the dispute with Hussyn Sūfy, the ruler of Khuarizm.† As it had been previously represented in my council, that Hussyn Sūfy had shewn signs of hostility by sending troops to plunder part of my territory, I received at this time a representation from the prelates and principal inhabitants of Khuarizm, containing complaints against their ruler, and stating that their country, with the districts of Khyuk and Kāt, had from time immemorial, belonged to the Jagtay family, but that Hussyn Sūfy having found them without a master, had taken possession of the kingdom, and exercised great tyranny and oppression over the inhabitants; it was therefore incumbent on me to deliver them from the hands of the oppressor.

In consequence of this intelligence, I deliberated with myself whether I should immediately march in person to deliver Khuarizm from the grasp of Hussyn Sūfy, or whether I should send an army under the command of another person. The determination that sprung from the east of my heart was this, that I should first turn my reins towards Khurasān; but as my mind was not quite at ease

* Timūr was married to his sister, Seray Mulk Khanūm, widow of Amyr Hussyn, and daughter of Kezān Khān.

† It is an extensive kingdom on the eastern shores of the Caspian Sea.

with regard to Badukhshān, I appointed Amyr Jakū to the governments of Kundez, Bukelān, and the boundaries of Kabūl, and sent with him a large army to protect these places.

CHAPTER V.

After having taken the necessary precautions for the defence of my own dominions, I appointed the Amyr Syf Addeen to be governor of Samerkund, and in the year 773, being the second of my reign, and the thirty-seventh of my age, I set out with the intention of subduing Khuarizm; when A.D. 1371. I reached the banks of the Jihūn, I halted, and was there joined by the ambassador of Melk Ghyās Addyn, son and successor of the late Aāzaddyn, ruler of Khurasān, of Ghur, and Ghirjistān, who brought a number of presents from his master to me; in return for which, I conferred a dress of honour, and many gifts on the ambassador, and sent a letter replete with condolence and congratulations to Melk Ghyās Addyn.

At this time it reached my ears that the troops of Hussyn Sūfy had entered the country of Maveralnaher, and had extended their hordes in plundering the inhabitants. I therefore issued orders that my (Keravul) advanced division should immediately march to oppose them, this they did in so vigorous a manner, that at the first charge they put the enemy to flight, and took a great number of them prisoners; those who escaped, took refuge in the fort of Kāt, the governor of which, whose name was Byrem Yusavul, and the Cazy Shykh Muvyd, both of whom shut themselves up in the fortress; my victorious army pursued the runaways, and laid siege to the place.

On receipt of this intelligence, I placed my foot in the stirrup, and proceeding with great celerity, arrived at the ditch of the fort, where I alighted. When my troops saw this action, all the cavalry dismounted and hastened to the attack. Shykh Behader threw a (Kumund) rope with a noose on the battlement, by help of which, he nearly mounted the wall; but at this time the garrison saluted us with a shower of arrows, and one of them cut the rope, so that Behader fell headlong to the bottom of the wall; he soon however recovered his footing, again threw the noose, and being supported by Jehān Pehlwān, they mounted the wall; I then ordered the drums to be beaten, and my troops having made a general assault, mounted the battlements: on seeing this, the governor called out for quarter, I gave him quarter, but all the wealth and property in the fort, became the plunder of the soldiers.

I spent three days in Kāt, I then sent off Ghyās Addyn and Aljaitū, with two divisions, to turn the flanks of Hussyn Sūfy's army, whilst I sent against him my main body, commanded by Ky Khuserū Khutelāny; I then ordered the drums to strike up, and having mounted my steed, I advanced with rapidity, and entered the plains of Khuarizm. When Hussyn Sūfy saw my victorious army, he sent an ambassador to request my forgiveness, and to say that he would in future place his head on the line of obedience. Although I did not believe him, I nevertheless pardoned him, but in order to try him, I said to Ky Khuserū, "as long as Hussyn keeps possession of the fort of Khuarizm, it is impossible to clear the country of sedition." In consequence of this hint, Ky Khuserū treacherously sent him a message, advising him not to trust to my promises, nor leave the fort, but if he would draw out his army, and come forth at the head of them, he Ky Khuserū would join him with all his troops.

The Khuarizm Prince fell into the snare laid for him, marched out with a large body of troops, and advanced to the bank of the river Karān, which is at the distance of two *Fersukh** from the fort, and drew up in battle array. At this period, Ky Khuserū waited on me and said, "I have outwitted the enemy, and have brought the prey into your toils;" I commanded him instantly to march with his troops, and cut off the communication with the fort: I then ordered my drums to be beaten, and having mounted my horse, proceeded towards the enemy, and while going along, determined on the plan of attack. I commanded Amyr Muvyd to go up the river with his division, and then cross over, and at the same time I sent Khetay Behader down the river, to effect his passage over it, and ordered Ak Timūr to cross with his division in front of the enemy; the three divisions swam their horses over the river, and reached the opposite bank with safety, except Aylchy Behader, who fell off his horse and was drowned. When I spurred my steed to enter the stream, Muhammed Seldūz caught hold of my stirrup, and entreated me not to proceed; he at the same time seized my standard, and rushed into the river. As soon as the divisions to the right and left, saw my standard, they made a desperate charge on the enemy, and a very severe conflict took place between the contending armies, in so much that the men engaged with knives and daggers, and pulled each other by their collars off their horses. Hussyn Sūfy seeing the desperate situation of his troops, fled alone into the fort. My victorious soldiers now laid siege to the fortress, and in a very short time they advanced their batteries so near, as greatly to harass the garrison: during the siege, Hussyn Sūfy was so terrified, that he departed this life.

On the death of Hussyn, he was succeeded by his brother Yusuf Sūfy, who

* Six miles.

immediately sent out his sword, and expressed his sorrow for the circumstances that had occurred, with protestations of his obedience and attachment to me. He further offered to give his niece, who was a descendant of the Khān of the Jetes, in marriage to one of my sons, so that a family connection might be cemented between us, which should serve as a bond of his fidelity. Having approved of this offer, I gave my consent, on condition that agents on the part of my son Jehangyr should remain in the districts of Khuarizm, to collect the tribute. Having written an edict on the above mentioned subject, I turned the reins of my steed towards Samerkund, and having arrived in that city, I caused the carpets of justice and happiness to be spread.

At this time, I discovered that Amyr Ky Khuserū Khutelāny, had during the siege of Khuarizm, carried on a secret correspondence with Hussyn Sūfy, and had encouraged him to oppose me, by promising to join him. It was in consequence of this negociation, and a renewal of the correspondence, that Yusuf Sūfy ventured to turn out the agents of Jehangyr, and to raise the standard of revolt. This was the sixth disturbance that took place during my reign, and was all owing to the want of loyalty of Ky Khuserū, whose ambitious spirit excited him to aim at the sovereignty; he therefore sent an agent named Shāh Mahmūd, to form a secret treaty with Yusuf Sūfy, by which they agreed to assist each other in my destruction; when I first received intelligence of this plot, I could not believe it, till one of their confidential agents shewed me a written copy of the treaty, I however kept the matter a secret.

In the year 774, being then thirty-eight years of age, I quitted Samerkund, under pretence of a hunting expedition, but resolving to make a sudden incursion into the Khuarizm territory, and to take my revenge both on Yusuf Sūfy and the traitor Ky Khuserū; when I arrived in the plain of Kārshy, I gave orders for a general assembly of the nobles and prelates to be summoned, and brought Ky Khuserū before it; I then produced the secret treaty, gave it into his hand, and desired him to read it; when he saw the writing, and his own seal affixed to it, he was ashamed and held down his head; I was much affected on seeing him in this situation, but he himself saved me the pain of passing sentence by saying, "I am guilty, and am deserving of any punishment your Highness may command." I therefore determined to give the (Toman) horde of Khutelān to Muhammed, the son of Shyr Behram, and as there existed a great enmity between them, I judged that there could not be a greater punishment than to deliver Ky Khuserū over to Muhammed, to do with him as he pleased, and ordered accordingly.* I then arose from the assembly, and having mounted my horse, proceeded towards Khuarizm. A. D. 1372.

* Here Timūr purposely omits the result, which was the death of the prisoner.

When I had crossed the sandy desert of Khuarizm, Yusuf Sūfy having heard of the fate of his confederate, and of my arrival, sent an ambassador to beseech the chiefs and my son Jehangyr, to intercede for his pardon; he also sent his niece Khān Zadē, who was bethrothed to Jehangyr, with a great retinue, and many presents to wait on me. As the young Princess was very eloquent, and had a charming address, she said to me at our first meeting, " an Emperor is he who pardons equally Kings and beggars, and does not severely criticise their actions, and if they have been guilty of faults, freely forgives them, because when an enemy asks for forgiveness, he should no longer be considered an enemy: also a great monarch, having elevated any person, does not again cast him down; and whatever he gives, does not seek for any return; he does not place implicit reliance on the friendship of any individual, nor does he behold with implacability the enmity of any person, but considers both equally beneath his notice." She then requested me to pardon her uncle, in return for this speech, I gave the kingdom of Khuarizm for her (Kabyn) marriage dower, to be managed by Yusuf Sūfy, as the agent of my son Jehangyr; I then returned to Samerkund, and shortly after deputed the Amyrs Yadgār Berlās and Aljaitū, to bring the bride Khān Zadē from Khuarizm. These noblemen were received by Yusuf Sūfy with the greatest respect, he professed his willing obedience to me, and gave to each of the ambassadors rich presents, and prepared a sumptuous banquet for them. After a few days he dismissed them with the bride and a suitable equipage.

When the Princess approached Samerkund, I ordered several of the chief ladies of my family, attended by a number of noblemen, to go and meet her, and bring her into the city with the greatest honour and pomp. I also commanded all the chiefs, Syeds, and prelates, to be assembled, and in their presence the marriage ceremony was performed according to the rites of the Muhammedan religion, may the Lord be praised for all his goodness.

CHAPTER VI.

A.D. 1373. In the year 775, being then thirty-nine years of age, I was informed that Kummer Addyn, the slave and commander-in-chief of the army of the Khān of the Jetes, had raised his scymitar and said, " by the force of my sword, I will take the kingdom of Maveralnaher from Amyr Timūr." On hearing of this, my honour was so roused that I could not sleep, and although the weather at this period was very cold, I nevertheless mounted my steed, and marching with great expedition, I arrived at the caravansery of Kutfān. At this place the cold was excessive, but my troops collected great quantities of wood, lighted fires, and dressed their provisions; unfortunately soon after, the snow began to fall with great violence, and the quadrupeds being much distressed, many of them died. On this my chiefs waited on me, and having bent the knee, represented that numbers of our followers and cattle were perishing from the severity of the winter; it would therefore be better to return to Samerkund.

As I had previously determined to erect huts for the army, and to remain out during the winter, I said to the chiefs, "we ought not to have commenced a campaign at this season of the year, but having done so, it would be very prejudicial to my interest to return, and very beneficial for me, to remain where we are; God be praised, that every requisite is here procurable, and when a King has resolved on any measure, he should not deviate from his purpose; I have determined not to return till I have made Kummer Addyn repent his boasting, or taken him prisoner." I therefore passed forty days at the (Rebat) caravansery, and when the cold had decreased, I gave the command of the advanced division to the Prince Jehangyr, but sent with him the Amyrs Muhammed Byan Seldūz, and Aādil Shāh Jelayr, at the head of the tribe of Jelayr, and many other troops.*

When the Prince and the illustrious chiefs reached Jarun, they learned that Kummer Addyn, with his army, were encamped at Kuruk Tupē, and were waiting there for reinforcements. On hearing this news, the Prince placing his trust in God, made a forced march, and beat up the Jete camp during the night; Kummer Addyn was much terrified, took to flight, and sought refuge in a pass called the Birkē Ghuryān.

When the day broke, my troops seized a number of the enemy's followers, and took much plunder, after which they proceeded towards the pass; that day the Jetes defended the pass, but when night came on, they again fled; a number of their soldiers and other infidels became the food of the swords and arrows of the Muselmāns.

As soon as the letters of the Prince Jehangyr reached me, I placed my foot in the stirrup, and marching with great rapidity, joined the advanced division, just after they had seized and plundered Kummer Addyn's followers.

I immediately ordered Amyr Daoūd, Hussyn Behader, and some other officers to pursue the fugitives, and not give them time to rest, or even draw their breath, and I encamped that night at Payāk; at this place I was grieved to learn that Amyr Hussyn Behader had been drowned in crossing a river, this I considered as an unlucky omen, but ordered the Prince Jehangyr to pursue, and use every endeavour to take the Jete commander prisoner; the Prince in obedience to my

* This differs considerably from Petis de la Croix's History.

commands, pursued him over hill and dale, took all his camels and baggage, and compelled him to wander with only seven persons among the mountains, even his women were all seized, together with all their jewels and ornaments.

The Prince being anxious to secure the fugitive, did not relax in the pursuit, but as the country was full of trees and caves, he dismounted and travelled on foot; at length he reached a spring of water, near to which Kummer Addyn had laid down with his head on a stone, and was only roused by some of my people approaching him; as they were about to seize him, a young man, who was one of his followers, but very much resembled him, called out, "I am Kummer Addyn," in consequence of which, they quitted the master and seized the servant; the other attendants being seized, also falsely swore that the latter was the personage we were in pursuit of; in the mean time Kummer Addyn escaped and hid himself in a cave.

When my victorious son returned triumphant with his prisoners to my camp, and they were brought into my presence, several of my people who knew Kummer Addyn, declared that the prisoner was not him, although very like him; the youth also acknowledged that being grateful to his master for his salt, he had devoted his life for his (Kummer Addyn's) preservation. I praised the young man exceedingly, and said, "as you have proved yourself a grateful servant, I forgive you for this meritorious action."

My people then wished me to return home, but I said, "although we have quenched the fire, we have left the sparks;" I therefore placed my foot in the stirrup, and proceeded to the mountain of Shemāk, from thence we marched to Azbehbary. As the plains of Azbehbary were very beautiful, and the season of spring was just now commencing, I passed two pleasant months in that delightful place, during which time Mubarik Shāh, the governor of that district, had the honour of being introduced, and performed all the duties of a host towards me; in return for his hospitality, I bestowed on him the command of the tribe of Salar Aghlān, and returned to Samerkund.

CHAPTER VII.

A. D. 1374. Of the circumstances that occurred in the year 776, my age being then forty, was the rebellion excited by Amyr Sārbugha and Aādil Shāh; these chiefs compassionating the distressed state of the Jete Commander, Kummer Addyn, went and joined him, and he having obtained a reinforcement from the Khān of Jetteh, proceeded at their instigation to invade Andijān; on their arrival there, they dispersed and plundered the horde of Kuzāk, who were under the protection of the Prince Omer Shykh.* My son thought it advisable to retreat before the enemy into the mountains, to effect this, he drew out his army and shewed himself, he then fell back, and by degrees having enticed them among the fastnesses, he cut off their retreat, and made a number of the Jetes the food of his victorious sword. He (Omer Shykh) then sent an express to inform me of all these circumstances; I immediately gave orders for the army to be assembled, and having placed my foot in the stirrup, set out to join my son. When we reached the village of Atbashy, I received intelligence that Kummer Addyn had again retreated, but this proved to be a stratagem of his, for having collected his dispersed troops, he waited in ambuscade, with a select party. In consequence of the false information I had received, I ordered Shykh Aly, Aktimūr, and two other chiefs, to pursue the Jetes with all their forces; my faithful generals having bent their knees, represented that they would not leave me unprotected, on which I was very angry with them; they in consequence set off with great expedition, but I having repented of my passion, followed them gently, not having with me more than three hundred horse.

When I had lost sight of my army, Kummer Addyn came out from his ambuscade, and approached me; my followers on seeing the enemy, were much alarmed, I however encouraged them, and put on my armour: when my troops saw that I was resolved on death or victory, they became of one heart, and I formed them into six divisions, and waited for the enemy.

Kummer Addyn having drawn out his army, and being desirous of revenge, attacked us, and in the second or third charge, came up close to me; I raised my sword, and gave him such a blow on the helmet that he was stunned; at this instant one of his servants seized his bridle, and led him out of the battle, upon which his army took to flight. After having been joined by my army, I pursued the enemy, and at the end of eight *Fersukh,* came up with them; I then gave orders to surround Kummer Addyn, but he continued fighting and retreating till only seven of his soldiers remained with him: as his horse was wounded, and he could not procure another, he dismounted, and for some time hid himself among the people on foot; he then threw off his armour, and concealed himself in a hole in a cave. The next morning his horse was brought to me, but we could not find the fugitive; my officers all said he had certainly gone to the other world, I did not coincide with them, and ordered the search to be continued on all sides; but as we could not discover any trace of him, I determined to return to Samerkund.

As I had left my eldest son the Prince Muhammed Jehangyr very ill at Samer-

* Timūr's second son.

kund, my mind was very anxious on his account; one night I dreamt that I was seated in a boat with the Prince, that the boat sunk, and although I endeavoured to catch the hand of my son, I could not effect it, and he was drowned; I was therefore much affected by this dream, nor could I obtain any intelligence of the Prince till after I had crossed the Sihūn.

When I arrived in the vicinity of Samerkund, I saw a number of the nobles, and the principal inhabitants of the city who had come out to meet me, clothed in black; as soon as I saw the procession, I was convinced that the fatal event had taken place, and was much distressed and afflicted: the Imperial Etiquette would not permit me to put on mourning, but I shut myself up for several days, and lamented extremely for two reasons; first, on my son's account, that so fine a young man of only twenty years of age, should so soon have been called to another world; secondly, on my own account, that such a tree, the support of my empire, should have been broken down. But I comforted myself by reflecting that two verdant branches of my son still flourished, the first, the Prince Peer Muhammed, to whom I gave the title of his father, Jehangyr;* the other, Muhammed Sultān, to both of whom I assigned a high place of honour in my public courts. Amyr Syf Addeen, who had been the preceptor of my son, was so much affected by his loss, that he forsook the world and became a hermit.

CHAPTER VIII.

A. D. 1375. In the year 777, and the forty-first of my age, the Jete commander, Kummer Addyn, who had escaped from the whirlpool of death, and had reached the shore of safety, finding by experience, that he could not effect any thing against me, repaired to the court of the Khān of Jetteh, where he collected a large army, and again advanced towards Maveralnaher. At this time, the Amyrs Sar Bughā and Aādil Shāh, who had deserted from me, and joined Kummer Addyn, having wandered for two years among the mountains of Jerahuk, and finding they had no remedy but to return to my court, sent a messenger to me, acknowledging their faults, and requesting my pardon. I therefore sent Khuajē Kukultāsh and Alchy Bughā, to bring them to my presence; when my agents arrived at Atrar, Aādil Shāh being alarmed, again fled and took refuge at Aksumā,† but the Tūrks who inhabited those plains, foolishly plundered all his

* Conqueror of the world.

† Atrar is the place where Timūr died, it is situated on the Sihūn, in the 44th degree of Latitude; Aksumā is said to have been a castle built on a mountain, overlooking the plains of Kipjak. Petis de la Croix, page 73.

wealth and property. Sar Bughā, who had been my declared and open enemy, advanced manfully, and came with great sincerity to my court, having his sword suspended round his neck; on entering into my presence, he placed the sword on the ground, and said, "there is the scymitar, and here is my neck, cut away, but still I am hopeful from the generosity of your Highness, for since I quitted your service, I have only experienced disgrace and ill luck, therefore I am returned to you." I encouraged him, and gave him the command of the horde of Jelayr, and as he was a courageous fellow, I liberally forgave him, and he undertook to be the guide of my forces against the Jetes.

I then sent off an army under the command of my son Omer Shykh, against Kummer Addyn, but I gave him strict injunctions that he was upon all occasions to consult with Sar Bughā. Previous to their marching, Ak Bughā advised, that as the Jetes were as watchful as crows, one division should make a detour, and get in the rear of their camp, while the main body should attack them in front; I therefore gave orders that my son Omer Shykh, accompanied by Sar Bughā, should march directly against the Jete army, whilst Ketay Behader should go round and plunder the horde. Omer Shykh, with the main body, reached the plain of Khuratū (encampment of the Jetes) at the moment that Kummer Addyn was sitting down to dinner; when he saw the victorious army approaching, he was confounded, vaulted on his horse, and turned his face towards the desert, and no one knew whither he was gone, but his whole army dispersed.

Omer Shykh continued to search for the fugitive for some time in the desert, but not being able to discover any trace of him, turned the reins of his steed towards Samerkund, and Khetay Behader having plundered the Jete horde, rejoined the Prince: the victorious army having returned to Samerkund, had the honour to kiss the royal carpet.

My mind being now quite at ease with regard to Kummer Addyn, I was informed that Beg Timūr, the son of Aurūs Khān of Kipchāk, had advanced with an army of five thousand horse into the territory, occupied by the tribe of Jujy, had plundered them of all their property, and compelled their Prince Tuktāmush * Khān, a descendant of the imperial family, to flee towards me for refuge. As Tuktāmush was an acquaintance of mine, he sent a messenger to me with his blessing (*Dwa*): † I in consequence sent out Tumen Timūr to meet the Prince,

* He was descended from Jengyz Khān by Tūshy, the eldest son, and succeeded to the throne of Kipchāk, on the death of Aurūs Khān, A. H. 778, A. D. 1376. See Abul Ghazy's History of the Tartars.

† Although a suppliant, he still considered himself as superior to Timūr, who never took any other title than (Amyr) commander; the same *hauteur* is still kept up by the (Delhy) royal family towards the *Nuwabs* of Hindūstān.

with orders to bring him to Samerkund with the greatest honour and respect: I also prepared a great banquet for him, and assembled all the chiefs, the Syeds, and the learned, to meet him, and gave to the whole assembly, abundance to eat and to drink, and conferred dresses of honour, and presents of jewels and horses on every one according to his rank, and having made them all happy, I dismissed them.—Farewell, Farewell.

Here ends the Book called the Tuarikh Mubarik Shāhy, (History of the illustrious Monarch) which contains the Military Regulations of Timūr Shāh Saheb Kerāny, compiled by himself. (See Appendix No. 9.)

Conclusion of Colonel Davy's MS. *

* This *Conclusion* is certainly a mistake of the copyist, as I have found in two other MSS. belonging to Colonel Davy, a further continuation of the history, but they both end in the following curious manner.

"Be it known that from this (Majlis) place, (page 284 of Petis de la Croix) to the time of the Emperor's making his last testament, in the plains of (Khetā) Tartary, together with his Institutes, nearly forty thousand (Byts) lines are deficient or obliterated."

"If it please God to grant me health and strength, it shall be compleated." (Appendix No. 10.)

CORRIGENDUM.

Page 133, for Book V. read Book VI.

APPENDIX I.

(Page 1.)

بسم الله الرّحمان الرّحيم

حَمد بليغ سبحاني‌را كه بمقتضاي كريمه انا جعلناك خليفةً في الارضِ عنقاي بقاي سلطنت صاحبقراني‌را ببال اقبال جهان گشاي بر قُلعه قاف گيتي ستاني اشيان فرمود سپاس بيقياس يزداني‌راكه صولت خلافت و دودمان تيموري‌را بجهت رواج دِين مبين مُحمدي وتجديد شريعت غراي مُصطفي برجميع سلاسل سلاطين عالم برترِ ومُعظمِ داشت وستايش بيشمار جهان افريني‌راكه همچنان دايره افلاك و عناصر وموالِيد بمركز عالم قوام داد و دايره سُلطنت عظمي‌را بذات كثير البركاتِ شهنشاهِ جم جاه بمصداق كريمهٔ اَلسُلطان العادل ظُل اللهِ حافظ بُلادُ اللهِ ثبات و بقا داده ·

APPENDIX II.

(Page 1.)

اما بعد المحتاج الي رحمة ربهِ الهادي ابو طالب الحسيني بعز عرض باريافتگان پایه سریر میرساند که در حرمین اشرفین درکُتب خانه جَعفر حاکمِ یمن کتابي ترُکي دیدم از مُلفظات عالي حضرت جنت مکاني فردوسِ اشیانه صاحب قراني غفران الله تعالي که وقایع خود

بیت

از سِن هفت سالگي
تاهفتاد ویک سالگي

كه بچه كيفيت خود بمرتبهٔ سلطنت راسانیدم

چون عبارات و الفاظ ترُکي و عربي قریب الفهم نبود عبارت شکسته ریختهٔ معلق انرا ازترُکي بفارسي نقل نمودم

الله تعالي ذات کاملُ الصفات عالي حضرت خاقاني صاحب قران ثاني را از حوادثِ دوران مَحفوظ و مَصیون داراد وظل سلطنت و عدالت این بادشاه عادل را برمفارق عالمیان گسترده داراد

APPENDIX III.

(Page 3.)

فرزندانِ مُلک گیر کامکار ونبایر ذوي القدر جهاندار وغیره معلوم

تُرکي

اُوسُن اوله کم عالي مقام او ندانستم کم روین

مقام یلقان اولمش کم ایتمش کشي برم

لوایم و قایع خودرا بنابر این بتُرکي انشاء نمودم که هریک از نبایرِ من که بر تخت سلطنت صعود نماید و دولت سلطنت مرا که برنجها و محنتها و قدا قیها وجنگها بتاید ربّاني و نصرت محمدي صلي الله الیه وسلم بچنگ اورده‌ام نگاه‌باني نموده بدین ترک عمل نمایند تا دولت وسلطنت ایشان از خلل وزوال ایمن گردد

APPENDIX IV.

(Page 7.)

Shykh (Sudder Addyn) Sefy was rendered famous by his posterity; he asserted that he was descended from Aly, son-in-law of Muhammed, and resided in the city of Ardebil, province of Azerbijān, and was reputed as a Saint. Tamerlane held him in such esteem, that at his request he gave him all the captives that he had taken in Asia Minor.

All these captives who owed their lives and liberty to the Shykh, evinced the greatest gratitude to him, and cultivated his friendship by rich presents, and frequently visiting him, in such a manner, that his reputation rose very high; he left several children, who became very powerful.

It was from Shykh Sefy that the royal family of Sophys of Persia were descended.

D'Herbelot, Bibliothèque Oriental.

APPENDIX V.

(Page 14.)

Syed Mahmūd, commonly known by the name of Geesū Derāz, (long hair) became a very celebrated *Saint* in Hindūstan; his tomb yet exists in the vicinity of Kulberga, in the Dekhan, and is still resorted to by numerous Muhammedan pilgrims. He wrote several treatises on *Sūfyism*, four of which are described in the Catalogue of Tippoo Sultān's Library, No. 17 to 20.

I take the opportunity of mentioning, that although Muhammed declared that he would have no monks in his religion, yet it abounds with more orders of them under the denomination of Fakeers, Dervishes, and Sūfies, than exist in any Catholic country, and the number of Saints equals that in the Roman Kalendar. The tenets of the Sūfies resemble those of the Mystics and Quietists of Europe. The Shykhs or Presidents of these monasteries are supposed to possess a prescience of events, and some of them the power of performing miracles.

APPENDIX VI.

(Page 21.)

The proper title of the 67th Chapter of the Korān, is *Al Mūlk*, but is more generally known by the name of *Tebarek Allezy*, and is very much admired by the Muselmāns, the following is the verse given in page 26.

اَمِنتُم مَن فِي السَّمَا آن يَخسِفَ بِكُم اَلاَرضَ فَاِذا هِي تَمُورُ

It is not meant by this, that he was the first who bore the name of *Timūr*, as it occurs previously to this period, in the Moghul history; Arab Shāh says that it means *Iron* in the Tūrky language; he employs two lines to give the true orthography of the word, but acknowledges that the pronunciation has been changed in the course of time.

APPENDIX VII.

(Page 23.)

We are not to understand by this expression, the plurality of worlds of the astronomers, but what the Asiatics term the invisible world of angels, spirits, genii, &c.

APPENDIX VIII.

(Page 30.)

در آن وقت مُنجمي از مُنجمانِ فارس بماوراُلنهر امده بود او در مجلسِ عُلماء زمان میکفت که ازگردش افلاك چنین مَعلوم میشود که در سنّه هفت صد و سي مولودي ازرحمِ مادر درعرصهٔ وجود خواهد امد که عالم گیر گردد

بیت

درهفت صد وسي درنهم ماه رجب
طالع شود آن کوکب فرخند لقب

APPENDIX IX.

(Page 154.)

تمت تمام شد هذا الکتاب تواریخ مُبارک شاهي که دستورالعمل محاربات تیمور صاحب قران خود تصنیف فرموده بودند

APPENDIX X.

(Page 154.)

معلوم باد که از این مجلس تا مجلسِ وصیت که امیر در دست انداز صحراي خطا نموده اند بایرلیغ تزک قریب بچهل هزار بیتِ دیکر خواهد بود از سواد بیاض رفته انشاء الله اگر دل و دماغ یاري دهد باتمام خواهد رسید

APPENDIX XI.

(Addenda.)

وصیت دیگر انکه تزوکاتي که در امور سلطنت خود نوشته ام انرا در ذیل وقایعِ من ثبت نموده احکام انرا دستور العمل خویش سازید و سرشته انرا در دست داشته باشید تا سلطنت و مملکت خودرا بحال خود توانید نگاه داشت و این وصیت که درین وقت بشما کرده ام و به نصایح و اموري که شمارا مامور گردانیده ام تادم واپسینِ من هرچه از گفتار و کردار من بوقوع اید در وقایع من از زبانِ من مُندرَج گردانید

APPENDIX XII.

ودر تقویت دین و مِلت مُحمدي صلي‌الله و الهُ و اصحابهُ و سلم و رواج مذهب برحقُ اهل سنّت و جماعت و محو ساختنِ مذاهِب باطله خواهید کوشید چه مُلک و دین از یک شکم زاده اند

APPENDIX XIII.

Continuation of the family of Timūr to the present time, with the contemporary Kings of England.

	Timūr,		Richard II. and Henry IV.
	Myran Hussyn,	Rulers of Ferghanā,	Henry IV.
	Muhammed Myrza,	Rulers of Ferghanā,	Henry V.
	Abū Saied,	Rulers of Ferghanā,	Henry VI.
	Omer Shykh,	Rulers of Ferghanā,	Edward IV.
Moghul Emperors of Hindūstān.	Baber,		Henry VII.
Moghul Emperors of Hindūstān.	Humayūn,		Henry VIII.
Moghul Emperors of Hindūstān.	Akber,		Elizabeth.
Moghul Emperors of Hindūstān.	Jehangyr,		James I.
Moghul Emperors of Hindūstān.	Shāh Jehān,		Charles I.
Moghul Emperors of Hindūstān.	Aalumgyr, Aurungzebe,		Charles II.
Moghul Emperors of Hindūstān.	Behader Shāh,		William III.
Moghul Emperors of Hindūstān.	Ferrukhsyr,		Anne.
Moghul Emperors of Hindūstān.	Muhammed Shāh,		George I.
Moghul Emperors of Hindūstān.	Aalumgyr II.		George II.
Moghul Emperors of Hindūstān.	Shāh Aalum,		George III.
Moghul Emperors of Hindūstān.	Akber Shāh,		George IV.

N. B. This is not meant to be a minute statement, but merely to give a general outline of the subject.

ADDENDA.

Several months after I had commenced this Translation, I procured from my friend Major William Yule of Edinburgh, many years First Assistant to the Resident (Ambassador) at the Court of Lucknow, an authentic transcript of the Delhy Imperial copy, mentioned in Major Davy's letter, prefixed to the printed volume of Timūr's Institutes, and noticed in the Preface of this work, which he, Major Yule, obtained as a special favour from the Emperor, or Great Moghul. I also received from my friend Lieutenant Colonel William Franklin, a second copy of the above work, which had been procured by General Sir David Ochterlony, while Resident at the Court of Delhy, and Commander of the northern provinces of India.

They are both large Quarto volumes, the former is neatly written, but the latter is most correct; they both contain the Memoirs of Timūr till his death, but they are too voluminous for *me* to undertake the translation of them. I shall however compare them with Petis de la Croix's version of Sherif Addyn's History, and if they contain any thing new, will notice it. I have minutely compared them with Colonel Davy's manuscript as far as it extends, and find that the only additions they contain, are extracts from Sherif Addyn's History; an explanation of some particulars omitted in the Memoirs, and an attempt to prove that Timūr was of the Sūny sect, although there is the strongest evidence that he was a very bigoted Shyā, (follower of Aly) as may be proved by his destruction of the cities of Aleppo and Damascus, the account of which is to be found in the 65th Chapter of Gibbon's Roman Empire.

In order to enable the Public, and especially the Oriental Translation Committee, to judge whether it may be worth while to employ some younger person to continue these Memoirs, by a translation of the transcript of the *Imperial edition*, I herewith subjoin the Editor's Preface to that work, also that part of the Book which has given rise to the report that Timūr had written an account of his own death, which has been erroneously quoted as a proof that the whole composition is a forgery.

THE

PREFACE OF THE EDITOR

TO THE MULFUZĀT TIMŪRY.

He commences with the usual form of praise of God, and blessings on Muhammed, on the four Khalifs, Abū Beker, Omer, Osman and Aly; he then repeats the account given by Abū Talib Hussyny of discovering the book in the library of Jāfer Pashā, and of its contents.

He then states that the Emperor Shāh Jehān of Hindūstān, having perused the book was not satisfied with it, and ordered him, Muhammed Afzel Bukhāry, to revise it.

" In the year 1047 of the Hejira, and tenth of his Majesty Shāh Jehān's reign, (A.D. 1637) the royal orders were issued to me, the meanest of the servants of the Imperial Court, (Muhammed Afzel Bukhāry) to read and revise this book from beginning to end, and to assimilate it with the *Zuffer Nameh*,* of the correctness of which no intelligent person can have a doubt, and compare it with some other trust-worthy histories, to omit some things which the translator had inserted, and to insert some occurrences which he had omitted; also to translate the Tūrky and Arabic sentences into Persian, and to correct several of the dates, which do not agree with the *Zuffer Nameh*."

" In submission to the royal order, the least of the servants of his Majesty, having bound round him the girdle of obedience, has exerted himself as much as possible in revising and correcting the said translation, and has thrown out all the unauthenticated passages which Abū Talib had inserted. He has inserted several passages that have been omitted by that translator, and he has thereby made the book conform with the Zuffer Nameh. Thus under the happy auspices of his Imperial Majesty, equal in dignity to Solomon, the Defender of the Faith, and the Protector of Princes, this work has been brought to a conclusion, and now only waits the stamp of approval of his Majesty (the King of the world)."

It appears in Dow's History of Hindostan, that Muhammed Afzel was the name of the Emperor, Shāh Jehān's preceptor; he was probably the person employed to revise this work, but he has not complied with his promise of translating all the Tūrky passages, although a native of Bokhārā, where that language was well understood.

* The Persian history by Sherif Addyn Aly Yezdy, and the work translated by Petis de la Croix.

The conclusion of the work states the arrival of the Emperor Timūr at *Atrar*,* on his route to China; of his last illness; of his having assembled all his family, his ministers, and other principal personages, and of his having in their presence made his will, consisting of four clauses.

The two first clauses are to recommend union among his descendants, and loyalty to his nobles; the third clause appoints his grandson Pyr Muhammed Jehāngyr to be his successor and possessor of the kingdom of Samerkund, and that all his descendants should consider Jehāngyr as their superior.† The fourth clause entreats his posterity to observe the rules and regulations that he had written during his reign, and to insert them as an Appendix to his Memoirs; he further desires that they will continue his Memoirs to the last moment of his existence as if written or spoken by himself;

"I desire that this my Testament, and whatever I shall say to the last moment of my existence, shall be written in my Memoirs as if proceeding from my own mouth." (Appendix 11.)

He repeats his exhortation to his descendants to observe union, "to support the religion of Muhammed, to give currency to the tenets of the *Sūnies*, and to exert themselves in eradicating every false religion." (Appendix 12.) He then forbids any one to speak to, or again disturb, him, but leave him to the mercy of God.

Shortly after this exhortation he resigned his soul to his Creator, on Tuesday the 17th of Shabān, A. H. 807, March 19th, A. D. 1405.

* Atrar was a large town situated two Parasangs or leagues north of the Sihūn, (Jaxartes).

† This distribution was conformable to the English law, Jehāngyr being the heir of his deceased eldest son, but the throne was taken possession of by Khelyl Sultān, another of Timūr's grandsons, the son of Mirān Shāh; he died at the end of three years, when Maveralnaher was taken possession of by Shāh Rūkh, the youngest son of Timūr, but the other Princes having also seized upon the different provinces under their command, the mighty empire fell to pieces.

It may be interesting to some persons to know that the dominions of Timūr were visited in the year 1812, by Izzet Allah, an intelligent native of India, whose journal has been published in the Asiatic Researches, from which we learn that the Chinese have extended their conquests as far as the Sihūn or Jaxartes, that the *towns* of Transoxiana are in possession of different Uzbek chiefs, and the *country* is occupied by the Nomade Kirghys hordes.

FINIS.

PRINTED BY W. NICOL, CLEVELAND ROW, ST. JAMES'S.

REPORT

OF THE

PROCEEDINGS

OF

THE THIRD ANNUAL MEETING

OF THE

SUBSCRIBERS

TO THE

ORIENTAL TRANSLATION FUND,

WITH THE

REPORT OF THE COMMITTEE,

LIST OF THE SUBSCRIBERS,

REGULATIONS,

&c. &c.

LONDON:

PRINTED BY J. L. COX, 75, GREAT QUEEN STREET.

1830.

CONTENTS.

Patron:

His Most Excellent Majesty

KING GEORGE THE FOURTH.

Vice-Patrons:

His Royal Highness the DUKE of CLARENCE.
His Royal Highness the DUKE of SUSSEX.
His Royal Highness the DUKE of CAMBRIDGE.
His Royal Highness the DUKE OF GLOUCESTER, Chancellor of the University of Cambridge.
His Royal Highness PRINCE LEOPOLD of SAXE COBURG.
His Grace the LORD ARCHBISHOP of CANTERBURY.
The Right Honourable the LORD HIGH CHANCELLOR.
His Grace the DUKE OF WELLINGTON.
The Most Noble the MARQUESS of LANSDOWNE.
The Right Honourable the EARL SPENCER.
The Right Honourable the EARL AMHERST, late Governor-General of India.
The Right Honourable LORD W. H. C. BENTINCK, G.C.B., Governor-General of India.
The Right Honourable LORD VISCOUNT MELVILLE.
The Right Honourable LORD VISCOUNT GODERICH.
The Right Honourable LORD GRENVILLE, Chancellor of the University of Oxford.
The Right Honourable LORD ELLENBOROUGH, President of the Board of Commissioners for the Affairs of India.
The Right Honourable C. W. WILLIAMS WYNN, M.P., President of the Royal Asiatic Society of Great Britain and Ireland.
The Right Honourable SIR ROBERT PEEL, Bart., M.P.
The Right Honourable HENRY GOULBOURN, M.P.
The Right Honourable S. R. LUSHINGTON, Governor of Madras.
Lieutenant-General SIR E. BARNES, K.C.B., Governor of Ceylon.
Major-General SIR JOHN MALCOLM, G.C.B., Governor of Bombay.
H. T. COLEBROOKE, Esq., Director of the Royal Asiatic Society of Great Britain and Ireland.

REPORT

OF

THE PROCEEDINGS

OF THE

THIRD ANNUAL MEETING OF THE SUBSCRIBERS

TO THE

ORIENTAL TRANSLATION FUND.

At a Meeting of the Subscribers to the Oriental Translation Fund, held on Monday, the 14th of June, 1830, at the House of the Royal Asiatic Society,

The Right Honourable the Earl AMHERST in the Chair:

The Right Honourable Sir Gore Ouseley, Bart., informed the Meeting, that he was authorized by His Royal Highness the Duke of Sussex, to express his sincere regret, that His Majesty's lamented illness prevented his taking the Chair on this occasion.

The Minutes of the Proceedings of the last Anniversary Meeting were then read by the Secretary, and confirmed.

The Right Honourable Sir Gore Ouseley, Bart., Chairman of the Oriental Translation Committee, having read the Report of the Committee's proceedings since the last anniversary, and the Auditor's Report of the Receipts and Expenditure of the Oriental Translation Fund for the year 1829:

It was moved by the Right Honourable Lord Selsey, seconded by D. Pollock, Esq., and Resolved Unanimously,

"That the Committee's and Auditor's Reports be approved and printed."

Some amendments in the Sixth and Ninth Regulations for the Committee having been proposed by Sir Alexander Johnston, and seconded by James Alexander, Esq., M.P.,

It was Resolved Unanimously,

"That the proposed amendments in the Regulations be adopted."

The Right Honourable the Earl Amherst, then, in His Majesty's name, and accompanied by appropriate addresses, presented one of the Royal Medals to the Rev. Professor Lee; and the other to the Chairman of the Committee, as the Representative of J. F. Davis, Esq.; and one of the Institution's Medals to Sir William Ouseley, as the Representative of Major David Price.

The Chairman having left the Chair,

It was moved by the Right Honourable the Earl of Carlisle, seconded by Count de Lasteyrie, Vice-President of the Asiatic Society of Paris, and

Resolved Unanimously,

"That the warmest thanks of this Meeting be given to the Right Honourable the "Earl Amherst, for his able conduct in the Chair."

WILLIAM HUTTMANN,
Secretary.

THIRD REPORT

OF THE

ORIENTAL TRANSLATION COMMITTEE.

1830.

The Members of the Oriental Translation Committee, in offering this their Third Annual Report to the Members of the Royal Family, the Nobility, and the Gentlemen who have so generously patronized and munificently supported this long-wished-for Institution, entertain sanguine hopes that the simple recital of the incidents, labours, and acts of the past year will convince the Subscribers, in a gratifying manner, that the interesting objects for which they have so nobly granted their fostering protection, are in as flourishing a state of progress as they could have hoped for, and will obviate the necessity of their soliciting the attention of the Subscribers to more than a simple statement of Facts.

In the first place, the Committee have the grateful task of announcing to the Subscribers the gracious and munificent act of His Majesty, who, shortly after the last Meeting, with his usual beneficent protection of literature, on being presented with the five Works then printed at their expense, ordered Two Gold Medals, of the value of Twenty-five Guineas each, to be annually bestowed upon those learned Translators who may be considered worthy of this royal gift. A suitable device and motto having been agreed on by the Committee, and submitted by the Chairman to His Majesty, they have now the honour of placing before the Subscribers, for their inspection, the Medal of which the King has graciously condescended to express his approbation.

Although the Committee feel and regret the absence of a most active and zealous colleague, Colonel Fitz-Clarence, they avail themselves of the circumstance of his not being present at this Meeting, to express to the Subscribers, without wounding his modesty, their unqualified admiration of the persevering zeal, successful exertions, and eminent talent with which he has advanced the dearest objects of the Institution, during his sojourn in the "Eternal City;" and they feel confident that the resolution of thanks for, and confirmation of, his acts, which the Committee have unanimously come to, will be joyously re-echoed by the Subscribers.

Although the Colonel suffered much at first from the climate of Rome, which disabled him for all exertion, he made up amply for it, as soon as the state of his health permitted. A copy of the learned Professor Lee's translation of Ibn Batuta's Travels, he presented, in person, to his Holiness the Pope; who not only received it most graciously and thankfully, but, to mark his approbation of the establishment of the Oriental Translation Fund, immediately gave orders that the literary treasures of the Vatican library should be thrown open to the Colonel's researches. To this was added every assistance from the celebrated scholar, Monseigneur Angelo Mai, who, by the well-judged selection of the Papal Government, since sanctioned by the approbation of the European Republic of Letters, had been constituted Librarian; with permission to transcribe any manuscript contained in it, at the wish of the Committee.

To avail himself of the fruits of this most desirable acquisition, and at the same time to fulfil the wishes of the Committee, in establishing a permanent connection with Rome, Colonel Fitz-Clarence exerted his best ingenuity towards selecting such individuals for a "Branch Corresponding Committee at Rome," as, in addition to their eligibility on the score of excellent character, profound learning, and high attainment in Oriental literature, were sure to be approved of by the Pontifical Government.

It naturally suggested itself to the Colonel that our countryman, the Reverend Dr. Wiseman, an accomplished Orientalist, and the Head of the English College at Rome, who besides his fitness for the office by station and talent, possesses a hearty zeal for the cultivation of Eastern lore, and every other qualification, should be solicited to accept the office of Chairman. In this grand desideratum he has been successful; as also in appointing two learned colleagues to Dr. Wiseman, *viz.* the Reverend Dr. Cullen, Sub-Rector of the Propagandâ Fide establishment, a gentleman equally well qualified by ability and learning; and an English gentleman, Mr. Lewis, an excellent Arabic scholar, who passes his time in the cultivation of literature, between Rome and Sienna.

Letters from the Committee, confirming the above arrangement, will be immediately forwarded to Rome, similar to those addressed to the Indian Presidencies, which are already before the Subscribers; and we entertain the most sanguine hopes that this appointment will be of the utmost utility to the main objects of the Society, as well as to our Lexicographers and Philologists, for whom we can obtain many lights in colloquial knowledge, from the natives of so many different Eastern countries as are assembled in that city.

It is almost unnecessary to draw the attention of the Subscribers to the very great advantages which this Institution must derive from the meritorious exertions of our zealous colleague at the Roman capital. It will at once suggest itself that Rome possesses many celebrated Orientalists; that its constant and direct communication with many parts of Western Asia, and the influx of learned natives of Syria, Palestine, Egypt, and Abyssinia, who flock to the Propagandâ Fide, to study for the priesthood, afford great facility for the attainment of the objects of this Society, and that the Vatican and other libraries offer almost inexhaustible means for the cultivation of Eastern literature.

The Committee feel bound in justice to add, that the zeal of Colonel Fitz-Clarence in advancing the objects of the Society, has been fully equalled by the address and talent with which he made the necessary arrangements—secured the sanction and approbation of the Roman Government, and obtained the active and willing co-operation of the various learned bodies in that city, and their erudite members, as also in acquiring the aid of that powerful institution the Propagandâ Fide.

The heads of that college, in a most liberal manner, expressed their willingness to proceed conjointly with us in our desirable undertaking, and placed at our disposal the use of their founts and presses for the Oriental texts of such works as we may wish to publish in the original character; and the assistance of their Professors and Resident Orientalists, for composition and correction. They have also presented the Committee with specimens of their various types; and from Colonel Fitz-Clarence's calculation, a great saving must accrue in our future publications of voluminous Eastern texts, as contrasted with the expense incurred in England.

The learned Members of the Corresponding Committee at Rome have promised to publish in Italian, in the various periodical works circulated in Italy, a concise Prospectus of the views of our Institution; and it may be expected that ere long we shall receive numerous offers of translations from all quarters of the European continent.

In general, Colonel Fitz-Clarence found that amongst the Oriental scholars, with whom he took pains to become acquainted at Rome, the Syriac and Hebrew were more known than the other Eastern languages. The chairs of Arabic, Syriac, and Hebrew at the Sapienza are well filled by Signors Lance, Motza, and Sarte. The latter gentleman for general Oriental erudition is not to be surpassed in Europe, and he has partly promised to Colonel Fitz-Clarence a translation from a Syriac manuscript of Abulfarage very shortly, which Dr. Nott, Prebend of Winchester, has most kindly undertaken to translate from Latin into English.

Our active colleague made the acquaintance of Signor Habaschi, a native of the neighbourhood of Barout, originally educated at the Propaganda Fide, and now a resident agent at Rome for one of the Syrian Bishops; and also of a young German Orientalist, Dr. Kleugh, who has acquired a good knowledge of Arabic during a five years' residence in Egypt.

Although most of the learned men in official situations at Rome are too much occupied for us to expect from them translations of a voluminous nature, still there is every reason to hope that Dr. Wiseman and Signor Sarte will have the kindness to employ their leisure hours occasionally in translations from Syriac authors. Dr. Kleugh has obligingly undertaken a translation from El Vakedi's account of the Conquest of Syria, from the Arabic; and Signor Habaschi has had the goodness to promise us a translation of a history of the Circassian dynasty of Mamlukes in Egypt.

Colonel Fitz-Clarence informs the Committee, that he found the Grand Duke of Tuscany very ardent in Oriental research, and employing a learned gentleman at Florence to translate a very valuable work from the Arabic, "The History of the Moors in Spain, by Muhammed al Moghrebi," into Italian; and the same gentleman has expressed a wish to be employed by this Institution. His Imperial Highness also requested Colonel Fitz-Clarence to enrol his name in the List of Subscribers to the Oriental Translation Fund.

The Subscribers will have learned from the public papers, that an establishment on a very liberal and encouraging plan, for the cultivation of Oriental literature, is nearly completed at St. Petersburg; and certainly since the establishment of the Oriental Translation Fund in England, Eastern learning has been more assiduously cultivated throughout the continent of Europe, than for many years before. This is as it should be, and the Committee feel convinced that the Subscribers will sympathize with them in the gratification which this amiable rivalry excites. The Russian Oriental University is on an extensive scale; almost all the living languages of the East are to be taught in it by natives of the respective countries, assisted by and under the entire management of European Professors.

The Committee have the gratification of informing the Subscribers, that the Corresponding Committee at Calcutta have already transmitted to them a list of subscriptions to the Oriental Translation Fund, and part of a Translation made by Dr. John Tytler of the Khazanat ul Ilm, a Persian system of Mathematics, of which the original is being printed at Calcutta at the expense of the Bengal Government.

The translation of a Tract written by a Buddhist against the Brahminical castes, has also been sent to this Committee by them, accompanied by the information that translations of the "Hedayet ul Islam," by W. T. Robertson, Esq., and of the "Book of Jasher," by the Rev. William Adam, have been tendered for their acceptance. On the subject of the latter work, the Committee are making such researches as may enable them to make further communications at a future opportunity.

The following works have been published by the Oriental Translation Fund since the last anniversary, *viz.*—

The Fortunate Union, a Chinese Romance; translated by Mr. Davis, in 2 vols.

Two Singhalese Poems, descriptive of the Demonology and Masques of Ceylon; translated by Mr. Callaway.

The Adventures of Hatim Taï, a Persian Romance; translated by Mr. Forbes.

The Autobiography of Sheikh Mohammed Ali Hazin, a Persian Poet; translated by Mr. Belfour.

Memoirs of a Malayan Family: written by themselves; translated by Mr. Marsden: and

The Turkish account of the War in Bosnia between the Austrians and Turks; translated by Mr. Fraser.

In addition to these works, which have been delivered to the Subscribers, the Committee have the pleasure of laying before this Meeting three other works, the printing of which is expected to be finished about the end of this month. They are—Professor Neumann's translation of the Armenian History of Vartan; Professor Rosen's translation of an Arabic System of Algebra; and Major Stewart's translation of the Autobiography of the Emperor Tamerlane.

The Committee regret extremely that the printing of the text and a translation of Idrisi's Geography, is at present suspended, through an accident that happened to the Rev. Mr. Renouard; from the effects of which, however, they are happy to announce, he is now recovering.

Mr. Mitchell's having been called to Constantinople, has also for a time suspended the printing of his translation of the Maritime Wars of the Turks; but it is expected that it will soon be resumed and completed.

The History of Georgia, that was included among the works preparing for publication, has been withdrawn from the list, in consequence of a translation of it in Russian and French having been recently published at St. Petersburg.

The publication of original texts being one of the objects for which the Oriental Translation Fund was established, the Committee have the pleasure of announcing that, in addition to the text of the Arabic work on Algebra which is already printed, the Persian text of the Autobiography of Sheikh Mohammed Ali Hazin is now in the press; and that Ibn Haukul's Geography, Haji Khalfa's Bibliographical Dictionary, the Sheref Nameh, and the History of Mazendaran and Tabaristan, will be accompanied by the Arabic or Persian texts.

The Committee feel much pleasure in informing this Meeting, that a translation of the History of Japan made by Mr. Titsingh, and revised by Mr. Klaproth, will go to press immediately, and will, they confidently expect, be delivered to the Subscribers before the next anniversary.

Professor Erdmann, of Cazan, having sent to the Committee a German poetical translation, accompanied by the Persian original, of a small portion of the Heft Peiker, it is intended that it shall be printed with the translation of that work that is preparing for publication by the Chairman of the Committee, the Right Honourable Sir Gore Ouseley, Bart.

Besides the works in the printed list, announced as preparing for publication, those offered to Colonel Fitz-Clarence in Italy, and those mentioned by the Corresponding Committee at Calcutta, the Committee have the pleasure of stating, that Professor Wilken of Berlin has offered a translation of Ibn Beitar's Botany; and Professor Moeller of Gotha, a translation of Ibn Koteiba's History of the Arabians.

Mr. Huttmann, the Secretary to the Committee, also has offered to translate the Chun tsew of Confucius from the Chinese. This work, which still remains untranslated, contains the History of the Kingdom of Loo, of which Confucius was some time prime minister, and is the only one of the works usually attributed to him which he really wrote.

Prince Hubboff, an Armenian, having spent many years in compiling a general history of his native country, which is still in manuscript, and expressed his willingness to allow it to be translated, the Committee have requested the Rev. Mr. Glen, of Astrachan, where the Prince resides, to get it translated into English for this Institution.

For the information of the Subscribers, the Committee have incorporated in this Report the two following Resolutions from their proceedings, which they confidently hope the Subscribers will confirm:—

" Resolved,

" THAT a sum, varying from 20 to 100 Sovereigns, at the discretion of the Committee, " be given to any person who shall point out the translation of a lost Greek or Latin " work which shall be so circumstanced that the Committee may be enabled to obtain it " for translation."

" Resolved,

" THAT the Committee be empowered to give a premium, not exceeding 100*l.*, at its " discretion, to any person who shall discover Dr. Hyde's 'Manuscript Catalogue of " the Names of many Ancient Books lost in the original Greek, and the same now found " translated into Arabic or Syriac;' and any of his Translations, not now in the British " Museum, which shall be so circumstanced that the Committee may be able to procure " them for publication, if upon examination they should think them deserving of it."

It is now the pleasing duty of the Committee to recommend the following gentlemen as worthy of the honour of the Subscribers' approbation, for their exertions in translating; and as the Regulations proposed and confirmed in the last year's Report will account for the rewards not being adjudged to translations of small extent, however ingeniously performed, it is unnecessary to assure the Subscribers that no invidious or partial distinction has operated on their recommendation.

It will be remembered by the Subscribers, with due appreciation of his liberal motives, that the Reverend Professor Lee, the highly-talented translator of a most interesting work from the Arabic—the Travels of Ibn Batuta—declined last year accepting any mark of their approbation, lest it might diminish the funds of an Institution which is devoted to the attainment of objects most interesting to himself and consonant to his literary pursuits. But since His Majesty has placed two Royal Medals annually at the disposal of the Oriental Translation Fund, the Committee are most happy to find that the Reverend Professor's objections no longer exist, and they strongly recommend him for the honourable distinction of one of the Royal Medals.

The Committee feel satisfied that the Subscribers will approve of the other Royal Medal being given to J. F. Davis, Esq., for his interesting translations from the Chinese language; and of one of the Institution's Medals being given to Major Price, the learned translator of the Autobiography of the Emperor Janhangueir.

They also propose that a pecuniary reward of 25*l.* be offered to C. Fraser, Esq., the able translator of the History of the War in Bosnia; and that 50*l.* be given to Professor Neumann, for his valuable translation of the History of Vartan; and 100*l.* to F. C. Belfour, Esq. for his very curious translation of the Life of Sheikh Mohammed Ali Hazin.

Having understood that a misapprehension has arisen in consequence of the placing of a paragraph in the last Annual Report—that the translation of Ferishta's History of India, by Colonel Briggs, was published with the pecuniary assistance of the Oriental Translation Fund—the Committee think it right to remove this erroneous impression by stating that their object in mentioning their learned colleague's work was solely for the purpose of calling the attention of the Subscribers to so valuable a desideratum as a complete version of that interesting work. They have now the gratification to announce, that this distinguished Orientalist has kindly undertaken to prepare for publication by the Oriental Translation Fund, a Continuation of the History of India, known as the Seyer ul Mutakherin, of which a translation was published in Calcutta about forty or fifty years ago, by a French Renegade Mussulman named Mustafa, in very indifferent English, and of which the greater part of the impression was lost in its passage to Europe.

The Committee have sincere satisfaction in announcing the following flattering additions to the list of Subscribers to the Oriental Translation Fund since the last anniversary; *viz.*—

His Most Gracious Majesty, Fifty Guineas.

His Majesty the King of the Netherlands, Twenty Guineas.

And the following distinguished Individuals and Institutions Ten Guineas each:

His Imperial Highness the Grand Duke of Tuscany
His Serene Highness the Grand Duke of Hesse Darmstadt
The Most Noble the Marquess of Hertford
The Most Noble the Marquess of Northampton
The Right Honourable the Earl of Shrewsbury
The Right Honourable the Earl of Lonsdale
The Right Honourable Lord Burghersh
The Right Honourable Lord Prudhoe
The Right Honourable Sir R. Gordon
The Right Honourable C. R. Vaughan
The Honourable Mount-Stuart Elphinstone
The Honourable George Fortescue
The Honourable Edward Monckton
Sir G. J. Duckett, Bart.
Sir Robert Lawley, Bart.
Sir C. T. Metcalfe, Bart.
Lady Chambers
The Imperial Library, Vienna
The Imperial University, Dorpat
The Royal Library, Berlin
The Royal Library, Dresden
The Royal Library, Hanover
The Royal Irish Academy
The Royal University, Leyden
The Literary Society, Bombay
The Provost of Trinity College, Dublin
The Rev. E. Burton, D.D.
Lieut. Col. Caulfield
J. L. Cox, Esq.
R. W. Cox, Esq.
J. B. Elliott, Esq.
Hudson Gurney, Esq. M.P.
F. J. Halliday, Esq.
Lieut. Col. Vans Kennedy
J. Leard, Esq.
Lieut. Col. J. Macdonald
W. H. Macnaghten, Esq.
Captain J. W. J. Ouseley
The Rev. Dr. Nott
John Penn, Esq.
H. Preston, Esq.
Professor Rosen
A. Stirling, Esq.
Dr. John Tytler
H. H. Wilson, Esq.

The Committee, in concluding their Report, hope that they may be allowed to offer their congratulations to the Subscribers upon the flourishing state of the Institution which their protection and encouragement has formed and fostered, not only in relation to the state of its funds and on the works already before them, but also on those most important works which are in progress of translation and publication.

THE AUDITOR'S REPORT

OF THE

RECEIPTS AND DISBURSEMENTS OF THE ORIENTAL TRANSLATION FUND,

From January 1 to December 31, 1829.

RECEIVED.	£	s.	d.
139 Subscriptions of 10 Guineas each	£ 1,459	10	0
2 .. Ditto .. of 20 .. ditto	42	0	0
5 .. Ditto .. of 5 .. ditto	26	5	0
2 .. Ditto .. of 5 Pounds each	10	0	0
For Books Sold	6	2	0
Balance in hand January 1st 1829	850	4	7
	£ 2,394	1	7

PAID.	£	s.	d.
For Printing	£ 1,067	8	6
Translating	100	0	0
Gold Medals and the Die for them	126	10	0
Books	9	9	0
Salary and Transcription	74	3	8
Petty Expenses	60	2	8
	£ 1,437	13	2
Balance	956	8	5
	£ 2,394	1	7

Audited June 11th 1830,

J. B. S. MORRITT.

SUPPLEMENTARY STATEMENT FROM JANUARY 1st TO JUNE 11th 1830.

	£	s.	d.
Balance in hand January 1st 1830	£ 956	8	5
Received since January 1st	1,072	10	0
	£ 2,028	18	5
Balance in hand June 11th	£ 1,453	13	11

	£	s.	d.
Expended since January 1st	£ 575	5	6
Balance in hand	1,453	13	11
	£ 2,028	18	5

LIST OF ANNUAL SUBSCRIPTIONS.

His Most Gracious Majesty KING GEORGE THE FOURTH, Fifty Guineas.

His Majesty the KING OF THE NETHERLANDS, Twenty Guineas.

	£.	s.	d.
His Royal Highness the Duke of Clarence	21	0	0
His Royal Highness the Duke of Sussex	10	10	0
His Royal Highness the Duke of Cambridge	10	10	0
His Royal Highness the Duke of Gloucester	10	10	0
His Royal Highness Prince Leopold of Saxe Coburg	21	0	0
His Imperial Highness the Grand Duke of Tuscany	10	10	0
His Royal Highness the Duke of Orleans	10	10	0
His Serene Highness the Grand Duke of Hesse D'Armstadt	10	10	0
His Highness Prince de Lieven	10	10	0
His Grace the Lord Archbishop of Canterbury	10	10	0
The Right Hon. the Lord High Chancellor	10	10	0
His Grace the Duke of Somerset	10	10	0
His Grace the Duke of Richmond	10	10	0
His Grace the Duke of Leeds	10	10	0
His Grace the Duke of Bedford	10	10	0
His Grace the Duke of Devonshire	10	10	0
His Grace the Duke of Northumberland	10	10	0
His Grace the Duke of Wellington	10	10	0
The Most Noble the Marquess of Lansdowne	10	10	0
The Most Noble the Marquess of Hertford	10	10	0
The Most Noble the Marquess of Bute	10	10	0
The Most Noble the Marquess of Northampton	10	10	0
The Most Noble the Marquess of Anglesey	10	10	0
The Most Noble the Marquess of Cholmondeley	10	10	0
The Most Noble the Marquess of Londonderry	10	10	0
The Most Noble the Marquess of Donegall	10	10	0
The Right Hon. the Earl of Shrewsbury	10	10	0
The Right Hon. the Earl of Cassilis	10	10	0
The Right Hon. the Earl of Darnley	10	10	0
The Right Hon. the Earl of Glasgow	10	10	0
The Right Hon. the Earl of Carlisle	10	10	0
The Right Hon. the Earl of Egremont	10	10	0
The Right Hon. the Earl of Hardwicke	10	10	0
The Right Hon. the Earl Spencer	10	10	0
The Right Hon. the Earl of Powis	10	10	0
The Right Hon. the Earl of Lonsdale	10	10	0
The Right Hon. the Earl Amherst	10	10	0
The Right Hon. the Earl Dudley	10	10	0
The Right Hon. Lord W. H. C. Bentinck	10	10	0
The Right Hon. Lord Viscount Melville	10	10	0
The Right Hon. Lord Viscount Strangford	10	10	0
The Right Hon. Lord Viscount Goderich	10	10	0

	£.	s.	d.
The Right Hon. Lord Burghersh	10	10	0
The Right Hon. Lord Ashley	10	10	0
The Right Hon. and Right Reverend the Lord Bishop of London	10	10	0
The Right Rev. the Lord Bishop of Winchester	10	10	0
The Right Rev. the Lord Bishop of Salisbury	10	10	0
The Right Reverend the Lord Bishop of Ely	10	10	0
The Right Reverend the Lord Bishop of Peterborough	10	10	0
The Right Hon. Lord Southampton	10	10	0
The Right Hon. Lord Grenville	10	10	0
The Right Hon. Lord Selsey	10	10	0
The Right Hon. Lord Ellenborough	10	10	0
The Right Hon. Lord Prudhoe	10	10	0
The Right Hon. Lord Bexley	10	10	0
The Hon. George Agar Ellis, M.P.	10	10	0
The Hon. Mount-Stuart Elphinstone	10	10	0
The Hon. George Fortescue	10	10	0
The Hon. Edward Monckton	10	10	0
General the Hon. R. Taylor	10	10	0
The Right Hon. Sir R. Gordon	10	10	0
The Right Hon. Henry Goulburn, M.P.	10	10	0
The Right Hon. Sir G. Murray, Bart., M.P. G.C.B.	10	10	0
The Right Hon. Sir Gore Ouseley, Bart.	10	10	0
The Right Hon. Sir Robert Peel, Bart., M.P.	10	10	0
The Right Hon. C. R. Vaughan	10	10	0
The Right Hon. Sir G. Warrender, Bart., M.P.	10	10	0
The Right Hon. C. W. Williams Wynn, M.P.	10	10	0
Sir Robert Lawley, Bart.	10	10	0
Sir G. T. Staunton, Bart., F.R.S.	10	10	0
Sir C. T. Metcalfe, Bart.	10	10	0
Sir G. J. Duckett, Bart.	10	10	0
Admiral Sir C. M. Pole, Bart., G.C.B. F.R.S.	10	10	0
Sir Culling Smith, Bart.	10	10	0
Sir H. Halford, Bart., M.D., F.R.S.	10	10	0
Sir Benjamin Hobhouse, Bart., F.R.S.	10	10	0
Sir J. W. Waller, Bart.	10	10	0
Sir Edw. Kerrison, Bart., M.P.	10	10	0
Sir E. H. East, Bart., M.P. F.R.S.	10	10	0
Sir Francis Freeling, Bart.	10	10	0
Lady Chambers	10	10	0
Lieut.-Gen. Sir Herbert Taylor, G.C.H.	10	10	0
Sir W. Sidney Smith, K.C.B. F.R.S.	10	10	0
Sir A. Johnston, Knt., F.R.S.	10	10	0

	£.	s.	d.
Sir James Scarlet, M.P.	10	10	0
The Imperial University of Casan	10	10	0
The Imperial Library, Vienna	10	10	0
The Royal Library, Berlin	10	10	0
The Royal Library, Dresden	10	10	0
The Royal Library, Hanover	10	10	0
The Royal Library, Munich	10	10	0
The Royal University, Leyden	10	10	0
The Royal College of Surgeons, London	10	10	0
The Royal Irish Academy	10	10	0
The Asiatic Society of Bengal	10	10	0
The Literary Society of Bombay	10	10	0
The Athenæum	10	10	0
The Oriental Club, London	10	10	0
The Principal and Fellows of Brazen-nose College, Oxford	10	10	0
The Library of Catharine Hall, Cambridge	10	10	0
The Library of Christ Church College, Oxford	10	10	0
The Library of Corpus Christi College, Cambridge	10	10	0
The Library of Exeter College, Oxford	10	10	0
The Library of Jesus College, Cambridge	10	10	0
The President and Fellows of Magdalen College, Oxford	10	10	0
The Library of Trinity College, Cambridge	10	10	0
The Dean and Chapter of Ely	10	10	0
The Methodist Missionary Society	10	10	0
The Provost of Trinity College, Dublin	10	10	0
H. Alexander, Esq., M.P.	10	10	0
Francis Baring, Esq., M.P.	10	10	0
R. S. Berry, Esq.	10	10	0
Colonel William Blackburne	10	10	0
J. Broadhurst, Esq.	10	10	0
The Reverend E. Burton, D.D.	10	10	0
Lieut.-Col. James Caulfield, Bengal Cavalry	10	10	0
The Rev. H. Coddington	10	10	0
John Lewis Cox, Esq.	10	10	0
Richard Waite Cox, Esq.	10	10	0
John Bardoe Elliott, Esq.	10	10	0
Lieutenant-Colonel Fitz-Clarence, F.R.S.	10	10	0
R. Gregory, Esq.	10	10	0
John Guillemard, Esq.	10	10	0
Hudson Gurney, Esq., M.P.	10	10	0
F. J. Halliday, Esq.	10	10	0
A. Hamilton, Esq.	10	10	0
Major-General Thomas Hardwicke	10	10	0
Prince Hoare, Esq., F.R.S.	10	10	0
Godfrey Higgins, Esq.	10	10	0
Thomas Hope, Esq., F.R.S.	10	10	0
R. Jenkins, Esq.	10	10	0
Peter Johnston, of Carnsalloch, Esq.	10	10	0
Lieutenant-Colonel Vans Kennedy	10	10	0
The Rev. Wyndham Knatchbull, D.D.	10	10	0
John Lee, Esq., D.C.L.	10	10	0
Major-General Colin Macauley, M.P.	10	10	0
Dr. J. D. Macbride	10	10	0
Lieutenant-Colonel John Macdonald, F.R.S. M.A.S. Cal.	10	10	0
W. H. Macnaghten, Esq.	10	10	0
Captain F. Marryat, R.N., C.B., F.R.S.	10	10	0
W. Marsden, Esq., LL.D. F.R.S.	10	10	0
J. B. S. Morritt, Esq.	10	10	0
John Murray, Esq.	10	10	0
The Rev. Dr. Nott	10	10	0
Colonel H. S. Osborne	10	10	0
Captain J. W. J. Ouseley	10	10	0
C. N. Pallmer, Esq., M.P.	10	10	0
John Story Penleaze, Esq.	10	10	0
John Penn, Esq.	10	10	0
Louis Hayes Petit, Esq., M.P. F.R.S.	10	10	0
D. Pollock, Esq., F.R.S.	10	10	0
Henry Preston, Esq.	10	10	0
The Rev. E. B. Pusey, A.M.	10	10	0
R. Simmons, Esq.	10	10	0
William Sotheby, Esq.	10	10	0
A. Spottiswoode, Esq., M.P.	10	10	0
A. Stirling, Esq.	10	10	0
Major-General J. H. Symons	10	10	0
G. Watson Taylor, Esq., M.P. F.R.S.	10	10	0
Lieutenant-Colonel James Tod	10	10	0
Dr. John Tytler	10	10	0
George Vivian, Esq.	10	10	0
H. H. Wilson, Esq.	10	10	0
Captain J. Woolmore	10	10	0
The Imperial University, Dorpat	5	5	0
John Leard, Esq.	5	5	0
Philip Pusey, Esq.	5	5	0
The Rev. G. C. Renouard, B.D.	5	5	0
Professor Rosen	5	5	0
R. J. Thomson, Esq.	5	5	0
The Rev. Archdeacon Wrangham	5	5	0

It is requested that those individuals or Institutions who are willing to subscribe to the Oriental Translation Fund, will send their names and addresses to the Secretary, Mr. WILLIAM HUTTMANN, at the house of the Royal Asiatic Society, No. 14, Grafton-street, Bond-street, London; and inform him where their subscriptions will be paid. Subscriptions will also be received by the Branch Committees at Calcutta, Madras, and Rome.

REGULATIONS

FOR

THE ORIENTAL TRANSLATION COMMITTEE.

1st. THE Committee which is attached to the Royal Asiatic Society, for the purpose of selecting and superintending the translation and printing of Oriental works, is to be called the "Oriental Translation Committee."

2d. The object of the Committee is to publish, free of expense to the authors, translations of the whole or parts of works in the Oriental languages, accompanied occasionally by the original texts, and such illustrations as may be considered necessary. These translations are to be generally printed in English, but in peculiar cases may be printed in Latin or French.

3d. The Committee is empowered to add to its number, to purchase Oriental MSS. or printed books, to present copies of the works printed at the expense of the Oriental Translation Fund to Learned Societies and individuals, and to adopt all the means that it may consider to be necessary for promoting the objects for which it was appointed. No payment, however, exceeding twenty-five pounds, is to be made, until approved at two successive Meetings of the Committee.

4th. The Meetings of the Committee will be held as often as the Chairman or Secretary, or any two other Members of it, signing a requisition for that purpose, deem it necessary. All the Members of the Committee, resident within one hundred miles of London, are to be summoned to attend each of its Meetings; and five Members, including the Chairman or a Deputy Chairman, and the Secretary, are to constitute a quorum.

5th. The Secretary is charged generally with the business of the Committee, and is to record all the votes of the Committee in a Minute-Book, which every Subscriber has the right of inspecting, on application to him.

6th. For the purpose of directing the attention of scholars to the literature of the East, and encouraging translations, the Committee is empowered to give annually, for such works as it may consider deserving of distinction, four rewards in money, in sums not exceeding £100 each, and four gold medals, of the value of twenty guineas each, inscribed with the names of the individuals to whom, and the titles of the translations for which, they are presented. Any Member of the Committee who sends a translation for approval, whether to obtain a reward or medal, or merely to have it printed at the expense of the Oriental Translation Fund, is to cease to act on the Committee until the adoption or rejection of his work is decided on.

7th. No work, although prepared for the press at the expense of the Oriental Translation Fund, is to be printed, until the imprimatur of the Chairman or a Deputy Chairman, and at least eight Members of the Committee, is obtained. The Translators of such works as are printed by the Committee are entitled to twenty-five copies of their Translations for presentation.

8th. Every individual or institution subscribing ten guineas or upwards, annually, to the Oriental Translation Fund, will be entitled to one fine paper copy of every work printed by the Committee, with the name of the individual or institution subscribing printed on an ornamental title-page. Individuals or institutions subscribing five guineas annually, will be entitled to common paper copies of any of the works published by the Committee, to the amount of their subscriptions, at half the price paid for them by Non-Subscribers.

9th. A General Meeting, to which every Subscriber and Member of the Committee, resident in the United Kingdom, shall be summoned, will be held annually some time in the month of June. At that meeting Regulations may be proposed or rescinded; the Auditor will report the receipts and disbursements of the past year; and the Secretary report the progress made in the works that have been commenced, and give an account of those that are proposed for publication in the following year. A copy of each of these Reports will be sent to every Subscriber.—A Special General Meeting shall be convened by the Secretary at any time it is required in writing by nine Subscribers, the requisition stating the subject that is to be proposed for consideration.

LIST
OF
THE ORIENTAL TRANSLATION COMMITTEE.

Chairman:

The Right Honourable Sir Gore Ouseley, Bart., Vice-President R.A.S.

Deputy Chairmen:

The Right Honourable Charles Watkin Williams Wynn, M.P., President R.A.S.
Sir G. T. Staunton, Bart., Vice-President R.A.S.
Sir E. H. East, Bart., M.P.
Sir A. Johnston, Vice-President R.A.S.
Col. Mark Wilks.
Lieut.-Col. Fitz-Clarence, Vice-President R.A.S.

Committee:

J. Aitken, Esq., M.D., Secretary to the Literary Society, Madras.
The Rev. R. Anderson, late Assistant Professor of Oriental Languages in the Hon. East-India Company's College, Haileybury.
The Right Honourable Lord Ashley, M.P., one of His Majesty's Commissioners for the Affairs of India.
James Atkinson, Esq., M.A.S.Cal.
B. G. Babington, Esq., M.B., F.R.S., M.Lit.Soc.Mad.
Col. J. Baillie, M.P., M.A.S.Cal.
The Rev. A. Baird, A.M., Professor of Hebrew, New College, St. Andrews.
J. Barker, Esq., Consul-General, Alexandria.
The Rev. J. Beighton, Prince of Wales's Island.
I. Bentley, Esq., A.M., Professor of Oriental Languages, King's College, Aberdeen.
F. Bernar, Esq., Sincapore.
Col. W. Blackburne, late Resident at the Court of the Rajah of Tanjore.
Lieut.-Col. J. Briggs, M.Lit.Soc.Bom.
Samuel Briggs, Esq., Alexandria.
Col. Thomas Duer Broughton.
The Rev. A. Brunton, D.D., Professor of Hebrew in the University of Edinburgh.
The Rev. John Callaway, late Missionary in Ceylon.
The Rev. W. Carey, D.D., Professor of Sanscrit, &c. in the College of Fort-William, Calcutta.
R. Clarke, Esq., M.Lit.Soc.Mad.
The Rev. B. Clough, Ceylon.
Sir J. E. Colebrooke, Bart., M.Lit.Soc.Cal.
Sir Robert Colquhoun, Bart., Kumaon.
Lieut.-Col. J. M. Coombs, M.Lit.Soc.Mad.
J. F. Davis, Esq., F.R.S., M.Lit.Soc.Bom. Canton.
Lieut.-Col. C. J. Doyle, M.A.S.Cal.
Henry Ellis, Esq., F.R.S.

W. Erskine, Esq., M. Lit. Soc. Bom.
Col. W. Farquhar, late Governor of Malacca.
The Rev. J. Forshall, A.M., Keeper of the Manuscripts in the British Museum.
The Rev. W. B. Fox, late Missionary in Ceylon.
J. Frazer, Esq., Consul, Bona.
The Rev. W. French, D.D., Master of Jesus College, Cambridge.
Capt. T. B. Gascoyne, Secretary to the Literary Society, Ceylon.
The Rev. Gavin Gibb, D.D., Professor of Oriental Languages in the University of Glasgow.
The Rev. William Glen, Astrachan.
Lieut. A. D. Gordon, late Examiner to the College of Fort-William, Calcutta.
Terrick Hamilton, Esq.
Richard Haughton, Esq., Professor of Oriental Languages in the Honourable East-India Company's Military Seminary, Addiscombe.
Graves C. Haughton, Esq., A.M. F.R.S., late Professor of Hindu Literature and the History of Asia in the Hon. East-India Company's College, Haileybury.
E. W. A. Drummond Hay, Esq., Consul General, Mogadore.
The Rev. Dr. Henderson, Tutor to the Mission College, Hoxton.
Godfrey Higgins, Esq.
Richard Jenkins, Esq., M. A. S. Cal.
Capt. Jervis, Secretary to the Literary Society of Bombay.
The Rev. A. Judson, Rangoon.
The Rev. H. G. Keene, A.M., Professor of Arabic, Persian, and Hindustani Literature, in the Honourable East-India Company's College, Haileybury.
Sir John Kennaway, Bart., M.A.S. Cal.
Lieut.-Col. Vans Kennedy, Vice President of the Literary Society, Bombay.
The Rev. J. Kidd, D.D., Professor of Oriental Languages, Mariachal College, Aberdeen.
The Rev. W. Knatchbull, D.D., Archbishop Laud's Professor of Arabic, Oxford.
E. W. Lane, Esq.
The Rev. S. Lee, B.D., Professor of Arabic in the University of Cambridge.
The Rev. H. D. Leeves, Corfu.
Capt. J. Low, Prince of Wales's Island.
Col. J. L. Lushington, C.B. M.P.
Capt. T. Macan, late Persian Interpreter to His Excellency the Commander-in-Chief in India.
Dr. J. D. Macbride, Lord Almoner's Reader of Arabic, and Principal of Magdalen Hall, Oxford.
Col. Sir J. Macdonald, Teheran.
W. Marsden, Esq., LL.D. M. A. S. Cal.
The Rev. J. Marshman, D.D., Serampore.
The Rev. W. H. Medhurst, Batavia.
Capt. J. Michael, Professor of Hindu Literature and the History of Asia in the Hon. East-India Company's College, Haileybury.
The Rev. W. H. Mill, D.D., Principal of Bishop's College, Calcutta.
Mirza Ibrahim, Assistant Professor of Oriental Languages in the Honourable East-India Company's College, Haileybury.
The Rev. R. Morrison, D.D., Canton.
The Rev. T. Musgrave, A.M., Lord Almoner's Reader of Arabic, Cambridge.
Colonel H. S. Osborne, formerly Malabar Translator on the Bombay Establishment.
Sir W. Ouseley, Knt., Hon. M. A. S. Cal.
Capt. J. W. J. Ouseley, Professor of the Arabic and Persian Languages in the College of Fort-William, Calcutta.
J. S. Penleaze, Esq.
T. P. Platt, Esq., A.M., Fellow of Trinity College, Cambridge, and Honorary Librarian to the British and Foreign Bible Society.
Major David Price, M. Lit. Soc. Bom.
Capt. W. Price, Professor of Hindustani in the College of Fort-William, Calcutta.
The Rev. E. B. Pusey, A.M., Regius Professor of Hebrew, and Canon of Christ-Church, Oxford.
Sir T. Reade, Consul-General, Tunis.
The Rev. G. C. Renouard, B.D., late Lord Almoner's Reader of Arabic, Cambridge.
Professor Rosen.
J. Ross, Esq., A.M., M. A. S. Cal.

Captain D. Ruddell, Secretary to the College of Fort-William, Calcutta.

Abraham Salamé, Esq.

E. V. Schalch, Esq., M.A.S.Cal., Assistant Professor of Oriental Languages in the Honourable East-India Company's College, Haileybury.

J. Shakespear, Esq., late Professor of Oriental Languages in the Hon. East-India Company's Military Seminary, Addiscombe.

The Rev. G. Skinner, A.M., Fellow and Tutor of Jesus College, Cambridge.

William Sotheby, Esq., F.R.S. F.A.S.

The Rev. E. Stallybrass, Selinginsk.

Major C. Stewart, late Professor of Arabic, Persian, and Hindustani Literature in the Honourable East-India Company's College, Haileybury.

Major-Gen. J. H. Symons.

Capt. Taylor, Political Agent at Bussora.

The Rev. C. H. Thomsen, Sincapore.

Lieut.-Col. J. Tod, M.A.S.Cal.

Lieut. H. Todd, Examiner to the College of Fort-William, Calcutta.

The Rev. D. G. Wait, LL.D., St. John's College, Cambridge.

C. Wilkins, Esq., LL.D., Oriental Librarian to the Hon. East-India Company.

Major Sir Henry Willock, Teheran.

H. H. Wilson, Esq., Secretary to the Asiatic Society of Bengal, Calcutta.

The Rev. Archdeacon Wrangham.

Auditor:

J. B. S. Morritt, Esq.

Treasurer:

Lieut.-Col. Fitz-Clarence, Hon. M.A.S.Cal.

Secretary:

Mr. William Huttmann.

BRANCH ORIENTAL TRANSLATION COMMITTEE, CALCUTTA.

PRESIDENT:
Sir C. T. METCALFE, Bart.

F. J. HALLIDAY, Esq.
W. H. MACNAGHTEN, Esq.
Captain MACAN.
Captain PRICE.
A. STIRLING, Esq.
H. H. WILSON, Esq.

SECRETARY:
JOHN TYTLER, Esq., M.D.

BRANCH ORIENTAL TRANSLATION COMMITTEE, MADRAS.

PRESIDENT:
The Venerable the Archdeacon T. ROBINSON, A.M.

J. AITKEN, Esq. M.D.
C. J. BROWN, Esq.
A. D. CAMPBELL, Esq.
H. CHAMIER, Esq.
Lieut.-Colonel COOMBS.
Captain H. HARKNESS.
Captain KEIGHLEY.
J. M. MACLEOD, Esq.
W. OLIVER, Esq.
Lieut.-Colonel ORMSBY.

SECRETARY:
J. LUSHINGTON, Esq.

BRANCH ORIENTAL TRANSLATION COMMITTEE, ROME.

PRESIDENT:
The Rev. Dr. WISEMAN, Principal of the English College.

The Rev. Dr. CULLEN, Sub Rector of the College de Propaganda Fide.
— LEWIS, Esq.
&c. &c.

The Tareki Afghan; translated by Dr. Bernhard Dorn. Part II.

This is a Persian History of the Afghans, who claim to be descended from the Jews. It will be accompanied by an account of the Afghan tribes.

The Annals of Elias, Metropolitan of Nisibis; translated by the Rev. Josiah Forshall, A.M.

This Syriac Chronicle contains chronological tables of the principal dynasties of the world, brief memoirs of the Patriarchs of the Nestorian church, and notices of the most remarkable events in the East, from the birth of our Saviour to the beginning of the eleventh century.

Ibn Haukul's Geography; translated by Professor Hamaker.

This Arabic work was compiled in the 10th century by a celebrated Mohammedan Traveller, and is not the same as the Oriental Geography of Ebn Haukal that was translated by Sir William Ouseley.

Naima's Annals; translated by the Rev. Dr. Henderson.

This Turkish History comprises the period between 1622 and 1692, and includes accounts of the Turkish invasion of Germany, the sieges of Buda, Vienna, &c.

The Chun tsew of Confucius; translated by Mr. William Huttmann.

This Chinese work, which still remains untranslated, contains the history of the Kingdom of Loo, of which Confucius was some time Prime-Minister, and is the only one of the works usually attributed to him that he really wrote.

The Asseba as Syar of Syed Mohammed Reza; translated by Mirza Alexander Kazem Beg.

This is a Turkish History of the Khans of the Crimea, written about A.D. 1740, and contains many interesting particulars relating to Turkey, Russia, Poland, and Germany.

Nipon " dai itsi ran; translated by Monsieur Jules de Klaproth.

This Japanese work contains the History of the Dairis or Ecclesiastical Emperors of Japan from the year 660 Ante Christum.

A Description of Tibet; translated by Monsieur Jules de Klaproth.

This will consist of extracts from various Chinese and Mandchu works, forming a complete account of Tibet, and of the Buddhic religion, of which it is the principal seat.

Ibn Khaldun's History of the Berbers; translated by the Rev. Professor Lee.

This is a rare and valuable Arabic work, containing an account of the origin, progress, and decline of the dynasties which governed the northern coast of Africa.

The great Geographical Work of Idrisi; translated by the Rev. G. C. Renouard, B.D.

This Arabic work was written A.D. 1153, to illustrate a large silver globe made for Roger, King of Sicily, and is divided into the seven climates described by the Greek Geographers.

Makrisi's Khitat, or History and Statistics of Egypt; translated by Abraham Salamé, Esq.

This Arabic work includes accounts of the conquest of Egypt by the Caliphs, A.D. 640; and of the cities, rivers, ancient and modern inhabitants of Egypt, &c.

Part of Mirkhond's Ruzet-al-Suffa; translated by David Shea, Esq.

The part of this Persian work selected for publication is that which contains the History of Persia from Kaiomurs to the death of Alexander the Great.

Class 3d.—Bibliography, Belles-Lettres, and Biography.

Haji Khalfa's Bibliographical Dictionary; translated by Monsieur Gustave Flügel.

This valuable Arabic work was written by the celebrated Kateb Chelebi al Marhoom, and contains accounts of above 13,000 Arabic, Persian, and Turkish works, arranged alphabetically.

Heft Peiker, an historical Romance of Behrám Gúr; translated by the Right Hon. Sir Gore Ouseley, Bart.

From the Persian of Nizámi of Ganjah, containing the romantic history of Behrám, the Vth of the Sassanian dynasty of Persian Kings.

Meher va Mushteri; translated by the Right Hon. Sir Gore Ouseley, Bart.

This Persian Poem, of which an abridgment will be published, was composed by Muhammed Assár, and celebrates the friendship and adventures of Meher and Mushteri, the sons of King Shapur and his grand Vizier.

Ibn Khalikan's Lives of Illustrious Men: translated by Dr. F. A. Rosen.

This is an Arabic Biographical Dictionary, arranged alphabetically, of the most celebrated Arabian historians, poets, warriors, &c. who lived in the seven first centuries of the era of Mahommed, A.D. 600 to A.D. 1300.

The Bustan of Sadi; translated by James Ross, Esq., A.M.

This is a much-admired Persian Poem, consisting of Tales, &c. illustrative of moral duties.